FRAGMENTS
of the SPIRIT

FRAGMENTS
of the SPIRIT

Nature, Violence,
and the Renewal
of Creation

Mark I. Wallace

TRINITY PRESS INTERNATIONAL
HARRISBURG, PENNSYLVANIA

To Ellen,
she walks in beauty

Trinity Press International, P.O. Box 1321, Harrisburg, PA 17105

Trinity Press International is a division of the Morehouse Group.

Cover art: *Field under Stormy Skies*, William W. Huggin. Private Collection/William Huggin/SuperStock.

Cover design: Laurie Westhafer

A catalog record for this book is available from the Library of Congress.

Printed in the United States of America

02 03 04 05 06   10 9 8 7 6 5 4 3 2 1

Contents

PART TWO: TOWARD A LIFE-CENTERED
THEOLOGY OF THE SPIRIT

Preface

On September 11, 2001, the twin towers of the World Trade Center in New York City were brought to the ground by a terrorist attack. The Pentagon in Washington, D.C. was attacked at the same time. Since then, the biological agent anthrax has seeped into government offices, mailrooms, and workplaces across America. As a result of these threats to national security, many Americans are both fearful about the future and coming to terms with our country's complicity in creating global structures of oppression that provide the context, if not the reason, for the terrorist attacks. In this stressful climate, I am reminded of the value of religious faith at a time when people fear for their safety and look for a meaningful and transformative response to these recent events.

I have written this book out of my own personal struggle to find God in a world scarred by violence—including the terrifying violence of recent weeks—and seemingly empty at times of any signs of divine presence. Friedrich Nietzsche writes that "one must have chaos in oneself in order to give birth to a dancing star." For me, the struggle to believe in God in the face of strong and troubling evidence to the contrary is the endeavor that has defined my life. At times, this struggle has seemed to me to be too self-centered; at other times, it has struck me as the only struggle worth living for.

As a boy growing up in Southern California in the 1960s, I found meaning in my family and friends, school activities and summer vacations, and the wide expanse of the chaparral foothills that surrounded my family's suburban home. Ecologically speaking, this was a world of roadrunners and screech owls and coyotes and horny toads. But as I entered my teens I lost connection to this world, and in the social upheaval of the times I went on a search for a moral compass. I found it in Christianity. The church took the place of my coyote friends, and well into my college years I wore the badge of evangelical religion with pride. But something happened along the way, and by the time I finished college and began to contemplate my future, I realized that I had lost my faith and that no amount of apologetic reasoning could restore it. In the words of Paul Ricoeur, I had lost my *first naïveté*, and I was beginning to enter that period of my life that he refers to as the desert of criticism. Since that time I have oscillated between belief and doubt, hope and despair. I am many different things—husband, parent, writer, teacher, mentor, activist—but what I have become is sometimes a mystery to myself. I am a theologian in a secular college, a Christian who is conflicted about his church identity, a religious writer who wonders whether there is a God.

This conflict—both inner and outer, both internal to my own religious doubts and specific to my professional identity—has led to the writing of this book. This book seeks to enact in writing a ground for religious hope in a world chronically devoid of hope. This ground—always unstable, never certain, shifting and changing like the biosphere itself—is my belief in the Spirit as the power of life and renewal within creation. I live now in the horizon of what Ricoeur calls the *second naïveté*—that tenuous religious hope that life can have meaning even in a world suffering from systemic violence and ecological degradation. But my sense of the second naïveté is hedged with caution and doubt, for while I live in the hope that belief in God's Spirit as the power of life itself is a belief worthy of my most passionate loyalty, I cannot be certain that such a belief is founded on anything more than my and others' intense desire that this belief have an ultimate referent. I live my life as a wager on the hope that this belief is true.

All writing is personal agony. While this book is written in academic prose style, I want it to be more than an intellectual exercise. The writing of this book has been a travail of the soul. I no longer possess the confidence of a bedrock faith, but I cannot join the ranks of those who have taken leave of faith and regard religious life and thought as an exercise in obscurantism. Instead, I hold out for something else: I seek to discover the gossamer thread of the Spirit's work in a world badly wounded by social and ecological violence. This search reflects my struggle to come to terms with the loss of my childhood coyote world and the pietistic subculture of my teenage years. Personally speaking, this is the reason for writing a book on the Spirit: it is my way of understanding and expressing how I now experience the presence of the sacred in the world today. My belief in the Spirit as the power of benevolent unity in all things has helped me to make sense of my memories of the heady fragrance of the sagebrush hills surrounding my family home and the steadying presence of Jesus in my heart amidst the whirling chaos of entitled American youth culture. Little of these two worlds remains for me now: the sagebrush has been plowed under and replanted with groundcover for tract homes, and my evangelical certainty has dissolved in the face of my personal and intellectual transformations.

Yet, as I seek to convey in this book, I do believe that the Spirit of Jesus, the Spirit of God, sustains every community of hope and resistance that seeks to discern God's will in its midst. In this book, then, I suggest that though the Jesus of history has passed before us in biblical time, the Spirit of creation abides with us daily in the people, animals, and places that make up our planet home. I ask, Is this not what the Gospel of John teaches in chapter 16, that unless Jesus goes away, the Advocate, the Counselor, the Spirit will not come and live among us, filling all creation with her presence? Unless Jesus takes his leave from the earth the long-awaited promise of the Spirit cannot be fulfilled. But if this is the case, then why has theology in our time been christocentric rather than pneumacentric?

Some final thoughts. First, a comment about the book's organization. While the book is structured in a sequential Part One-Part Two fashion, in fact the two parts can be read independently of one another. Not every reader will want to dwell on the methodological material in Part One and will prefer to move on to the book's constructive vision in Part Two. The book can be read and understood in this way, though the integrity of its overall argument, and its relevance to current issues in philosophy and theology, may not be as apparent to the reader who only peruses Part One.

Second, some material in this book is borrowed and reworked from my previously published articles, and I thank the relevant copyright holders for permission to use my work in this format. "Ricoeur, Rorty, and the Question of Revelation," in *Meanings in Texts and Actions: Questioning Paul Ricoeur*, ed. David E. Klemm and William Schweiker, Studies in Religion and Culture (Charlottesville: The University Press of Virginia, 1993), 234–54, has been used in part for chapter 2; "Performative Truth and the Witness of the Spirit," *Southwestern Journal of Theology* 35 (1993): 29–36, has been used in part for chapter 3; "Postmodern Biblicism: The Challenge of René Girard for Contemporary Theology," *Modern Theology* 5 (July 1989): 309–25, has been used in part for chapter 4; "The Wild Bird Who Heals: Recovering the Spirit in Nature," *Theology Today* 50 (April 1993): 13–28, has been used in part for chapter 5; and "Can God Be Named Without Being Known? The Problem of Revelation in Ogden, Thiemann, and Ricoeur," *Journal of the American Academy of Religion* 59 (Summer

1991): 201–28, has been used in part for chapter 6.

In conclusion, I want to express my deepest gratitude to my family, friends, and the institutions that have sustained me and supported this project in a spirit of friendship and generosity. My parents, Homer and Shirley, and my sister, Darice, early in my life wove around me the web of connections that continues to nurture my growth and development. Ben Bryson, my student assistant at Swarthmore College, helpfully assisted in the preparation of chapter drafts and the bibliography. Stephen Dunning read the entire manuscript and offered many thoughtful criticisms that helped me to refine, and in some instances overhaul, the book's argument. Many friends from two discussion forums I have been privileged to be a part of in recent years—the Colloquium on Violence and Religion and the Constructive Theology Workgroup—have been faithful conversation-partners and have helped me to sharpen my line of thinking on many occasions. I am grateful to my editor at Trinity Press, Henry Carrigan, who has invested considerable time and effort to insuring that this book will continue to be read. Swarthmore College has played a defining role in supporting this endeavor. Swarthmore embodies the liberal arts ideal of a rigorous and convivial learning community where faculty and students alike are encouraged to be scholar-teachers. After receiving small grants from the National Endowment for the Humanities and the American Academy of Religion, Swarthmore funded me for a sabbatical leave in order to write and finish this book. Informed by its Quaker heritage, Swarthmore has been a sort of Cassiciacum where I have been sustained in my teaching and research.

I express my final words of gratitude to my wife, Ellen Ross. The contributions of Ellen to this book are incalculable. She patiently read and re-read the manuscript, suggested numerous revisions, and helped me to hone my articulation of the book's thesis. Along with sharing with me our home, our faculty appointment, and the recent chairing of our department, Ellen always found the time to study the manuscript with the same probity and good cheer that she brings to life in general. Along with our two young children, Katie and Christopher, Ellen is a loving reminder to me that the Spirit is always at play in the circle-drama of daily life.

Introduction

Many people now sense that we live in the "age of the Spirit," a time in which a fragile connection with the earth and one another is being felt in friendship with a power anterior to ourselves. The medieval mystic Joachim of Fiore prophesied that humankind has lived through the periods of the Father and the Son and has now entered the age of the Spirit. Karl Barth remarked at the end of his life that the Holy Spirit is the proper focus for a theology that is right for the present situation. And practitioners of nature-based religion, from native peoples to modern neopagans, claim that a reverence for the Spirit in all life-forms, from people and animals to trees and watersheds, is the most promising response to the threat of global ecological collapse at the end of the twentieth century.

This book interrogates the nature of the Spirit in relation to recent work in theology, philosophy, critical theory, and environmental studies. My orienting thesis is that the Spirit is the power of life-giving breath (*rûaḥ*) within the cosmos who continually works to transform and renew all forms of life—both human and nonhuman. The Nicene Creed in 325 C.E. named the Spirit as "the Lord, the Giver of Life"; the purpose of this book is to contemporize this ancient appellation by reenvisioning the Holy Spirit as God's invigorating presence within the society of all living beings. This life-centered model of the Spirit expands the understanding of the Spirit beyond its *intratrinitarian* role (traditionally expressed as the bond of unity between the Father and the Son) to include the Spirit's *cosmic* role as the power of healing and renewal within all creation. To facilitate this exposition, I seek to establish a conversation about the Spirit among a group of contemporary religious thinkers (Søren Kierkegaard, Paul Ricoeur, Schubert Ogden, René Girard, Jürgen Moltmann,

1

Ronald Thiemann, Richard Swinburne) and a number of representative post-modern theorists (Friedrich Nietzsche, Jacques Derrida, Michel Foucault, Julia Kristeva, Emmanuel Levinas, Richard Rorty). The book is divided into seven chapters, with each chapter taking up a theme—postmodernism, metaphysics, truth, violence, nature, and evil—that is central to the contemporary discussion.

ECOLOGICAL PNEUMATOLOGY

My methodological approach is rhetorical rather than philosophical. No attempt to *prove* the reality of the Spirit is offered here; instead the focus is on recovering and constructing *imaginative discourses* about the Spirit that are transformative for earth-identified communities who have risked following the Spirit's inner promptings. In labeling my approach "rhetorical" I seek to examine the problem of the Spirit in a manner that is self-reflexively aware of my own commitments and passions. I will not defend a model of the Spirit through appeals to unbiased and value-free modes of argumentation; instead, I will offer a very particular and concrete theology of the Spirit that uses imaginative-symbolic discourses as well as argumentative-propositional analyses.

My position is that the Spirit is best understood not as a metaphysical entity but as a healing life-force that engenders human flourishing as well as the welfare of the planet. I label this approach "ecological pneumatology" in order to distinguish it from metaphysically based notions of the Spirit characteristic of normative Western thought. I want this distinction to relocate understandings of the Spirit outside the philosophical question of being and squarely within a nature-based desire for the integrity and health of all life-forms—human and nonhuman. This model understands the Spirit not as divine intellect or the principle of consciousness but as a healing and subversive *life-form*—as water, light, dove, mother, fire, breath, and wind—on the basis of different biblical and literary figurations of the Spirit in nature. Philosophers of consciousness (for example, G. W. F. Hegel) have bequeathed to contemporary theology a metaphysically burdened idea of the Spirit that has little purchase on the role of the Spirit in creation as the power of unity between all natural kinds. The wager of this book is that a rhetorical understanding of the Spirit (beyond the categories of being) can provide resources for confronting the cultural and environmental violence that marks our time.

My basic source for a life-centered portrait of the Spirit is the Bible. I use the scriptures to craft a postmetaphysical model of the Spirit in the struggle for social justice and ecological renewal. I note, however, that since the Bible is *conflicted* about its depictions of the divine life—God is alternately portrayed as healing and life-giving, on the one hand, and as capricious and judgmental, on the other—a biblically informed pneumatology must guard against an overly positive and one-sided view of the Spirit's ministry of renewal and reconciliation. Throughout the Gospels, for example, the Spirit is figured as empowering Jesus' followers to live in solidarity with the poor and oppressed. But this is not the whole story when it comes to the Spirit in the Bible. In Acts, for example, the Spirit is portrayed in a different light as a terrifying judge who condemns to death two renegade disciples, Ananias and Sapphira, for their lying and disobedience. A well-rounded understanding of the Spirit for our time must account for the Spirit's Janus-faced role as both healing and exacerbating the plight of victims within the stories of the Bible. Unfortunately, however, the virtual absence of discussion about this double-edged portrait of the Holy Spirit in the current literature is symptomatic, I fear, of a studied ignorance concerning the "dark side" of the divine life within contemporary theology.[1]

The idea of the Spirit has existed in the borderlands of the academy since Hegel's masterful but flawed attempts to subsume all philosophical inquiry under this rubric. Recent studies of the nature of Spirit (or spirit) have reawakened Hegel's concern, but both conventional usage of and residual philosophical prejudice against spirit-language have prevented an overturning of the traditional biases.[2] "In Western theology and philosophy the very

---

1. The exceptions to this trend are the work of feminist biblical and theological scholarship, and post-Holocaust Jewish thought. See, for example, Phyllis Trible, *Texts of Terror: Literary-Feminist Readings of Biblical Narratives* (Philadelphia: Fortress Press, 1984); and Arthur Cohen, *The Tremendum: A Theological Interpretation of the Holocaust* (New York: Crossroad, 1988). In both cases, these analysts have critiqued the biblical God of terror and abandonment as a deity whose credibility must be radically questioned in a violent and unfeeling universe. This suspicion toward the God of the Bible has had little impact on contemporary Christian theology, however. My hunch is that the theological silence on this point is an index to the uneasy conscience many Christian thinkers feel over the embarrassing malevolence characteristic of the divine life within the Bible.

2. A number of recent texts have initiated recoveries of discourse about "spirit," "the Spirit," or "the spiritual" in a variety of genres. In theology, see Michael Welker, *God the Spirit*, trans. John F. Hoffmeyer (Minneapolis: Fortress Press, 1994); Peter C. Hodgson, *Winds of the Spirit: A Constructive Christian Theology* (Louisville: Westminster John Knox Press, 1994); Elizabeth A. Johnson, *She Who Is: The Mystery of God in Feminist Theological Discourse* (New York: Crossroad, 1992); Jürgen Moltmann, *God in Creation: A New Theology of Creation and*

concept of 'spirit' has for the most part been fraught with difficulties, convey-
ing something vapid and dualistic, implying a separation of and a hierarchy
between the mental and the physical, the soul and the body, the human and
the natural, the male and the female, the holy and the profane."³ Discourse
about spirit remains saddled with ethereal and pejorative connotations, con-
juring images of ghosts, phantoms, and other incorporeal forces; of vaporous
clouds and gaseous substances; of whatever is airy, immaterial, invisible, non-
substantial, bloodless, bodiless, passionless, and unearthly.

A nature-based pneumatology challenges these conventional assumptions
by figuring the Spirit, in the economies of confronting violence and healing
the earth, as a living embodied being who works for healthy communities
within our shared planet home. An ecological pneumatology that is right for
the current crisis will recapture the disorienting freedom of the Spirit as a wild
and insurgent natural force in the healing of human persons' violence toward
nature and one another. As the divine wind in Genesis, the dove in the
Gospels, or the tongues of flame in Acts, the Spirit reveals herself in the biblical literatures as a *life-form* who labors to create, sustain, and renew humans
and otherkind in solidarity with one another. An earth-based understanding
of the Spirit will not domesticate the Spirit by locating her activity simply
alongside nature; rather, nature itself in all its variety and diversity will be
construed as the primary mode of being for the Spirit's work in the world. In
this framework, the earth's waters and winds and birds and fires will be
regarded not merely as *symbols* of the Spirit, but rather as sharing in her very
being as the Spirit is enfleshed and embodied through natural organisms and
processes.⁴

---

the Spirit of God, trans. Margaret Kohl (San Francisco: Harper & Row, 1985); idem, *The Spirit
of Life: A Universal Affirmation,* trans. Margaret Kohl (Minneapolis: Fortress Press, 1992); and
José Comblin, *The Holy Spirit and Liberation,* trans. Paul Burns (Maryknoll, N.Y.: Orbis
Books, 1989); in philosophy, see Jacques Derrida, *Of Spirit: Heidegger and the Question,* trans.
Geoffrey Bennington and Rachel Bowlby (Chicago: University of Chicago Press, 1989); and
Steven G. Smith, *The Concept of the Spiritual: An Essay in First Philosophy* (Philadelphia:
Temple University Press, 1988); and in cultural studies, see Joel Kovel, *History and Spirit: An
Inquiry into the Philosophy of Liberation* (Boston: Beacon Press, 1991).

3. Hodgson, *Winds of the Spirit,* 276.

4. A note on some issues of style. I have capitalized "Spirit" throughout in order to distinguish the divine personality (Holy Spirit or Spirit of the Lord) from other similar spirit-term
significations (spirit of the times, public spirit, and so forth). I also use the female pronoun for
the Spirit in order rhetorically to realize aspects of the transgressive freedom the Spirit promises,
including the freedom to complicate and confuse her/his/its gender. This complication is not
original to me: the term for Spirit in Hebrew is feminine (*rûah*), neuter in Greek (*pneuma*), and

Part of the burden of this book will be to demonstrate that the Spirit is the power of revolutionary transgression. I believe that the Spirit forges unity among enemies and opposites by eradicating the dysfunctional differences that define personal and communal identity. Like a purgative fire, the Spirit empowers her followers to disrupt many of the classification systems and secure structures that have ensured stable social identity since time immemorial. Most societies fear a loss of hierarchy and distinctions; they live by separations and divisions and fear intermixing of opposites at all costs. Stable societies fear change and often persecute the "dangerous" person or groups "responsible" for disrupting the normal order and rendering indeterminate and undefinable the structures that have been culturally sacrosanct since *illo tempore.* "Danger lies in transitional states, simply because transition is neither one state nor the next, it is undefinable. The person who must pass from one to another is himself in danger and emanates danger to others."[5]

Some persons, however, feel prompted by the Spirit to violate and crisscross the time-honored limits that unjustly separate and define many social groups even though such transgressions unleash the nightmare of non-differentiation among societies that rely on guaranteed boundaries for their internal cohesion. In this vein, René Girard maintains that it is not the *preservation* of cultural differences and classifications but their *eradication* that leads to social chaos. Fundamental challenges to the cultural order dissolve the critical distinctions that societies rely on for organizing their social space.[6] Girard argues that any change in the hierarchical systems of difference between, for example, the pure and the impure, or the normal and the abnormal, upsets social equilibrium and inevitably results in violent attempts to reinscribe the differences and restore order. Many who follow the Spirit, however, are intentional about challenging the social order's false and debilitating systems of difference—even at great cost to themselves. For these risk-takers, to follow the Spirit's promptings is to enact category-confusing values and

---

masculine in Latin (*spiritus*) and its derivative Romance languages. On the history of woman-identified language for the Spirit, see Gary Steven Kinkel, *Our Dear Mother the Spirit: An Investigation of Count Zinzendorf's Theology and Praxis* (Lanham, Md.: University Press of America, 1990); and Johnson, *She Who Is,* 128–31. Finally, I refer to divine, human, and nonhuman realities simultaneously as "life-forms" or "natural beings" in order to signal the value of construing all entities as interdependent members of a common biotic community.

5. Mary Douglas, *Purity and Danger: An Analysis of the Concepts of Pollution and Taboo* (London: Routledge, Ark Paperbacks, 1966), 96.

6. See René Girard, *Violence and the Sacred,* trans. Patrick Gregory (Baltimore: Johns Hopkins University Press, 1977), 39–88.

life-styles that challenge and undermine the dominant order. To follow the Spirit's revolutionary promptings is to risk living a liminal existence vulnerable to attack by mainstream members of society who bitterly resist the mixing of opposites and the crossing of cultural boundaries.

From the perspective of ecological pneumatology, persons who are bearers of the Spirit's nature-based desire for the integrity of *all* biotic populations blur the human/nonhuman distinction and thereby engender what Girard calls a "muddy mass" or Kristeva a "transitional swarming" that undermines the taxonomic hierarchies of anthropocentric thought and practice.[7] Responding to the subversive earth-love of the Spirit, prophets of biocentrism challenge our regnant sense of biological order in the name of biotic equality: all natural entities possess *equal* value and worth and should be allowed to exercise their *full* potential with minimal human interference. Followers of the Spirit challenge the received system of distinctions that classify some life-forms as valuable, pure, and sacred and others as worthless, unclean, and profane. Inevitably, however, persons who question the normative pattern are labeled dangerous outsiders and threats to social, even cosmic, order. They are vulnerable to the charge of sowing confusion and disorder by dismantling the common assumptions and forms of social organization that support and maintain human dominance over other living things. But I argue here that the Spirit's distinctive work is to do just that: namely, blur customary boundaries, challenge life-denying taxonomies, promote unity among all species, and thereby set free new patterns of reciprocity and cobelonging in spite of the danger to the web of beliefs and institutions that have bound human societies together for generations.

In historic Christian thought the work of the Holy Spirit has always been understood in terms of communion, mutuality, and the overcoming of divisions. The early Latin fathers conceived of the Spirit in the bosom of the Trinity as the divine power that unites the Father and the Son in a bond of mutual love. Basil of Caesarea wrote that the Holy Spirit is the agent of inseparable union within the Trinity. The Spirit labors alongside the Creator and the Redeemer as the Perfector who strengthens and completes the divine work of salvation in the world.[8] Similarly, Augustine analyzed the role of the Spirit in terms of the *vinculum caritatis* or the *vinculum Trinitatis*, the communion

---

7. Girard, *Violence and the Sacred*, 51; Julia Kristeva, "Semiotics of Biblical Abomination," in *Powers of Horror: An Essay on Abjection*, trans. Leon S. Roudiez (New York: Columbia University Press, 1982), 109.

8. Basil of Caesarea *De Spiritu Sancto* bk. 16.

that binds the other two members of the Godhead together in dynamic unity.[9] The Spirit enables the mutual indwelling of each divine person in the other. Moreover, as the bond of peace and love universal, the Spirit is the power of relation not only between the other members of the Trinity but also between God and the whole creation.

Later medieval iconographers make a similar point but in a pictorial medium. The doctrine of the Spirit as the *vinculum caritatis* is graphically set forth in the trinitarian miniatures of the medieval *Rothschild Canticles,* in which the Spirit is pictured as a giant encircling "dove" whose wings enfold the Father and Son, and whose large talons and tail provide points of intersection for all three figures. In the *Canticles* the Spirit is represented less like the domesticated birds or pigeons of traditional church art than like the wild raptors of the mountain wildernesses. The Spirit-Bird in the *Canticles* spins and twirls the other two members of the Godhead into amorous and novel combinations and permutations. As the *Canticles* progress, each life-form within the Trinity loses its separate identity in a blur of erotic passion and movement and color. As the Trinity twists and turns into surprising recombinations, the human Father and Son smile and twirl and dance around the aviary Spirit, symbolizing the union of each figure in the sacred bird—as well as the union of all life-forms in a common biotic order.[10]

According to the patristic authors and later medieval art, the Spirit ensures the interrelationship of each divine person in perichoretic harmony.[11] Likewise in the economies of creation and salvation, the Spirit is regarded as "the Lord, the Giver of Life" (so the Creed), who as wind or dove or *charism* is the power of innovation and fecundity in creation. The Spirit's goal is to transform and renew all life-forms by healing pain and division within communities that have broken apart. Eternally giving of herself, the Spirit is the life-restoring breath of God who mediates differences with an eye toward mutuality and reciprocity. Thus, as the Spirit exists perichoretically within the Godhead to foster communion between the divine persons, so the Spirit

---

9. Augustine *De Trinitate* bk. 15.

10. For reproductions and commentary, see Jeffrey F. Hamburger, *The Rothschild Canticles: Art and Mysticism in Flanders and the Rhineland Circa 1300* (New Haven: Yale University Press, 1990), 118–42. I am grateful to Ellen Ross for directing my attention to this volume.

11. *Perichoresis* is the doctrine that teaches the coinherence of each member of the Trinity in each other. For a fuller discussion of this term and its relevance to contemporary theology, see Catherine Mowry LaCugna, *God For Us: The Trinity and Christian Life* (San Francisco: HarperSanFrancisco, 1991), 270–78.

comes to us "with healing in its wings" (Malachi 4:2) in order to restore unity and cooperation between all living things.

OUTLINE OF THE PROJECT

This book is made up of two parts. After chapter 1, where I make a case for the rhetorical nature of theology in a postmodern culture, Part One is broadly methodological and consists of an initial articulation of God as Spirit beyond the philosophical categories of metaphysics and empiricism. My overriding concern is to defend a *performative* understanding of theological truth-claims in which the ascription of "truth" to a belief or practice in religion is deemed valid whenever the belief or practice enables commitment to the welfare of the other. I ask, Can a recovery of the idea of Spirit avoid the impasse of understanding truth either in terms of the metaphysical quest for absolutes or in terms of the historicist judgment that all claims to truth are exercises in personal preference and nothing more? My question is whether one can responsibly wager belief in the Spirit even though the reality of the Spirit is neither a deliverance of universal reason, on the one hand, nor a defensible idea within neoempiricist philosophy, on the other.

In chapter 2, I consider how some analysts seek to reestablish theological reflection on the basis of a metaphysics of human subjectivity (for example, Schubert Ogden), while others maintain that it is impossible to talk about transcendence (and notions like Spirit) after the death of the metaphysically certain God of Christian theism (for example, Richard Rorty). In the space between these two approaches, I use in chapter 3 Wittgenstein's, Levinas's, and Kierkegaard's practice-based philosophies as models for tracing the interior work of the Spirit in the journey toward self-understanding and other-regard. Insofar as the Spirit in biblical literature is said to "blow where it wills," the Spirit is a never guaranteed but always potential aid in working toward the "performance of the truth," that is, caring for the self and other life-forms.

The book's major transition occurs between Parts One and Two, where my interest shifts from a general study of claims to truth in theology to a concrete analysis of a body of particular claims concerning the role of the Spirit in the current situation. Specifically, Part Two moves to a substantive analysis of the problem of violence in contemporary culture from the perspective of a non-sacrificial and earth-centered notion of the Spirit. The topics that are studied in each chapter of Part Two—violence against other people (chapter 4), violence against the earth (chapter 5), and the problem of divine violence in the Bible (chapter 6)—form a theological triptych that is centered by a life-affirming portrait of the Spirit.

Chapter 4 analyzes René Girard's theory concerning the foundation and unity of culture and religion in the play between desire and violence. Girard maintains that the basic human drive to own or imitate what the other person has or is—what he calls "mimetic desire"—inevitably threatens to tear apart a society by fomenting unchecked rivalry between individuals and groups. Eventually, however, the threat of cultural disorder is contained by the society's invention of a "scapegoat" who is said to be the cause of its problems. Convenient scapegoats are those individuals (Jesus, Martin Luther King, Jr.) or groups (poor people of color, persons with AIDS) that are perceived to be a "threat" to the society's collective identity because they are marginal to and different from its sense of hierarchy and order. Since violence toward the outsider initially checks the corrosion of mimetic rivalry by reuniting (at least temporarily) warring factions under a common sacrificial vision, such violence is a permanent fixture of all world cultures.

Girard's pessimistic thesis is balanced by his writings about the Spirit, the God of Victims, who in the Bible advocates on behalf of the scapegoats who are unjustly accused of creating social chaos. In the Christian Gospels the Spirit empowers Jesus and others to risk lives of nonviolent compassion for the other in opposition to the culture's structures of domination. I suggest that this construal of the Spirit as the defender of victims contains critical moral and spiritual resources for responding to the needs of oppressed communities in today's world.

Biblical religion postulates the Spirit as the dynamic life-giving force within the universe. "In the beginning, God created the heavens and the earth . . . and the Spirit of God hovered over the waters" (Genesis 1:1, 2). In chapter 5, I suggest that whereas historic Western religious thought defined nature as the object of humankind's domination and control, ecological pneumatology construes humankind and otherkind as members of a common ecosystem in which no one species (including the human species) is more valuable and worthy of protection than another. Since all life-forms possess intrinsic worth as embodiments of the Creator Spirit, the traditional idea of Christian "stewardship" of nature must be challenged in the contemporary setting. I consider the nonanthropocentric theologies in the Genesis creation story, the book of Job, and John Muir's writings as alternatives to the ideal of so-called "resource conservation" (that is, managing nature as a consumable "resource" to meet human needs) within mainstream religious environmentalism. This earth-centered approach figures all beings as temporary sojourners within fragile bioregions; it avoids defining human beings as stewards who have the right to arrogate to themselves the role of adjudicating how the earth and its bounty are to be used and developed.

Chapter 4 makes reference to the corrosive effects of interpersonal mimetic violence, while chapter 5 addresses the legacy of earth violence. In chapter 6, I turn again to the problem of violence, but now by way of analyzing the problem of evil in biblical wisdom discourse. I argue that biblical wisdom provides a "therapeutic" resource for confronting the question of how evil flourishes in a world purportedly under the governance of a good God. Christian theology has generally offered two responses to the problem of evil: either evil is rationalized as a necessary condition for moral growth and maturity, or it is devalued as a momentary aberration within God's master plan of reconciling all things to the divine order. I use Richard Swinburne's work as an expression of the first tack, and Ronald Thiemann's for the second approach. I maintain in dialogue with Paul Ricoeur and some post-Holocaust theologians (such as Arthur Cohen) that the tenacity of certain forms of recalcitrant violence and evil is not adequately addressed by the two standard approaches. Instead of a philosophical *solution* to the problem of unjust suffering, I offer a practical *response* to evil in terms of catharsis, anger, protest, and irony. This response is drawn from the vocabulary of biblical wisdom writings in which the figure of the agonistic contestant—the one who struggles with and against God—is retrieved in the face of the absurdity of unmerited violence and suffering. While the Spirit is generally not explicitly thematized in biblical wisdom discourse, I suggest that a "sapiential sensibility" is an important resource for recovering the presence of the Spirit in a world fragmented by gratuitous evil.

The Spirit is the divine healer who consistently insinuates herself into situations where renewal and rehabilitation are chronically needed. By empowering the erasure of false boundaries between self and other, the Spirit seeks to overcome the systematic distortions that define contemporary culture. As the breath of God who animates all life, the Spirit becomes present in the spaces opened up between persons who risk themselves for the other. "Spirit is not in the I but between I and You. It is not like the blood that circulates in you but like the air in which you breathe."[12] To say with Martin Buber that the Spirit is "not in the I but between I and You" is to say, as Peter Hodgson puts it, that

---

12. Martin Buber, *I and Thou*, trans. Walter Kaufmann (New York: Scribners, 1970), 89.

the Spirit is an *emergent* reality.[13] The Spirit is not a static entity but a potential modality of divine presence that becomes actual in the co-partnerships of persons with one another and other life-forms. In general, the Spirit does not gate-crash into reality but rather becomes present whenever persons create mutually open spaces for the Spirit to inhabit. These open spaces are generated by persons who intentionally nurture a bound(ary)less desire for the integrity of the other person and the other life-form. In this gesture of openness, the ego boundaries a person uses to insulate herself from others break down, and the self passes over, as it were, into the reality of the other. Outside approved cultural limits and in-spir(it)ed in the margins of dynamic openness to the other, one gives of oneself to the other in an attitude of reciprocity, coparticipation, and joy.

13. Hodgson, *Winds of the Spirit,* 46–50, 171–72.

PART ONE

Methodological Overtures

CHAPTER ONE

Theology, Rhetoric, and Postmodernism

WRITING THE SPIRIT

This book is a wager on the possibility of transcendence. It is a wager on the belief that all life is charged with the presence of the Spirit, and that a life so understood carries the promise of renewal in a world at risk. I am well aware, however, of the naïveté of such hope. I am aware that such hope can easily degenerate into the false comfort of otherworldly promises of salvation and render one incapable of finding meaning in one's here-and-now endeavors. I am aware, for example, of Nietzsche's telling denunciations of religious belief as flight into the "false world" of the Platonic Beyond—a flight that leads one away from the "true world" of everyday existence. But I am also intrigued by Nietzsche's own deconstructions of his antitheological rhetoric —his calls for new "festivals of atonement and sacred games" that the person-against-the-mob can perform through a life lived with singular attention to one's innermost drives and desires.[1] I am intrigued by Nietzsche's attempts to craft a religion of earth-wisdom that eschews the virulent hostility to nature and the body promulgated by repressive Jewish and Christian priestcraft. "I beseech you, my brothers, *remain faithful to the earth*, and do not believe those who speak to you of otherworldly hopes! Poison-mixers are they, whether they know it or not. Despisers of life are they, decaying and poisoned themselves, of whom the earth is weary: so let them go."[2]

1. Friedrich Nietzsche, *The Gay Science*, trans. Walter Kaufmann (New York: Random House, 1974), 125.
2. Friedrich Nietzsche, "Thus Spoke Zarathustra," in *The Portable Nietzsche*, ed. and trans. Walter Kaufmann (New York: Viking Press, 1980), 125.

A book that wagers on the Spirit must pass through and not around thinkers such as Nietzsche. Nietzsche puts to us the question whether there can be a spirituality that is earth-centered, sensual, and passionate, or whether apprenticeship to the Spirit must always remain freighted with body-hating and world-denying beliefs and practices. *Can a life lived out of one's deepest instinctual passions coexist with belief in a divine Other? Can belief in God give depth and meaning to one's this-worldly endeavors?* Nietzsche himself is provocatively conflicted on this question. He alternately decries the debilitating dualisms of anti-body and otherworldly religion while still invoking the need for a joyous, spontaneous, iconoclastic, and earthy spirituality that allows one to live according to the dictates of one's own root impulses rather than the moral codes sacralized by religious authorities. It is this Nietzschean conflict that generates the unstable hope that I labor under in this project: the fragile experience of *epiphany* in my encounters with certain works of art, the partial sense that some *power* underlies the rhythms of nature, the uncomfortable feeling of being *addressed* by an obligation greater than myself in my relations with others. In these discrete realms of experience—art, nature, ethics—I am brought up short by a vision or a presence or a voice that I can neither fully affirm nor easily deny.

As a *wager*, my argument is directed to readers who are willing to risk a thought experiment concerning a possibility that is unlikely if not impossible for many in our culture. And as a wager on the *Spirit*, it is aimed at the reader's self-conscious or latent desire for belonging to a meaningful whole in a world seemingly evacuated of divine presence. Certainly for readers who have decided that such a wager is an exercise in false consciousness the bet is off, and both parties, those who risk the thought experiment and those who do not, go their separate ways. In writing this book, however, I have tried not to divide potential readers into "believers" and "nonbelievers," nor, by the same token, have I sought to paper over important individual differences by insisting that, in the long run, we are all in communion with the Spirit, whether we realize it or not, by virtue of an innate transcendental knowledge of God that we all share. To make the first move is to be unnecessarily divisive, while the second gesture is theologically imperialistic. Most of us, I suspect, would situate ourselves somewhere in the middle of the spectrum between belief and unbelief. Like the father of the epileptic boy in the Gospel who, when confronted with Jesus' potential to heal his son, cries out "I believe; help my unbelief!" many of us are tethered between possibility and doubt, hope and despair, vision and confusion.

This book is an attempt to *write* the meaning of the Spirit for a world on edge. What does it mean for the Spirit to be present in and to all life-forms in a shared struggle for a just and sustainable future? On one level this focus places this project in a long-standing theological conversation about the nature of the Spirit and the Spirit's work in the world. But I would like this book to go beyond a discussion of theological doctrine by being a self-consciously *constructive* exercise in crafting an understanding of the Spirit that speaks directly to the cultural and environmental violence that marks our time. Where this book seeks to depart from the mainstream theological tradition is in its recognition that theology, like most other academic disciplines, is a particular type of rhetorical art that uses a variety of aesthetic conventions and imaginative tropes to figure its subject matter. As a figural activity, theology is an imaginative (rather than descriptive) activity insofar as all forms of writing (including theological writing) are imperfect mirrors that only partially reflect the realities they signify. We see through a glass darkly—even our most privileged forms of discourse are bounded by their origins in the perspectival biases of the interpreter. Such a banal claim as this should not be controversial. The point here is not to deny objectivity but to point out that objectivity is always arrived at (if at all) in a particular time and place. To say that theological knowledge is constructed and situated is to underscore its provenance in the economies of class, race, gender, and ideology that generate all systems of discourse. It is to say that there is no theory-free, detached, commonsensical, and unbiased inventory of "reality" that exists apart from the contingent perspectives of the interpreter. But as Robert Solow remarks, just because no medical operation is perfectly sterile it does not follow that all surgical procedures might as well be conducted in a sewer.[3] There is no discourse of pure innocence, theological or otherwise, but that does not mean that all language is irredeemably subjective and provincial.

As a type of writing, Christian theology is not the witness to the presence of the divine life but rather a sustained inquiry into the representations of that witness. As such it is a second-order, once-removed discipline that interprets the discourses of representation within a variety of Christian traditions. This sensibility was first initiated by Friedrich Schleiermacher's phenomenology of religion: the turn to understanding *how* the objects of religious belief are present to consciousness and away from adjudicating *whether* such objects really exist. Schleiermacher's systematic inquiries into the nature of the divine life only in relation to its bearing on religious self-consciousness signify an

---

3. Noted in Clifford Geertz, "Thick Description: An Interpretive Theory of Culture," in *The Interpretation of Cultures* (New York: Harper Basic Books, 1973), 30.

epochal change in modern theological method. His famous maxim that "Christian doctrines are accounts of the Christian religious affections set forth in speech" marks the critical shift from defining theology as providing "descriptions of," to reconceiving it as offering "interpretations about" its distinctive subject matter, God.[4] Schleiermacher's program set in motion the move away from (1) *metaphysical* questions about God's essence to (2) *phenomenal* construals of how God is experienced in the world and now to (3) *hermeneutical* inquiries into how these construals are inscribed in discourse. This does not mean that the traditional subject matter of theology is displaced by a concern with the strategies for signifying this subject matter, but it does mean that the study of the signifying process is now as important to postmodern theological reflection as the understanding of the realities to which this process refers. The question then becomes not, Does this description of God get it right? but rather, With which aesthetic devices, and under what cultural conditions, was this particular depiction of the divine life produced, and for what purpose?

The turn to examining the process of theological signification announces the space, indeed sometimes the yawning chasm, between the representations and their referents. This is especially disturbing for theologians who seek for the right "fit" between word and object—for a perfect isomorphism between signifier and signified. Such thinkers would like to establish an incorrigible test for whether this or that particular representation rightly corresponds to the reality of God. They are uncomfortable with claims concerning the embeddedness of theological discourse in culture and ideology, preferring to see themselves as something like "safely-detached observation-posts" who have the ability to articulate the right and timeless understanding of the divine life for the religious community.[5] Indeed, traditional theologians envisioned their role as adjudicators over which religious reality claims were (or were not) true to the revealed data of the Christian religion. But ongoing disputes as to the exact content and status of such putative "revealed truths," and the acknowledgment of the constructed nature of knowledge in general, have landed theology in the same epistemological quandary in which all other forms of postmodern intellectual inquiry now find themselves: by abandoning the Myth of the Given, contemporary theology, like other disciplines, is

---

4. Friedrich Schleiermacher, *The Christian Faith*, ed. H. R. MacKintosh and J. S. Stewart (Edinburgh: T. & T. Clark, 1976), 76.

5. The phrase belongs to Steven Connor in *Postmodernist Culture: An Introduction to Theories of the Contemporary* (Oxford: Basil Blackwell, 1989), 5.

seeking for a postmetaphysical, antifoundational footing upon which to base its enterprise.

The result of this search is that theology today is beginning to understand itself as a self-consciously fictive enterprise with an emancipatory intent. It is a discipline consisting of value judgments and rhetorical persuasion; it is not an argumentative calculus free from the bias of the author. It is an activity (like most intellectual disciplines) where authors have opinions and make decisions, not a (so-called) hard science in which nonpartisan observers interrogate facts and then organize their findings in a format free of interpretive bias. Contemporary theology, like contemporary postpositivist philosophy or literary theory or cultural studies, is increasingly recognizing itself to be an exercise in persuasion and pragmatics, a conversation partner in many persons' collective search for meaning and understanding, not a royal road to a reality immediately and incorrigibly self-present to the subject.

Theology, therefore, is a thoroughly *value-oriented* and *perspectival* form of reasoning; in a word, theology is *rhetoric*, that is, a mode of critical inquiry acutely aware of the literary styles and personal passions that make up particular visions of the world. Paul de Man's work on rhetoric provides a helpful analysis of the deliberative *and* imaginative character of humanistic disciplines, including the discipline of theology. In this vein, consider de Man's important distinction between figural and metafigural writing.[6] Figural works are straight-ahead poems or novels that rely on various figures of speech, while metafigural texts consist of self-reflexive (but still imaginative) writing about which figures are or are not most adequate to the subject matter at hand. The advantage of this distinction is that it preserves the poetic character of all writing while identifying the rhetorical strategies operative in metafigural, discursive writing as deliberative and adjudicative. Using this distinction, on one level theology is best described as metafigural insofar as it makes considered judgments about which figures best represent particular understandings of the divine life. On another level, however, theology is clearly figural writing *as such* because it invents tropes and manipulates modes of discourse in new ways in order to redescribe its subject matter.

Rhetorically conscious theology, then, blurs the de Manian distinction between figural and metafigural writing. More often than not, good theologians not only step back from other people's writing and decide on its merits, but they also rhetorize the whole theological writing process by making novel

---

6. Paul de Man, *Allegories of Reading: Figural Language in Rousseau, Nietzsche, Rilke, and Proust* (New Haven: Yale University Press, 1979), 14–19.

advances in conceptualizing and articulating the meaning of the Christian tradition for the current situation. As a cross-fertilization of figural and metafigural styles, de Man's point (now applied to theology) is well taken. De Man's approach allows us to recognize theology as a literary-philosophical enterprise that alternately creates original imagery *and* normatively shapes other thinkers' rhetoric into new patterns of organization and explanation.[7]

The understanding of theology as a rhetorical task has important consequences. Its object of study is now better understood as "that by which" communities of interpretation have figured their religious experience, not "that which" they have worshiped, prayed to, and adored. By characterizing theology in this way I am not saying that there is no transcendent Other who grounds existence, but simply that theology is no longer (nor was it ever) the supreme guarantor of sure access to this Other. A variety of discourses are potentially able to produce transformative life maps for the spiritually itinerant. It is the theologian's task to track these potentially transformative pathways, evaluate their origins, contours, and destinies, and help the traveler to decide whether any of these courses should be adopted as productive routes toward growth and understanding. But if theology is a cartographical enterprise, so to speak, then it should remember that the map is not the territory.[8] The territory is not the proper domain of the theologian but is rather the "promised land" to which the discourses she studies and adopts are avowedly directed. There may or may not be a final territory on the other side of existence—and only faith can secure the knowledge that there is such a place—but there are a plethora of road maps for the journey ahead and the theologian can serve as a spirited conversation partner along the way.

POSTMODERN PRESUPPOSITIONS

Construing the theological task as a rhetorical discipline serves as a challenge to the traditional understanding of normative theological discourse. In this section, I lay out the baseline presuppositions that have formed the back-

---

7. For discussions of the rhetorical character of theology, see Stephen H. Webb, *Re-figuring Theology: The Rhetoric of Karl Barth* (Albany: SUNY Press, 1991), 1–45, 149–78; Rebecca S. Chopp, *The Power to Speak: Feminism, Language, God* (New York: Crossroad, 1989), 90–98; and David E. Klemm, "Toward a Rhetoric of Postmodern Theology: Through Barth and Heidegger," *Journal of the American Academy of Religion* 55 (1987): 443–69.

8. See Jonathan Z. Smith, *Map is Not Territory: Studies in the History of Religion* (Leiden: Brill, 1978).

bone of this postmodern challenge to mainstream Western thought, including Western theology. I am in broad agreement with this challenge because I believe it offers Christian theology a productive mind-set and vocabulary for understanding the radical otherness of the divine presence in contemporary culture. Indeed, I would say that certain emphases within postmodernism provide theology today with a *praeparatio evangelica* for articulating the power and mystery of God in a world racked by chronic interhuman violence and ecological abuse.[9] Such a claim at first glance may appear at best paradoxical, since postmodernism, particularly as practiced as a type of a/theological deconstruction, is often regarded as hostile to religious belief. Indeed, many radical postmodern theologians have made the point that "*deconstruction is the 'hermeneutic' of the death of God.*"[10] On the one hand, then, deconstructive postmodernism does pose a disturbing challenge to *traditional* religious belief by virtue of its sustained argument against a transcendental signified, a stable

---

9. My case is that *some* aspects of postmodern thought can be pressed into the service of explicating contemporary religious belief and practice. The utilization of a postmodern sensibility for theological reflection is positively developed in a number of recent works. Note particularly the recent studies of the structural affinities between Derridean deconstruction, negative theology, and mysticism in Kevin Hart, *The Trespass of the Sign: Deconstruction, Theology and Philosophy* (Cambridge: Cambridge University Press, 1989); Susan A. Handelman, *The Slayers of Moses: The Emergence of Rabbinic Interpretation in Modern Literary Theory* (Albany: SUNY Press, 1982), 15–25, 123–78; Jean-Luc Marion, *God Without Being: Hors-Texte*, trans. Thomas A. Carlson (Chicago: University of Chicago Press, 1991), 53–107; Joseph S. O'Leary, *Questioning Back: The Overcoming of Metaphysics in Christian Tradition* (Minneapolis: Winston Press, 1985), 1–55, 156–61; John D. Caputo, *Radical Hermeneutics: Repetition, Deconstruction, and the Hermeneutic Project* (Bloomington, Ind.: Indiana University Press, 1987), 95–206, 268–94; and the articles by Toby Foshay, Michel Despland, Mark C. Taylor, and Morny Joy in *Derrida and Negative Theology*, ed. Howard Coward and Toby Foshay (Albany: SUNY Press, 1992). Derrida himself has explored the structural relationship between deconstruction and apophatic thought, though he rejects the essentially positive presumption of classical negative theology that God is a hyperessential reality without "Being." See Derrida, "Of An Apocalyptic Tone Newly Adopted in Philosophy" and "How To Avoid Speaking: Denials," in *Derrida and Negative Theology*, ed. Coward and Foshay, 25–71, 73–142.

10. Mark C. Taylor, *Erring: A Postmodern A/theology* (Chicago: University of Chicago Press, 1984), 6. In this vein, see also *Deconstruction and Theology*, ed. Thomas J. J. Altizer (New York: Crossroad, 1982); and Charles E. Winquist, *Epiphanies of Darkness: Deconstruction in Theology* (Philadelphia: Fortress Press, 1986). The position of the a/theologians that radical deconstruction is generally inimical to religious belief has been similarly argued by other authors, though for different reasons. See Ernest Gellner, *Postmodernism, Reason and Religion* (London: Routledge, 1992); and George Steiner, *Real Presences* (Chicago: University of Chicago Press, 1989).

center, a "God" that can secure the loss of presence and the freeplay of meaning. On the other hand, however, deconstruction embodies the promise of a countermetaphysical and nontotalizing approach to religious faith that resists the temptation to secure faith on the basis of a philosophical foundation. In this sense, deconstruction is best understood not as a pernicious nihilism at war with the possibility of faith but as an exercise in philosophical hygiene that serves to purify theology of its perennial quest for metaphysical security. My contention, therefore, is that postmodernism is best understood when positioned dialectically in relation to theology: postmodernism is both a resource for criticizing the nostalgia for unmediated presence in theology, and an ally in thematizing the possibility of God beyond the categories of traditional philosophy and metaphysics.

By patiently tracking the heterogeneity and alterity that underlie our culture's privileged texts and philosophies, postmodern thought has created intellectual space for the theological claim that there may be a divine Other, beyond our categories of understanding, who indwells all living things. To live and love in openness to the possibility of such an Other is not an expression of longing for pure presence but rather a willingness to acknowledge the (im)possibility of a Wholly Other beyond "Being," even beyond "God." I call this Other the "Spirit" in critical fidelity to the Christian tradition and in dialogue with the attention to alterity so characteristic of postmodern discourse.

Insofar as postmodern thought takes issue with the basic classical and Enlightenment axioms that have undergirded Western thought and culture, it is a resource for constructing a postmetaphysical model of the Spirit sensitive to the crises that define our era. In what follows I articulate a number of my presuppositions, indebted to postmodernism, as a preamble to the book's overall argument. These presuppositions are discussed in terms of five interwoven rubrics: the erasure of the stable self, the deprivileging of the metaphysics of light, the breakdown of totalizing narratives, the restoration of value to nature, and the failure of theodicy. The articulation of these rubrics at this point in the argument provides the baseline for my subsequent understanding of the Spirit as an agent of transformation in a world characterized by violence and ecological degradation.

Erasure of Self

Ancient and classical thought begins with the assumption that there is a permanent, reliable, interior entity called the "self" which has direct access to the visible world of objects and the invisible world of God or Mind. Whether by way of Neoplatonic emanation or the decree of Yahweh, the self is created out of (or by) the divine essence (or voice), is always already in relationship with the divine; and it is in return to God that the self discovers its true nature and destiny. This *exitus-reditus* schema is the master narrative of the Christian West: the ideal of authentic selfhood is to discover (whether through philosophical analysis or spiritual practice) the return path back to the Source from which the self originated. As the privileged site of transcendence, the awakening of the true self in the interior life of the individual is the assumed goal of all classical philosophical theories of moral formation.[11]

That such a powerful and all-encompassing perspective could be questioned, even abandoned, by contemporary thinkers is an index to the breakdown of the regnant theories of personhood in the West since the time of the Greeks. In fact, many persons today are as likely to embrace the non-Western, Buddhist idea of the no-self (*anatta*), in which there is no entitative noumenal ego that underlies human beings, as they are to accept the normative discourse about an occult substratum anterior to all particular individuals. Indeed, the Buddhist provenance of the no-self idea does not undermine its appeal in the late capitalist West because the credibility of such non-Western ideas rises in inverse proportion to the decline of the intellectual and cultural plausibility structures that once supported the traditional model. Disillusionment with the Platonic and Augustinian orientation has set in motion the "Pacific shift" toward more nonsubstantive and less atomistic understandings of personhood.[12] The West is enduring a legitimation crisis of historic dimensions, and the growing dissatisfaction with traditional Western philosophy and patterns of social organization has become the negative condition for many persons' attraction to Asian philosophies of personal identity.

The Buddhist *anatta* doctrine and corollary idea that the "self" is always interdependently "arising" have deep resonances with postmodern notions of intersubjectivity and its criticisms of the entitative Cartesian subject. The elective affinities between these two positions—Buddhism and postmodernism— deepen the appeal of both thought currents and widen their distinct but related credibility bases. The conclusion of both perspectives is the same: there is no essentialist "self" that underlies all humankind; selfhood, rather, is an ongoing task that requires the active construction of a life by each individual.

11. See Plato *Phaedrus* 245–59; and Augustine *The Confessions* 7–10.
12. See William Irwin Thompson, "Pacific Shift," in *Nature in Asian Traditions of Thought: Essays in Environmental Philosophy*, ed. J. Baird Callicott and Roger T. Ames (Albany: SUNY Press, 1989), 25–36.

The quest for a universal core "self" or "mind" that can provide incorrigible access to reality has been abandoned by poststructuralist theory (even as it was by historic Buddhism). "There is and can be no transcendental mind; on the contrary postmodernists claim that what we call the mind or reason is only an effect of discourse. There are no immediate or indubitable features of mental life. Sense data, ideas, intentions, or perceptions are already preconstituted."[13] Since there is little evidence for the idea of a permanent mental substratum underlying the subject, the corresponding notion that the self is hardwired, so to speak, with innate ideas of goodness and justice has been difficult to justify in the light of vertiginous cultural diversity and historical consciousness. If every person possesses a deep common self that intuitively knows the nature of the "good life," then why is there such fundamental disagreement as to what constitutes this self and its best interests? If, as it now seems, diverse communities do operate with incommensurate truth-claims and moral values, are not ideas about selfhood and virtue culturally constructed rather than transcendentally self-given?

Both perspectives—that there is a noumenal self and that it is transparent upon eternal truths—are variations of *classical foundationalism*. Foundationalism is the epistemological theory that maintains that knowledge is a product of noninferential beliefs which are the basis of all other beliefs and are themselves not founded on any other beliefs.[14] The criterion for such basic beliefs is that they be immediately self-evident either to reason (for example, simple mathematical axioms or universal ideas of the just and the good) or to the senses (for example, direct perceptual experiences or facts of memory). Foundationalist assumptions provide intellectual justification for rationalist models of human nature by construing the subject as a disinterested interrogator of self-subsistent facts that are independent of theoretical frameworks. But the collapse of confidence in philosophical rationalism has opened up considerable space for newer (postmodern) vocabularies about personal identity and social organization that run counter to the once-dominant assumptions. Today we seem less and less convinced that we are free, rational "monads" who have direct access to a self-evident and/or empirically given body of truths that can be used as an incorrigible philosophical foundation for understanding all reality. Our time is marked by an erosion of

13. Jane Flax, *Thinking Fragments: Psychoanalysis, Feminism, and Postmodernism in the Contemporary West* (Berkeley: University of California Press, 1990), 35.

14. See Alvin Plantinga, "Reason and Belief in God," in *Faith and Rationality: Reason and Belief in God*, ed. Alvin Plantinga and Nicholas Wolterstorff (Notre Dame: University of Notre Dame Press, 1983), 44–63.

confidence in the atomistic subject who stands in ready openness to the transcendental ideas of beauty, truth, and justice that float free of the culture and history each of us inhabits.

In a culture increasingly characterized by perspectivalism and historicism, the supreme self of the West has been humbled, if not extinguished altogether, by the antitotalizing impulses of postmetaphysical thought and global (non-Western) cultures. In postmodernism, the self is a *relay* for the exchange of conflicting discourses, not a stable *site* of timeless transcendence. The self is a dynamic within an artistic process where it must craft and script its own identity in its regular commerce with the cultures and languages it inhabits. The self is a social construct, a product of its various relationships, not a preexisting interior reality.[15] It exists in a complex web of discourses and relationships and is continually challenged to remake itself in this web without the benefit of any epistemic foundations on which to ground this creative process. Here the self does not discover itself once and for all by locating its return path back to the source, but by inventing itself daily in its interactions with the discursive practices and exercises of power within which it is constituted.

Deprivileging of Metaphysics

The theory of illumination is the second axiom of Western thought that is questioned by the current climate. Insofar as Anglo-European philosophy is founded on its Greek origins, it has operated in accord with a metaphysics of light. Reality—dumb and dark—is illuminated by the light of the agent intellect which itself is a participation in the Active Intellect of God. Originating in the divine intelligence, the human mind assimilates to its categories of understanding any object that can be comprehended. It renders transparent the other under the limpid horizon of consciousness by representing what was novel and distant as familiar and proximate.

Postmodernism maintains constant opposition to such metaphysical theories of illumination because they violently subject the alterity and integrity of the other to the luminous grasping of the knowing subject. Though very different in other respects, both Emmanuel Levinas and Jacques Derrida argue against the violence of metaphysics: the suppression of difference by assimilating the novelty of the other to the self's conceptual activity. Classical epistemology argues that the other can only be known—made visible—through

---

15. See Kenneth J. Gergen, *The Saturated Self: Dilemmas of Identity in Contemporary Life* (New York: Basic Books, 1991).

the natural light of the agent intellect. But if the other in its unforeseeable strangeness can only become intelligible on the basis of its being illuminated by my intellect, then the other is always captive to my theoretical, categorizing, homogenizing activity. The theory of illumination posits a "horizon within which alterity is amortized as soon as it is announced precisely because it has let itself be foreseen. [But] the infinitely-other cannot be bound by a concept, cannot be thought on the basis of a horizon; for a horizon is always a horizon of the same. . . ."[16] The problem with the classical model is that because the other must first submit itself to the subject's organizing activity, no eruptions of radical alterity and novelty are permitted since they cannot be contained within the horizon of consciousness.

The metaphysics of light is the metaphysics of totality. Light is the medium that allows whatever is to presence itself to the knower; it illuminates the "mind's eye" so that it can "see" the world.[17] This ocular operation binds the other to the knower's luminous horizon—and in so doing the other is reduced to the same. This model neutralizes radical alterity by positing a common ontological reciprocity between self and other. But for postmodernism there is no reconciliatory third term or analogy of being that mediates the other's exteriority by bringing it under the control of a middle category. "This mode of depriving the known being of its alterity can be accomplished only if it is aimed at through a third term, a neutral term, which itself is not a being; in it the shock of the encounter of the same with the other is deadened."[18] The other resists all categories, all middles, all possessive strategies under the banner of "being," "light," "spirit," "the inbetween," or "God." Kant's common root between sensibility and intuitions, or Hegel's inevitable return of the self to its origins through *Geist*—all such mediatorial strategies encompass and attenuate the freedom and particularity of the other under the canopy of the same, the common, the knowable, the universal.

If the mind is a mirror that accurately represents the world, then truth consists in the correspondence of thought with its object. Truth is a property of statements that correctly apprehend (or "match") the realities they signify. The problem with such a correspondence theory of truth, however, is that it

16. Jacques Derrida, "Violence and Metaphysics," in *Writing and Difference*, trans. Alan Bass (Chicago: University of Chicago Press, 1978), 95.

17. For an analysis of the development of visual metaphors for understanding the mind as a "mirror" in the history of Western philosophy, see Richard Rorty, *Philosophy and the Mirror of Nature* (Princeton: Princeton University Press, 1979), 1–164, 357–94.

18. Emmanuel Levinas, *Totality and Infinity*, trans. Alphonso Lingis (Pittsburgh: Duquesne University Press, 1969), 42.

cannot account for the interpretive and perspectival nature of experience. There are no apprehensions of the world free of the control of a particular description; there are no immediate perceptual givens apart from the conceptual frameworks that make all knowledge possible in the first place. The alternative to classical epistemology is to allow space for disclosures and displacements in one's experience that resist and defy the categorizing limitations of the luminous mind. The alternative is to permit creativity and otherness in one's commerce with the world even if the realization of such possibilities overturns the received categories of understanding. The alternative, in sum, is to refuse to foreclose possibilities in experience that might challenge and subvert the regnant paradigm of truth as the fit between the mind's eye and compliant reality.

Breakdown of Metanarratives

Jean-François Lyotard's notion of "incredulity toward metanarratives" is a third distinctive of postmodern culture.[19] His point is that most of us are suspicious toward the claims of our culture's once-dominant "master narratives" to explain the inner meaning of historical events. This suspicion stems, in part, from growing disenchantment with the biblical myth as the regnant narrative framework for understanding the purpose and logic of history. The overarching historical sensibility of the modern West has been a gloss on the stories of creation, exile, redemption and apocalypse as narrated in the Bible. This narrative sensibility has been undergirded by the axiomatic notions of the stable self and the illuminating mind—through our powers of reason, we all have the ability to trace the unified pattern of history amidst the change and flux of daily events. Most premodern and modern literary classics from the *Divine Comedy* and *Paradise Lost* to *Moby Dick* and *Crime and Punishment* have been variations on what Northrop Frye, borrowing from William Blake, calls the "Great Code."[20] The "Great Code" is the coherent mythological universe of the Bible that has provided Western thought with a unified temporality for interpreting the sweep of human history. Though the Bible is a compilation of disparate texts, it has traditionally been read as a unified whole; in turn, this reading has enabled history to be understood not as a

19. Jean-François Lyotard, *The Postmodern Condition: A Report on Knowledge*, trans. Geoffrey Bennington and Brian Massumi (Minneapolis: University of Minnesota Press, 1984), xxiv.
20. See Northrop Frye, *The Great Code: The Bible and Literature* (New York: Harcourt Brace Jovanovich, 1981).

cacophony of random events but as a progressive unfolding of humankind's growth toward a predetermined telos. Analogous to the biblical chronology of creation, covenant, and apocalypse, history is regarded as following a trajectory from a reliable time of origins through a coherent middle period and onward to a long-predicted destination point.

While the hegemony of the master plot for understanding historical change is questioned today, earlier nineteenth-century thinkers operated within this imaginative framework irrespective of whether they considered their projects biblical or not. Hegel conjured the trope of the "slaughter-bench" to explain that history is the sometimes violent actualization of the Idea through and in spite of the intentions of particular historical subjects.[21] And Marx argued that the revolution of the working class is a necessary precondition for the demise of the capitalist state and the formation of a utopian, classless society.[22] In both cases history is understood as possessing an interior order that rational analysis could discover and make known; once seemingly random events now "make sense" to the philosopher who knows the inner logic of historical development.

The reading of history through the template of a totalizing master plan suppresses the differences resistant to the narrative whole. The imposition of narrative coherence onto the flux of time and events denies any differences that are an exception to the inner truth that underlies the flow of history. The imposition of coherence foists false closure onto open-ended story lines, silencing the voices of those outside of the organizing myths of origin and destiny. "Like every effort to dominate, history and its narration represent a colonial enterprise. . . . Historical narration reflects the effort to ease the trauma of dislocation by weaving scattered events into a seamless web."[23] Alternatively, a postcolonial reading of history consists of sustained attention to the differences introduced by the "other" who stands outside the coherence of the master plot. Heterogeneity and alterity replace unity and identity; a new sensitivity to the local and particular replaces the quixotic hope of uncovering the supreme plot underneath the ebb and flow of events.

The specter of *violence* has always haunted the writing of master stories. The project of totalizing events betrays a repressive gesture toward the other—a gesture that subsumes the cry for freedom, the drive for individua-

21. G. W. F. Hegel, *Reason in History: A General Introduction to the Philosophy of History*, trans. Robert S. Hartman (Indianapolis: Bobbs-Merrill, 1953), 25-43.

22. Karl Marx, *Capital: A Critique of Political Economy*, trans. Samuel Moore and Edward Aveling; rev. Ernest Untermann (New York: Modern Library, 1950).

23. Taylor, *Erring*, 70-71.

tion, and the politics of identity under the universalizing logic of the supreme plot. A history without zones of indeterminacy and regions of difference finally destroys the hopes and dreams of those who do not benefit from the master plan.

> The nineteenth and twentieth centuries have given us as much terror as we can take. We have paid a high enough price for the nostalgia of the whole and the one, for the reconciliation of the concept and the sensible, of the transparent and the communicable experience. Under the general demand for slackening and for appeasement, we can hear the mutterings of the desire for a return of terror, for the realization of the fantasy to seize reality. The answer is: Let us wage a war on totality; let us be witnesses to the unpresentable; let us activate the differences and save the honor of the name.[24]

The master narratives of our time are soaked in the blood of victims. Consider the regnant American myth of redemption as a case in point. The quasi-biblical American myth is that through collective military sacrifices the covenant community is cleansed and renewed. For example, Abraham Lincoln, America's greatest civic theologian, preached a message of blood atonement to heal the wounds of civil war: the internecine conflict between North and South served the higher purpose of blotting out for a nation the great sin of slavery.[25] The American myth of redemptive violence promulgates the doctrine that the death of a few is often a prerequisite for the salvation of the many. Thus, occasional cycles of purgative violence are necessary for preserving the health and well-being of the body politic.

All those who exist on the fringes of Western culture—whether for economic, ethnic, or religious reasons—are potential victims of the American monomyth's logic that blood forges unity, that death generates life. Many such marginal persons are branded as insidious outsiders who must be quarantined, if not destroyed, in order to preserve the health of the larger whole. The high priests of the myth theologize that the good of the commonweal is best served when certain individuals volunteer, or are "picked," to sacrifice their lives for the welfare of the system. The postmodern cry against the tyranny of the whole—the cry of thinkers such as Kierkegaard, Derrida, Levinas, Lyotard, and Girard—is the cry for the integrity of individual life over and against the demands of the totality for more sacrifice and more blood. In

---

24. Lyotard, *Postmodern Condition*, 81–82.
25. See Robert N. Bellah, "Civil Religion in America," *Daedalus* 96 (1967): 1–21; idem, *The Broken Covenant: American Civil Religion in Time of Trial* (New York: Seabury Press, 1975).

this vein we will see especially in Girard that theologies of victimage *are* efficacious in forging (albeit temporarily) national and corporate unity, but that
such "unity" should be resisted *at all costs* because it traffics, quite literally, in
human flesh.

Revalorization of Nature

The metanarrative model we examined above not only marginalizes differences; it also works against the valuation of natural processes. The normative
approach operates according to a series of debilitating hierarchical oppositions: history/nature, order/chaos, progress/stagnation, unity/diffusion,
man/woman, spirit/matter. In this oppositional schema *history* is the stage
where intelligent human agents make rational decisions about the future,
while *nature* is construed as an inferior mass of directionless energy in need of
human subjugation and oversight. As understood in much of ancient philosophy and theology, and on the basis of the successes of Western technology,
nature at best is regarded as having instrumental value as a standing-reserve of
raw power for the maintenance of energy-intensive human societies.[26] While
history is viewed as malleable and receptive to the initiatives offered by reason, nature is devalued as inert and mechanical and always in need of human
stewardship. James Watt, Ronald Reagan's first Secretary of the Interior, summarized the frightening implications of this mind-set when he said that the
preservation of nature is irrelevant in the long run because environmental cataclysm is an inevitable consequence of God's master plan for history. Watt
and other fundamentalists' theocratic attitudes are extreme versions of the
well-entrenched understanding of nature as a transitory mass of dumb matter
in need of completion, if not annihilation, by God's viceroy, humankind. The
purpose of human history in harmony with the divine plan is to make perfect
the creation that remains unfulfilled.[27]

In this model, nature is devalued as brute force in relation to the rational
character of history, which is viewed as susceptible to human control. Analogously, the classical model defines *woman* as inferior to *man* because women,

26. See Martin Heidegger's well-known essay "The Question Concerning Technology," in
The Question Concerning Technology and Other Essays, ed. William Lovitt (New York: Harper
& Row, 1977), 3–35.
27. See the analysis of this mind-set in Susan Griffin, "Split Culture," in *Healing the
Wounds: The Promise of Ecofeminism*, ed. Judith Plant (Philadelphia: New Society Publishers,
1989), 7–17.

understood according to their customary procreative and domestic roles, are considered to be more "bodily" and "nature-identified" than men. Here nature or matter is "feminine" and spirit or mind is "masculine." Women are symbolized as childbearers who live according to their instinctual drives, while men are regarded as power brokers and decision makers who operate according to their linear reason.

Plato gave paradigmatic expression to this bipartite anthropology in the *Timaeus*. He figured archetypal woman as weighed down and tied to the earth because of her animal-like passion for procreative sex, while primordial man is pictured as relatively free of heavy earthly passions by virtue of the power of his nonmaterial reason, which is like God's. For Plato, woman's generative organs exercise a strong downward pull on her reason, while man tends to be a purer and relatively unsexed medium for the actualization of invisible reason.[28] "That regarding the understanding of spiritual things, women have a different nature than men, it is observed, and it is stated that women are 'intellectually like children.' That women are feebler of body and mind than men, it is said: 'Frailty, thy name is woman.'"[29] This schema was not lost on later Christian writers such as Paul or Origen or Augustine, who also at times essentialized woman as "flesh" and "other."[30]

Though both "man" and "woman" are an admixture of spirit and matter, in the final analysis body/woman is irreparably divorced from soul/man. The soul only resides temporarily in the body—a ghost in a machine—because of its otherworldly intellectual nature, which can never take permanent residence in that which is mortal and finally illusory. Correspondingly, paradigmatic man can find earthly pleasure in the woman's flesh but should guard against too intimate a union between his reasoned nature and her consuming physical drives lest his higher spiritual identity be compromised by her quintessentially bodily nature. Thus, in the normative tradition nature/woman is devalued, even inveighed against, as dumb matter/flesh to be disciplined by God's hu(man) representative.

The postmodern alternative to the classical denigration of woman, nature, and the body is the ideal of biocentrism. Biocentrism teaches that all life-forms possess intrinsic value as enfleshed members of a common biotic order,

---

28. Plato *Timaeus* 42, 89–92.

29. Susan Griffin, *Woman and Nature: The Roaring Inside Her* (New York: Harper & Row, 1978), 8.

30. See Rosemary Radford Ruether, *Sexism and God-Talk: Toward a Feminist Theology* (Boston: Beacon Press, 1983), 72–115.

and that no one species, including the human community, enjoys natural priority over any other species.[31] This model of interspecies equality entails that gendered human persons are of equal value and worth since all natural beings—plants and animals, women and men—are comembers with each other in the web of life.[32] In this model, the natural world is rehabilitated as the giver and sustainer of life itself and not devalued as mere matter to be overcome by the return of "pure reason" to its disembodied origin in the Godhead.

Failure of Theodicy

A fifth leitmotif of postmodernism is the loss of faith in the interruptive God of biblical history as the guarantor of human triumph over evil in this life and the world to come. In spite of the tenacity of systemic suffering and injustice, the classical viewpoint is that the world is justly and benignly ordered under the active governance of a compassionate God. The point of the cosmos, in short, is to enable human flourishing. Evil, therefore, is not the final word in the universe; rather, it is the Refiner's Fire wherein personal integrity and virtue are forged. Traditionally understood, the world is a proving ground for the development of character, where individuals learn the values of self-sacrifice, noble suffering, and communal responsibility through pain and misfortune. Since a necessary condition for individual moral maturity is the possibility of real moral choices with calculable consequences, God has good reason for creating a world in which these choices, for good or evil, can be realized by persons. In this schema God and world are justified—so the ideal of traditional theodicy—insofar as God is seen as the *supreme ensurer* of the development of personal growth and responsibility, and the world is regarded as the *constructive environment* within which these values can be realized.[33] Even the Bible, however, raises disturbing questions about naïve

---

31. For an early expression of this ideal within deep ecology philosophy, see Arne Naess, "The Shallow and the Deep, Long-Range Ecology Movement: A Summary," *Inquiry* 16 (1973): 95–100; also see the list of eight principles of egalitarian biocentrism in Bill Devall and George Sessions, *Deep Ecology: Living as if Nature Mattered* (Layton, Ut.: Gibbs M. Smith, 1985), chap. 5.

32. On the relationship between biocentrism and feminism, see Michael E. Zimmerman, "Feminism, Deep Ecology, and Environmental Ethics," *Environmental Ethics* 9 (1987): 21–44.

33. See John Hick's defense of evil and suffering as necessary conditions for the process of "soul-making" in *Evil and the God of Love*, rev. ed. (San Francisco: Harper & Row, 1978),

trust in the world as a safe place where healthy character formation can take place under the watchful eye of a good God. The wisdom books of Job, Ecclesiastes, Proverbs, Psalms, and Lamentations, for example, are a sustained *cri de coeur* against the facile logic of deuteronomic theologies which teach that keeping the covenant will result in life and health while disobedience will cause death and disease. For Job et al. the burden of faith is to remain faithful and *still* endure the ambiguities of history with no guarantee that there is a benevolent deity "on the other side" ready to deliver one from pain and confusion and destruction. The burden of faith nurtured by wisdom discourse is to confront the terrors of history as well as the (seeming) malevolence within the divine life itself. Sapiential literature reminds the follower of the covenant that the Bible's promises concerning human well-being are not inviolable safeguards against the loss of meaning and hope in a world that is brute and unfeeling, even Godless.

James M. Gustafson questions whether a contemporary doctrine of God's goodness must include the notion that the universe is anthropocentrically ordered to serve the interests of human flourishing. He suggests that a revised idea of God sensitive to the current ecological crisis need no longer assume that the preservation and development of humankind are the central focus of God's concern for the cosmos. "Imaginatively, a scenario can be developed in which the divine benevolence will lead to the extinction of our species when conditions for its sustenance no longer exist on this planet; this, however, is not the sense in which the certainty of divine benevolence has been fostered in the mainstream of the Christian tradition."[34] God may be good, Gustafson continues, but this goodness may have little if anything to do with our conventional understandings of the same. Gustafson's thought allows us to question whether God's goodness implies a cosmology in which the universe is organized according to the interests of human moral development and species flourishing. His point is that there is no guarantee that the universe has been ordered to serve the values of human growth or even human survival.

Gustafson's revaluation of divine benevolence is analogous to wisdom writers' analysis of history's vicissitudes. Both positions put the purpose of tradi-

---

201–61, and Richard Swinburne's similar argument that the world provides the right "opportunities for the exercise of the higher virtues" in *The Existence of God* (Oxford: Clarendon Press, 1979), chaps. 9–11.

34. James M. Gustafson, *Ethics from a Theocentric Perspective*, 2 vols. (Chicago: University of Chicago Press, 1981, 1984), 1:202.

tional theodicy in grave doubt: to defend God's power and goodness in the light of widespread suffering and injustice. What we learn, rather, is that life is sometimes fragmented by irruptions of an evil that resists assimilation to any totalizing system of explanation. Against the classical perspective, a post-modern spirituality tempered by the horrors of late modern existence postulates that radical evil finally stands as a *surd* outside all attempts to assimilate it to an overarching theological rationale. In this schema theodicy is bankrupt.

CONCLUSION

Inspired by postmodern thought and culture, these five contested positions provide the baseline for my subsequent discussion of the Holy Spirit. In the chapters that follow I will seek to defend the transgressive freedom of the Spirit to promote healing and renewal in a violent world without the security of the normative ideas about self, mind, history, nature, and God that have characterized Western Christian culture. The argument will make the following points. First, if there is no secure noumenal "self" that grounds existence, then selfhood is a task to be performed with the aid of the Spirit, not a *fait accompli* that awaits passive reception by the subject. Second, if the "mind's eye" is a philosophical invention and not the common underlying substrate that makes experience possible, then the "other" is not reduced to the gaze of the "same," and the Spirit can freely enable transformative encounters that preserve each subject's alterity and integrity. Third, if there is no single meta-narrative to which all human and nonhuman beings must conform, then the Spirit can be recovered as an advocate for the particular and the different, and as a defender of persons who resist the tyranny of hegemonistic plot lines and coercive forms of social organization. Fourth, if anthropocentrism is found wanting, then the Spirit can be reimagined as a healing life-force in the mending of the breach between humankind and nature, body and soul, and man and woman. And fifth, if belief in God and world as warrant and locale for human growth and preservation is contradicted by suffering irreducible to any theological system of justification, then a refiguring of the Spirit as the divine agon who struggles alongside the marginalized and oppressed may be possible as a performative response to the problem of fundamental evil.

These five theses adumbrate the sensibility that will underlie what follows in subsequent chapters. My intent is to articulate an understanding of the Spirit that will nourish and empower the nonviolent care of the other, both in terms of the other person and the nonhuman other within the natural world. Prior to the full explication of such a pneumatology, however, I turn my attention in the next two chapters to the methodological problems surrounding the making of truth-claims in religion. My reason for this methodological propaedeutic is that it will make little sense to make a number of subsequent claims about the Spirit in relation to violence if theological discourse as such cannot be defended as a credible mode of understanding the world.

CHAPTER TWO

Metaphysics, Neoempiricism, and the Possibility of Religious Belief

That the Christian faith does its reflective thought with the language of the metaphysical tradition is not really what is so aporetical. Faith must speak with the language of the world if it does not want to become dumb.[1]

God and Being are not identical, and I would never attempt to think the essence of God by means of being. . . . If I still sought to write a theology, an idea to which I am sometimes inclined, then the word "being" ought not to figure in it. Faith does not need the thinking of being. If it needs it, it is already no longer faith.[2]

For in its ideal form, the culture of liberalism would be one which was enlightened, secular, through and through. It would be one in which no trace of divinity remained, either in the form of a divinized world or a divinized self. Such a culture would have no room for the notion that there are nonhuman forces to which human beings should be responsible. It would drop, or drastically reinterpret, not only the idea of holiness but those of "devotion to truth" and of "fulfillment of the deepest needs of the spirit."[3]

This chapter evaluates critics and defenders of the role of metaphysics in theology. In relation to chapter 3, this focus foregrounds my subsequent anal-

---

1. Eberhard Jüngel, *God as the Mystery of the World: On the Foundation of the Theology of the Crucified One in the Dispute Between Theism and Atheism*, trans. Darrell L. Guder (Grand Rapids, Mich.: Eerdmans, 1983), 39.

2. Martin Heidegger, quoted in Joseph S. O'Leary, *Questioning Back: The Overcoming of Metaphysics in Christian Tradition* (Minneapolis: Winston Press, 1985), 18.

3. Richard Rorty, *Contingency, Irony, and Solidarity* (Cambridge: Cambridge University Press, 1989), 45.

ysis of the Spirit beyond the metaphysical question of being, that is, beyond the power of transcendental reason to discern the fundamental structures of reality. Most analyses of the Spirit in the history of Western thought have been dominated by metaphysical speculation.[4] In the metaphysical tradition, the Spirit is the divine principle of identity where being and knowing are brought together in original unity. Spirit is the all-encompassing ground of reality, the foundation of unity within all difference. From this perspective, human consciousness is intentionally directed toward its supreme source and ground, Absolute Spirit.

As Hegel put it, the aim of consciousness is always toward the Spirit, which is the ultimate condition for the possibility of being becoming self-present to itself and for itself. Hegel summarizes well the metaphysical concept of the Spirit. He maintains that Spirit is the reality of Being becoming conscious of itself *as Spirit*. Spirit becomes fully aware of its own inner life by becoming other than itself and then returning to itself in a supreme reconciliation of self and other. For Hegel all history presses toward this goal: the self-realization of Spirit as the final reconciliation of all oppositions in absolute unity.[5] From Aristotle to Hegel, from Thomas to Rahner, the question about being in Western philosophy and theology has generally been answered by a transcendental analysis of the unity of all being in Being-itself, that is, the Spirit.

Part of the task of this chapter is to critique the role of metaphysics in theology in order to undermine the philosophical concept of the Spirit that has held sway in Western thought, including Western theology. My goal is to preserve the distinction between the radically mysterious God of biblical faith, on the one hand, and the God of metaphysical theism that is always already known as the universal ground of human experience, on the other. In this vein I take up the promise of neoempiricist thought as an alternative to metaphysical theology, but conclude that this option is also wanting. In the contest between metaphysics and the empiricist revival, my hope is to "set the

---

4. On the history of the relation between pneumatology and metaphysics, see Steven G. Smith, *The Concept of the Spiritual: An Essay in First Philosophy* (Philadelphia: Temple University Press, 1988), 9–71; Michael Welker, *God the Spirit*, trans. John F. Hoffmeyer (Minneapolis: Fortress Press, 1994), 279–303; Alan M. Olson, *Hegel and the Spirit: Philosophy as Pneumatology* (Princeton: Princeton University Press, 1992), 3–35, 107–62; and Yves M. J. Congar, *I Believe in the Holy Spirit: Revelation and Experience of the Spirit*, trans. David Smith, 3 vols. (New York: Seabury, 1983).

5. See G. W. F. Hegel, *Reason in History: A General Introduction to the Philosophy of History*, trans. Robert S. Hartman (Indianapolis: Bobbs-Merrill, 1953), 20–49.

table" for the development, in subsequent chapters, of a postmetaphysical notion of God as Spirit unfettered by the language of being.

The long-held desire of metaphysical theology has been to develop a field-encompassing system of beliefs with enough certitude to be considered a science. As the natural sciences have been able to secure foundational knowledge about the order and predictability of physical objects, so theology has sought to specify the transcendental conditions for the possibility of every form of being and existence, including the being and existence of God. The dream of theology has always been the ideal of metaphysics, that is, "inquiry beyond or over beings which claims to recover them as such and as a whole for our grasp."[6] It is the ideal of a systematic transcendental investigation, as Kant put it, into the conditions of thought and experience built into the nature of reality itself. The various practitioners of metaphysical theology have hoped to articulate a body of intuitive beliefs—beliefs that are incorrigibly self-evident—the denial of which would fundamentally alter the received understandings of reality with which we all operate. Insofar as the task of metaphysics is to explicate the conditions constitutive of being as such, theology, properly understood, is the highest form of metaphysics because it interrogates the nature of the one strictly necessary being, God, who is the source and end of all possible beings.

In metaphysical theology God is the common ground, the ultimate presupposition, of our common experiences as contingent selves. And it is this experience of contingent selfhood—the sense that my existence is fundamentally related to other beings and even to Being as such—that is the privileged site for the disclosure of God as the absolutely necessary being whose essence is not dependent on others for existence. In Thomistic metaphysics, for example, God's being (*ens*) is God's existence (*esse*)—God's essence is to-be—whereas other beings exist not in themselves but only by virtue of their participation in God.[7] Thus, the reality of contingent existence leads one back to self-subsistent Being-itself as the noncontingent source of all particular beings. In this project theology's status as the supreme interrogator of the nature of being is secured, and all other forms of inquiry, as Thomas puts it, are "handmaidens" pressed into the service of metaphysical theology's articulation of the conditions for understanding reality per se.[8]

---

6. Martin Heidegger, "What is Metaphysics?" in *Basic Writings*, trans. David Ferrell Krell (New York: Harper & Row, 1977), 109.

7. Thomas Aquinas *Summa Theologica* 1.Q.3.art.4.

8. Ibid., 1.Q.1.art.5.

cates claims to truth in theological discourse (are these claims sufficiently universal?), theology articulates a fuller understanding of the nature of God than philosophy is able to do (are these claims appropriate to the biblical text?). Since, for example, "metaphysics has always had difficulties in conceiving the absolute One as personal," theology must press beyond its reliance on metaphysics for a comprehensive and agential interpretation of God within the Christian tradition.[15]

The compatibility between metaphysical theology and philosophy stems from an agreement that genuine thought about God follows the classical trajectory of intellectual *ascent* beyond the plurality of everyday objects and experiences toward the One who grounds all things in itself. Philosophy and theology share the same metaphysical content, since both disciplines articulate the return path back to the Source who is above the created order: our destiny is our origin as we recover the reality of God as the ground and end of all existence. The call to thought to "rise above" and "ascend" to the Absolute beyond the finite is the proper telos of all religious reflection, theological or philosophical. "Whenever philosophy uses the label 'God' for the absolute One—the goal of the metaphysical ascent above everyday experience—it already makes use of the language of religion . . . [thus] there is a thematic unity between the absolute One of philosophy and the one God of the monotheistic religions."[16] While the existence of God cannot be proven per se according to Pannenberg, reason pressed to its limits entails the reality of God as its "term" or "whence," rendering the complementary modes of identifying God in both disciplines flip sides of the same metaphysical coin.

For Whitehead, Pannenberg, and others the assumed goal of metaphysical inquiry is the critical correlation between general philosophical truth and special revealed truth in order to provide an account of the truth of being as such. "If," as Whitehead argues, "our trust is in the ultimate power of reason as a discipline for the discernment of truth," then appeals to truth in religion must be brought to the bar of universal reason where the question is adjudicated concerning which truth-claims are demonstrably constitutive of all reality.[17] Unless theology labors to ground its affirmations on the conclusions of a general philosophy, it threatens to degenerate into a private language game, a confessionalist ghetto, inadequate to the public criteria for meaning and truth to which all forms of rational inquiry must subscribe. Balkanized as

15. Ibid., 19.
16. Ibid., 20.
17. Whitehead, *Religion in the Making*, 74.

an exercise in religious subjectivism, theology has no place in the academy unless it can establish the validity of its claims on the basis of universal, metaphysical reflection.

The called-for reliance of theology on metaphysical presuppositions raises a number of questions, however, for a theology of the Spirit that seeks primary fidelity to the biblical witness. Should theology seek to ground its proposals on a metaphysical foundation, or should it cut its moorings to such foundations? Even if theology chooses the latter, can it do so? Can theology and metaphysics be disentangled so easily? As Heidegger asks, can theology "overcome" or "step back" beyond metaphysics by asserting its independence from any and all extratheological influences? Even if theology could ensure its autonomy from the question of being, should it do so? Will theology not slide into tribalism and privatism unless it is conceived as homologous to metaphysics? Or does the practice of theology under the horizon of being threaten to ignore or deny the novelty and heterogeneity that are peculiar to all modes of religious life and discourse?

To use God-language, does God need the openings that a metaphysical vocabulary can provide? Or are the openings proffered by such vocabularies in fact foreclosings of the presence of the Other who transgresses all categories and concepts? Given the historic elision of God and Being, how is the divine life to be understood in a contemporary setting? Is God a metaphysically certain *existent* within common human experience, or is God the unknowable (but not unspeakable) *Other* who is absolutely free of all metaphysical delimitations? Is God the necessary Being, the *ens realissimum*, who is knowable as the supreme origin of our beings, or is God, as the one who is *not-being* but still *is*, the violation of all categories and determinations? Is God best understood as the necessary ground of universal and contingent selfhood, the one who as Being-itself renders all derivative existence possible, or is God a reality anterior to and beyond all determinations (metaphysical or otherwise), a reality who meets us in ironic faith and discordant hope as we seek to encounter this reality in lives of openness to others? Is God, in short, not the *Being* known within the horizon of metaphysics, but the *occasion* for fostering new modes of existence that are no longer founded on the metaphysical securities of Western thought?

TRANSCENDENTAL THEOLOGY AND THE QUEST FOR CERTAINTY:
SCHUBERT OGDEN

Today the question of God in relation to "being" is asked by two different groups of theologians. On the one hand, there are those thinkers who argue for the viability of theological discourse on the basis of a metaphysics of human subjectivity, while on the other, there are theologians who propose a countermetaphysical understanding of religion that is not secured by appeals to a bedrock reality such as "being" or "truth" or even "God." This debate claims a distinguished provenance within the history of Western religious thought. Beginning with the first apologists, Christian thought has generally found itself divided between theologians who stress the timeless and universal character of the Judeo-Christian tradition's language about reality and those who accent the particular and more biblical nature of the tradition's distinctive vision of God. Indeed, the current debate between so-called revisionist and postliberal theologians can be construed along these lines. The former stress the need for theology to abide by academe's standards of rational public discourse, while the latter underscore the importance of strict adherence to the vocabulary and worldview of the Bible.[18]

While David Tracy is probably the best-known theological revisionist in the current discussion, Schubert Ogden is a more consistent exponent of revisionism than Tracy.[19] Ogden's defense of the existence of God as a necessary implication of our natural experience of the world as a meaningful whole, the

---

18. For a discussion of the relevant issues and bibliographies in this debate, see James J. Buckley, "Revisionists and Liberals," in *The Modern Theologians: An Introduction to Christian Theology in the Twentieth Century*, ed. David F. Ford, 2 vols. (Oxford: Basil Blackwell, 1989), 2:89–102; William C. Placher, "Postliberal Theology," in ibid., 115–28; and idem, *Unapologetic Theology: A Christian Voice in a Pluralistic Conversation* (Louisville: Westminster/John Knox Press, 1989), 123–74.

19. Tracy's thought has undergone such a sea change from his earlier process metaphysics to his current interests in hermeneutics and deconstruction that he is now not the best representative of liberal theology (in spite of some interpretations to the contrary; so Hans W. Frei, "The 'Literal Reading' of Biblical Narrative in the Christian Tradition: Does It Stretch or Will It Break?" in *The Bible and the Narrative Tradition*, ed. Frank McConnell [New York: Oxford University Press, 1986], 36–77). Tracy appears in his recent writing less interested in critically *correlating* religious reflection with Enlightenment standards of rationality than in theologically *interpreting* the challenge of postmodern discourse and the problems of global suffering. For the articulation of this shift, cf. Tracy's *Blessed Rage for Order: The New Pluralism in Theology* (New York: Seabury Press, 1975) with his *Plurality and Ambiguity: Hermeneutics, Religion, Hope* (New York: Harper & Row, 1988).

God presupposed by our generic self-understandings as human beings, is a model expression of the universalizing tendency in classic liberal theology. For Ogden, the reality of God is the fundamental and universal presupposition of the basic existential faith that is the ground for our common life and thought. Moreover, he argues that without the assurance of the transcendental experience of God as *the* constitutive event of human existence, Christian theology loses its status as a public, university discipline and becomes simply the self-enclosed witness to private faith. Thus Ogden's defense of the constitutive reality of God in all experience is *mutatis mutandis* a defense of the intellectual integrity of religious faith.

Ogden's project begins with a metaphysical axiom: the self's always already relationship to an ultimate referent is the ground for the possibility of authentic existence.[20] In this respect Ogden's theological thought is fundamentally optimistic about the human capacity for knowledge about and experience of God. Because human persons possess an a priori "innate faith" in the purpose and meaning of life, a genuine response to the Christian message is both possible and meaningful. The universe is benignly ordered, and to be human is to enjoy an original faith in the goodness of life and the value of human existence. This prethematic faith is fully actualized when the individual reunderstands herself in the light of the biblical message. Thus, it is in this sense that the individual respondent to the Christian message becomes a "new person"—not in the sense that she is changed into a different entity (a metaphysical impossibility), but in the sense that she now realizes what she always was, albeit in the depths of her being (namely, a person with the implicit predisposition to hear and respond to God's word).

Ogden's confidence in the structural certainty of this original faith emerges from "a general observation about human existence—namely, that to be human at all is both to live by faith and to seek understanding. . . . The faith to which I refer in observing that each of us lives by faith is our basic confidence or assurance simply as human beings that life is worth living."[21] In the face of our corporate inhumanity in everyday relations and the haunting prospect of mass environmental and nuclear death, this indeed is a remarkable claim. Ogden continues, however, that whereas nonhuman creatures have a basic "animal faith" in the receptivity of the universe to their wants and needs, human beings go beyond this by virtue of our "inalienable trust that

20. Schubert Ogden, *On Theology* (New York: Harper & Row, 1986), 22–44.

21. Ogden, *On Theology,* 106; see also idem, *The Reality of God and Other Essays* (New York: Harper & Row, 1963), 36–46.

our own existence and existence generally are somehow justified and made meaningful by the whole to which we know ourselves to belong."[22] This transcendental confidence in the worth of existence is what Ogden calls "original revelation."[23] It is expressed in our living, or attempting to live, according to the timeless values of truth, beauty, and goodness; in our philosophical attempts to understand conceptually the "ground" to which our questions about the meaning of life are directed; and in our historic beliefs that certain religious symbols and practices can give us access to that loving source, that ultimate mystery, toward which all of our yearnings are directed.

In this scheme theistic belief is constitutive of being human insofar as we realize that "faith in God as the ground of confidence in life's ultimate meaning is the necessary condition for our existence as selves."[24] This instinctive belief is twofold: *prethematic originary revelation* is our always already deep awareness of the kinship between worthwhile existence and the reality of God, while *special biblical revelation* makes explicit our preapprehension of the reality and love of God as the precondition of authentic selfhood. Indeed, Ogden maintains that special revelation adds no new content to original revelation since it essentially makes explicit the "eternal truths" that I already know, if only inchoately and implicitly, namely, that the world is ordered according to the loving governance of a good and gracious God.[25] The disclosure of truth in religion, therefore, operates on two registers. It consists in "what we can originally know of the nature and existence of God,"[26] and it is the decisive event in my life by means of which the divine source and end of my existence are now recognized and embraced. As with Rudolf Bultmann's theology, the importance of the *event character* of revealed truth is critical to Ogden's project: revelation is the event of God's self-presentation that brings about my realization of authentic existence. Special revelation, then, is the occasion for *me* to own and acknowledge what I already possess, to become what I already am; it is my personal awareness of the gift and demand of God's love in *my* life.

> In sum, *what* Christian revelation reveals to us is nothing new, since such truths as it makes explicit must already be known to us implicitly in every moment of

22. Ogden, *On Theology*, 107.
23. Ibid., 28.
24. Ogden, *The Reality of God*, 43; see also idem, *The Point of Christology* (New York: Harper & Row, 1982), 20–40.
25. Ogden, *On Theology*, 43.
26. Ibid., 35.

our existence. But *that* this revelation occurs does reveal something new to us in that, as itself event, it is the occurrence in our history of the transcendent event of God's love.[27]

Ogden suggests that his fundamental anthropology—a metatheory about human nature that is situation-neutral—sheds much-needed light on certain Christian doctrines (like the ideas of truth and revelation) that are generally misunderstood; in addition, it ensures the intellectual credibility of Christian faith. He contends that his understanding of revelation as the condition for the possibility of human authenticity secures theology's rightful claim to university status—a claim that allies it with other disciplines, such as philosophy and science, whose truth-claims are also generalizable and universal in scope. Since one of the tasks of theology (like science or philosophy or other disciplines) is to thematize and defend certain necessary truths, then theology too can operate with confidence that its place in the academy is assured. By rendering publicly credible the anthropological *fundamentum* that there is an all-encompassing ground to our lives that makes human existence worthwhile, theology is accorded the academic due that rightly belongs to it. Thus, only with the protection and advancement of theology's capacity to thematize certain incorrigible primary truths can theology hope to attain the status of public, academic *inquiry* and be something more than a type of *witness* to the Christian symbol system (notwithstanding, as Ogden always maintains, the importance of the activity of witness itself).[28]

With theology's claim to disciplinary status secure, the perennial question is answered as to whether theology should appeal to special criteria of truth in order to establish its assertions about reality. Ogden argues that it should not. He maintains that the use of special theological standards of truth "runs into contemporary counterclaims with respect to what alone can count as legitimate reflection. According to such counterclaims, no form of reflection appealing to special criteria of truth can to this extent be legitimate, since no assertion can possibly be established as true except by appealing to completely general criteria applicable to any other assertion of the same logical type."[29] Consistent with most revisionary theologians, Ogden upholds the critical correlation method for theological reflection. Theology should operate according to the dual criteria of *appropriateness* to the normative documents

27. Ibid., 43.
28. Schubert Ogden, *Faith and Freedom: Toward a Theology of Liberation* (Nashville: Abingdon, 1979), 17–39; idem, *On Theology*, 121–33.
29. Ogden, *On Theology*, 103.

of historic Christianity and of *credibility* as determined by the invariant standards of meaning and truth assumed by all liberal studies.[30] Theology, then, must always guard against a criteriology peculiar to its own erstwhile parochial origins and history. This does not mean that theological reflection should not be appropriate to its distinctive scriptural and confessional sources (it certainly should be because these sources provide the "datum discourse" for theology), but it does mean that this reflection should be "credible, in that it meets the relevant conditions of truth universally established with human existence."[31]

But what exactly does Ogden mean by the criterion of "credibility" in theological reflection? He means that Christian theology's standards of argument and verification are no different in principle from the rational standards that operate in all other areas of academic inquiry. Ogden's fear is that if theology divorces itself from the general principles of reason and argument operative in other disciplines it renders itself inaccessible to public scrutiny and runs the risk of becoming a private form of self-expression. The difference, therefore, between theology and other disciplines is not the *mode* of rational inquiry, which they share in common, but the *object* of this inquiry. The object of Christian theology is the witness of faith to authentic human existence, but the standards by which the meaning and truth of this claim are assessed are universal and situation-invariant. Credibility demands that theology should never be content with simply rationalizing and handing on the truths already accepted by historic Christian witness.[32] Theology properly understood is not the defense of assumed truths but the systematic investigation and criticism of those positions the Christian community has taken to be true; it is not merely the interpretation of the classical tenets of Christian faith but the process of critically reflecting on the intelligibility of these tenets in a fully public and methodologically conscious manner. This process of "critical reflection" on the credibility of faith is the "process of determining in a deliberate, methodical, and reasoned way whether something that appears to be the case, or, alternatively, is said to be the case, really is so."[33]

The difficulty with this approach, however, is that the criterion of credibility seems unable to address whether many religious beliefs really have a purchase on reality or not. The credibility criterion can assist the decision as to whether certain theological claims are formally valid by virtue of their follow-

30. Ibid., 4–6; cf. Tracy, *Blessed Rage*, 64–87.
31. Ogden, *On Theology*, 5.
32. Ibid., 1–21.
33. Ogden, *Faith and Freedom*, 116.

ing logically from this or that presupposition. But as to the presuppositions themselves, as to the question whether this particular cluster of beliefs is not simply *logically valid* but also *ontologically sound*—this question appears beyond the reach of the credibility condition as articulated by Ogden. It appears that the standards of rationality assumed by liberal studies can specify whether a specific truth-claim in religion is entailed by a particular first premise. Yet such standards appear woefully inadequate to establish whether many of Christianity's privileged premises and beliefs are true in the first place.[34] Ogden implies that the credibility criterion is a necessary condition for arbitrating the truth status of all originary religious beliefs, but the status of some of these beliefs cannot be decided upon with reference to situation-neutral criteria for meaning and truth. While this does not mean that such first beliefs are thereby untrue, it does mean that their rationality and truth are not subject to the criterion that Ogden argues is indispensable for the intellectual integrity of Christian thought.

A RHETORICAL RESPONSE

Attention to the rhetorical character of religious belief provides an alternative to Ogden's grounding of theology on transcendental analysis. From the perspective of rhetorical analysis, beliefs in religion (or any other mode of experience) rest on an *imaginative construal* of the world—a constellation of root metaphors about what one takes to be "reality"—that is the basis of all other related beliefs and cannot be proven in and of itself. Insofar as basic knowledge is derived from founding presumptions that admit of no external justification, fundamental claims to truth rely on tacit presumptions that cannot be proven on the basis of independent arguments. Presumably, however, Ogden would maintain that this approach to the structure of belief would render theology unable to establish and articulate the transcendental truths of religion that meet the universal truth-conditions established by the other disciplines. We have observed that one such truth Ogden has in mind is the reality of human persons' inalienable and fundamental trust in the worthwhileness of existence; the task incumbent upon the theologian is to defend this transcendental trust as a metaphysical first principle, thereby ensuring the intellectual credibility of theology. Theologians, therefore, should no more question

34. The Christian witness to the triunity of God, for example, is appropriate to certain elements within the New Testament. But the truth of this witness cannot be readily adjudicated by an appeal to the standards of rationality within the academy.

"*whether* there is a ground of basic confidence in life's worth" than the scientist should question "*whether* there is a world of fact somehow sufficiently ordered" to meet the needs of our empirical demands and expectations.[35]

But is this really the case? Does or should the religionist and scientist function according to axiomatic beliefs in the ultimate value of existence and the uniformity of nature? It seems to me that the assumption that the theologian operates with a priori confidence in "life's worth" and that the scientist proceeds according to an apodictic belief in an "ordered world of fact" is difficult to sustain in a post-Holocaust and post-Kuhnian world where religion is no longer understood as the self-evident belief in the innate meaningfulness of existence, and science is no longer viewed as the prediction and control of a uniform world of physical objects. On the contrary, we have in both disciplines related forms of storytelling and theory construction that seek successfully to "fit" their own narratives and paradigms to what the theologian and scientist construe as "reality." Postmodern religion and science have less to do with defending universal truths or securing particular facts about the physical world than with articulating a story that is coherent and flexible enough to accommodate a wide range of experiences and observations.[36]

Thus, it seems highly appropriate, even necessary, for the theologian and the scientist to question the metaphysical axioms Ogden deems self-evident and necessary for the intellectual integrity of their respective disciplines. In the face of the world's radical evil and the universe's fundamental mystery, the theologian does wonder whether there is a benevolent ground to human existence and the scientist does question the ordered mechanics of traditional physics. What for Ogden is the *sine qua non* of academic theology—its presumption concerning the worth of existence as such—is the very presupposition the theologian *must* question if she is to be responsible to a gospel and a situation that understand existence in the cosmos in highly fragile, enigmatic, and ambiguous terms.

What might a theology look like that understands itself in rhetorical rather than philosophical terms? A full explication of this alternative is part of the burden of this book. Whereas Ogden emphasizes the transcendental necessity of God as the constitutive ground of personal authenticity, a rhetorical

---

35. Ogden, *On Theology*, 108.

36. See Stephen Toulmin, *Human Understanding: The Collective Use of and Evolution of Concepts* (Princeton: Princeton University Press, 1972), 93–130; and Mary Gerhart and Allan Russell, *Metaphoric Process: The Creation of Scientific and Religious Understanding* (Fort Worth: Texas Christian University Press, 1984).

approach suggests how the language and imagery of the biblical witness could be interpreted to enable personal and social transformation. A rhetorical approach has less to do with philosophical attempts to *defend* the cognitive value of religious claims through appeals to generic experience than with hermeneutical strategies for *interpreting* particular figurations of God that might foster growth and renewal. Ogden's theistic metaphysics offers answers to such questions as, Is God the basic presupposition of human existence as such? while a rhetorical approach focuses on the imaginative power of religious beliefs to illuminate questions such as, Is God possible in a world charged with the absence of final hope and absolute meaning? In this schema the reality of God is a matter of rhetorical possibility and existential risk and not a necessary feature of our native noetic structure.

My model of a rhetorically conscious theology is indebted to Paul Ricoeur's hermeneutical philosophy of religion. For Ricoeur, the reality of God is most adequately described (or "figured") by the different modalities of discourse within the biblical texts. "To be brief, I will say that the confession of faith expressed in the biblical documents is directly modulated by the forms of discourse wherein it is expressed. . . . The religious 'saying' is only constituted in the interplay between story and prophecy, history and legislation, legislation and wisdom, and finally wisdom and lyricism."[37] Ricoeur argues that these texts open the reader to new possibilities of existence through the confluence and clash of the Bible's diverse literary genres. Instead, then, of abstracting philosophical concepts from the Bible's rich fermentation of meaning in the manner of theistic philosophy, Ricoeur focuses on the intertextual dynamics embodied in the originary literary expressions of biblical faith. Though Ricoeur uses a variety of conceptual and philosophical tools to analyze the plurality of biblical discourses, his approach does not sit well with current trends in philosophy of religion and philosophical theology.[38] There is a significant difference between his rhetorical model for analyzing originary scriptural discourses and the analytic model of Anglo-American philosophy of religion. It is the difference between the hermeneutical task of understanding a religious symbol or idea as a possible mode of experience and the philosophical attempt to justify the cognitive claims of

37. Paul Ricoeur, "Toward a Hermeneutic of the Idea of Revelation," in *Essays on Biblical Interpretation*, ed. Lewis S. Mudge (Philadelphia: Fortress Press, 1980), 91–92.

38. Representatives of these trends include, among others, the Reformed epistemologists Alvin Plantinga and Nicholas Wolterstorff and British analytic philosophers such as Anthony Flew and Richard Swinburne.

religious thought.[39] While transcendental philosophy of religion interrogates the question of God's existence and identity through formal *arguments* that are indifferent to the image-laden language of confessional and scriptural traditions, Ricoeur's rhetorical model analyzes the rich *descriptions* of God within the Bible through a literary-philosophical analysis of the text's crisscrossing patterns of meaning. Mainstream philosophy of religion asks whether the *truth* of certain formalized, second-order propositions can be apodictically demonstrated (for example, Does God exist? Is the soul immortal? Are theism and evil incompatible?), whereas Ricoeur's rhetorical approach focuses on the question of the *meaning* of certain figural depictions of God, self, and world within the first-order discourse of biblical literature (for example, How is God present and absent within biblical narratives? Can the testimony of the prophets be trusted? Is selfhood a present possession or future gift?).

Ricoeur maintains that the rhetorical approach avoids the ontotheological siren calls of Western thought that have lured thinkers about religion into a certain metaphysical comfort by convincing them that because they have mastered the standard analytic arguments and proofs *for and against* religious belief they have therefore finished the task of thinking *about* religion. Ricoeur's alternative is to sidestep this "temptation" altogether. His point is that the reality of God is not a deliverance of universal reason (as Ogden, Pannenberg, and others maintain) but, rather, the supreme trope within a series of genred texts that invite the reader to think and live alongside their creative mimesis of the world.

If, as Ricoeur argues, the identity of the Divine is rendered through the polyphonic discourses of the Bible, then the rhetoric of the Bible is not an incidental façade that needs dismantling in order to extract a series of speculative concepts. Rather, this rhetoric constitutes a generative poetics that "names God" through the interplay of the Bible's conflicting and complementary modes of discourse. "The naming of God, in the originary expressions of faith, is not simple but multiple. It is not a single tone, but polyphonic. The originary expressions of faith are complex forms of discourse as diverse as narratives, prophecies, laws, proverbs, prayers, hymns, liturgical formulas, and wisdom writings. As a whole, these forms of discourse name God."[40] Far from the textual identity of the divine life being indifferent to the

---

39. For a model similar to Ricoeur's, cf. Merold Westphal, *God, Guilt and Death* (Bloomington: Indiana University Press, 1984), esp. 1–13.

40. Paul Ricoeur, "Naming God," in *Figuring the Sacred: Religion, Narrative, and Imagination*, ed. Mark I. Wallace, trans. David Pellauer (Minneapolis: Fortress Press, 1995), 217–35.

originary discourses of the Bible, Ricoeur maintains that God is "named" through the intersections between this plurality of discourses—from narratives to laws and from wisdom to apocalyptic writings.

From the rhetorical perspective, religious commitment opens up a world of possibilities that the one who takes the risk of belief is asked to inhabit; it opens up imaginative space for articulating new modes of existence in which one's relations to self and other are fundamentally refigured. Such new figurations render knowledge of God through appeals to universal transcendental structures to be unnecessary flights of speculative theorizing. The rhetorical alternative is to wager one's existence on a network of textually mediated ideals and values in spite of the fact that one can never know with rational certitude whether the values in question are worthy of one's apprenticeship. In making this fundamental wager, it is impossible to eliminate "the element of risk."

> We wager on a certain set of values and then try to be consistent with them; verification is therefore a question of our whole life. No one can escape this. . . . In a certain sense my answer is fideist, but for me it is only an avowal of honesty to admit that. I do not see how we can say that our values are better than all others except that by risking our whole life on them we expect to achieve a better life, to see and to understand things better than others.[41]

Beyond, then, the certainty of metaphysical knowledge, the rhetorical approach in theology enjoins us to risk ourselves by performing the task of existence in response to an Other who is beyond the deliverances of reason.

The move from metaphysics to rhetoric does not, however, sacrifice the intellectual integrity of theological reflection; on the contrary, it places theology on the same antifoundational footing that all forms of liberal inquiry are now recognizing to be the place on which they in fact stand. Knowledge in the human and natural sciences is never achieved in a wholly objective or neutral fashion. All forms of human inquiry into the natural world or the "worlds" of culture and texts are governed by the interpreter's organizing tropes concerning the nature of the "reality" under question. Indeed, such schemata produce knowledge and understanding because without them the world remains impenetrably opaque—or "blind," to use Kant's famous metaphor.[42] The acknowledgment that there is no knowledge of the innocent eye that can secure an incorrigible foundation for this or that particular disci-

---

41. Paul Ricoeur, *Lectures on Ideology and Utopia*, ed. George H. Taylor (New York: Columbia University Press, 1986), 312.

42. The ideal of a neutral method of inquiry devoid of interpretive bias—the ideal of a pure nonrhetorical philosophy or science—is quixotic. This case is made by, among others, Hayden

pline (be it science or philosophy or theology) is the acknowledgment that all forms of intellectual inquiry are complicated exercises in argument and persuasion and not pipelines to universal certitude.

Ogden's difficulty emerges from his ontotheological attempt to demonstrate the necessity of God's existence as a datum of fundamental theological anthropology. At first glance this formula appears entirely plausible: What else is theology if it is not the rational explication of that tacit religious faith all people possess independent of their explicit knowledge of this faith? But if "original revelation" is what we always already possess so that "special revelation" communicates to us nothing new, then there is little space for genuine novelty and alterity in our experience of God. The fundamental problem with metaphysics in theology is that it cannot account for the ambiguity and indeterminacy of the referent of religious belief. Sometimes the divine life appeals quietly to a person or community according to the received canons of reason, and sometimes the Divine is the shattering force of rupture and opening to new forms of existence—alternative ways of being in the world—to which one would have no reliable access apart from this shock of the new and the different. Metaphysical theology betrays a totalizing and rationalistic impulse that cannot account for the novelty, even absurdity, of the interruption of the Other into human experience. Such an approach undermines the radical exteriority and excess of the Other who resists being thought under the conditions of metaphysical anthropology. *Whatever else God is, God is not subject to the gaze of the philosopher or the theologian.* The reality of God cannot be subsumed under a universal metaphysical system, in the manner of Ogden, because disclosures of this reality set free possibilities previously unthought and unimagined. Such disclosures are more dialectical and subversive than transcendental self-analysis can acknowledge. Outside the confines of conceptual thought systems, disclosures of God beyond being open up new resources for encountering the pathos and irony of existence in a world devoid of any assurances, theological or otherwise.

PRIVATE TRUTH AND STRONG POETS:
RICHARD RORTY

In the current discussion, one of the best-known counterpoints to Ogden's and others' quest for universal truth is the neopragmatism of philosophers

---

White, in *Metahistory: The Historical Imagination in Nineteenth-Century Europe* (Baltimore: Johns Hopkins University Press, 1973); idem, *Tropics of Discourse: Essays in Cultural Criticism* (Baltimore: Johns Hopkins University Press, 1978).

such as Richard Rorty. Rorty and others argue that metaphysical thought (in its classical and contemporary forms) suffers from an awkward circularity in which it assumes as transcendentally necessary a ground of Being (like God) that provides stability in a world of contingency and change. For Rorty, however, this assumption begs the fundamental question, and for analysts like himself who have accepted their lot as historically formed artisans of new vocabularies, not discoverers of ancient truths, the need for the security of Being has evaporated. In a culture no longer in need of metaphysical certainties, Ogden-like appeals to Truth or God as the object of universal finite experience appear as vestiges of a bygone era.

Today, postmodernism is divided between thinkers like Rorty, who argue against the traditional religious belief in God as the ultimate ground for all reality, and thinkers such as Derrida, who admit, albeit elliptically, the possibility of an Other beyond the philosophical categories that have dominated Western thought.[43] In this section, I turn to the antitheological skepticism of Rorty's philosophy as the most widely discussed and clearly defined counterpart to the metaphysical optimism of thinkers like Ogden.

Rorty has been lauded as the most important American philosopher in a generation.[44] This accolade is an index to his status as a thinker who has successfully translated the often arcane vocabularies of Anglo-American and Continental philosophies into a sensible and readable idiom. Such praise also points to Rorty's success at synthesizing traditional philosophical language with current work in a variety of cognate disciplines such as cultural studies, new historicism, literary criticism, and social thought. The result is a truly integrative "postphilosophical" perspective that stresses the fragile tasks of practicing democratic conversation and appropriating the communal values

43. Derrida's invocation of an Other outside metaphysics allows for a reading of his recent philosophy as a sort of postmodern theology of social responsibility. In *Specters of Marx*, he writes that the spirit of Marxism survives in Western culture just insofar as we live according to the messianic idea of *justice*. This "idea of justice" is the "experience of an emancipatory promise" specific to "a messianism without religion" that "remains irreducible to any deconstruction." See Jacques Derrida, *Specters of Marx: The State of the Debt, the Work of Mourning, and the New International*, trans. Peggy Kamuf (New York: Routledge, 1994), 59 and passim. Also see idem, *The Gift of Death*, trans. David Wills (Chicago: University of Chicago Press, 1995). The undeconstructible idea of justice or responsibility in Derrida's recent work functions similarly to the religious wager central to my project: the hope that there might be something alongside our everyday existence, call it justice or God, that could provide hope for a better future for ourselves and other life-forms as well.

44. See L. S. Klepp, "Every Man a Philosopher-King," *The New York Times Magazine* (2 December 1990): 117.

embodied in literature and art over and against the time-honored metaphysical quest for rational certitude and moral absolutes.

Rorty's irritation with the pretensions and irrelevancies of high philosophical culture and his concern for relocating intellectual life and moral reasoning within the contingencies and ironies of daily lived existence have spoken volumes to people who long ago abandoned the classical notions of truth and morality they inherited but have been left with little in their place. Rorty writes that the new breed of philosopher plays the role of "the informed dilettante, the polypragmatic, Socratic intermediary between various discourses. In his salon, so to speak, hermetic thinkers are charmed out of their self-enclosed practices."[45] The old-style philosopher, however, continues to emulate the classical model "of the cultural overseer who knows everyone's common ground—the Platonic philosopher-king who knows what everybody else is really doing whether *they* know it or not, because he knows about the ultimate context (the Forms, the Mind, Language) within which they are doing it."[46] Rorty styles his own project after the first model. His posture as a self-avowed dilettante and apologist for conversation and community is an attractive alternative to the flight from ambiguity and historicity so characteristic of Western philosophy's quest for certainty.[47]

Rorty writes in the wake of the death of God, the distrust in language as a medium of representation, and the demise of the transcendental self as a source of epistemically privileged beliefs. He claims that "[a]bout two hundred years ago, the idea that truth was made rather than found began to take hold of the imagination of Europe."[48] For Rorty, language is not a royal road to a self-subsistent Truth or God that exists independent of the human mind and lying ready-made for discovery through the right philosophical vocabulary. Language is not a reliable medium for mediating the relationship between the knowing subject and the so-called objective world outside of the subject; rather, language is a coping device that meets particular needs under certain conditions and circumstances. "Think of the term 'mind' or 'lan-

---

45. Richard Rorty, *Philosophy and the Mirror of Nature* (Princeton: Princeton University Press, 1979), 317.

46. Ibid., 317–18.

47. See Richard Rorty, "Pragmatism, Relativism, and Irrationalism," in *Consequences of Pragmatism* (Madison: University of Wisconsin Press, 1982), 160–75; idem, *Philosophy and the Mirror of Nature*, 315–94.

48. Rorty, *Contingency, Irony, and Solidarity*, 3. Also see his "Solidarity or Objectivity?" in *Objectivity, Relativism, and Truth* (Cambridge: Cambridge University Press, 1991), 21–34.

guage' not as the name of a medium between self and reality but simply as a flag which signals the desirability of using a certain vocabulary when trying to cope with certain kinds of organisms."[49] The old subject–object, inner–outer schema is an unhelpful remnant of classical coherence and correspondence theories of truth—theories that cannot account for the highly volatile factors of passion, desire, and power in deciding what is and is not deemed "truth" or "knowledge" or "morality" by particular communities of interpretation. The question is not, Is this language true to reality? but Is this language efficacious in meeting certain needs and performing certain functions for a contingent and perspectival group of inquirers?

If truth is a matter of constructing a vocabulary that one finds useful for coping with lived experience, then selfhood consists of developing a set of personal metaphors that allows one to craft a self-definition freed from the received wisdom of past traditions. Rorty asks us to write our lives as fictions which have overcome the inherited descriptions of the world that impede our progress toward free and responsible self-actualization. Borrowing from Nietzsche, he maintains that the journey toward selfhood is marked by the exclamation "thus I willed it!" over and against one's allegiance to the putative certainties of the philosophers.

> [Nietzsche] thinks a human life triumphant just insofar as it escapes from inherited descriptions of the contingencies of its existence and finds new descriptions. This is the difference between . . . thinking of redemption as making contact with something larger and more enduring than oneself and redemption as Nietzsche describes it: recreating all "it was" into a "thus I willed it."[50]

Authentic individuality is a product of aesthetic self-creation in defiance of the inherited assumptions of the philosophical mandarins; the strong poet, the maker of fiction, the artist who spins out worlds—these are the true individuals.

Platonists, Kantians, and Christians have blinded thinkers to the sheer contingency and perspectival nature of their traditional visions of the self. Such philosophers and theologians have upheld the metaphysical quest for a core self or deep common essence that all persons share—a transcendental orientation toward God as the ground of all experience, as Ogden puts it. The discovery of this generic human nature—what Rorty says Plato and Chris-

49. Rorty, *Contingency, Irony, and Solidarity*, 15.
50. Ibid., 29.

tians call the self or the soul—is championed as a universal reference point for making decisions about truth and moral obligation. This core self is said to be in communion with a power greater than ourselves, a transpersonal reality like Plato's Ideas or the God of Jews and Christians that can provide a stable warrant for adjudicating competing truth-claims and moral judgments.[51] But the trust in the invisible world of the soul and the reality of God is inimical to the development of liberal inquiry and Nietzschean self-construction. "For in its ideal form, the culture of liberalism would be one which was enlightened, secular, through and through. It would be one in which no trace of divinity remained, either in the form of a divinized world or a divinized self. Such a culture would have no room for the notion that there are nonhuman forces to which human beings should be responsible."[52]

The strong poet is an ironist. She realizes that there is no noncircular justification for the vocabulary she uses as basic and fundamental in the process of forging self-identity. Rorty acknowledges, therefore, that while the private task of constructing "true" individuality is of a piece with a thoroughgoing historicism and nominalism, this ironic mind-set is generally irrelevant to the public task of promoting human solidarity. On the surface it seems that the sense of solidarity and community with other people—the necessary social glue for maintaining stable human society—is not aided by the acquisition of this or that vocabulary for the process of self-creation. Writing the script of one's life ("Was that life? Well then! Once more!"[53]) is not the uncovering of

---

51. Rorty consistently criticizes traditional philosophy for accepting as given some larger reality with which all persons are connected. There are, however, many tradition-friendly contemporary theories of self-actualization that do not rely on classical metaphysical assumptions. Charles Taylor, for example, maintains that all persons possess a "deep moral sense" concerning a body of "higher goods" for giving meaning and direction to human existence, even though this moral sense cannot be proven on the basis of universal reason. See Charles Taylor, *Sources of the Self: The Making of the Modern Identity* (Cambridge, Mass.: Harvard University Press, 1989). For Taylor's reaction to Rorty's criticisms of his and similar philosophies of transcendence, see Charles Taylor, "Rorty in the Epistemological Tradition," in *Reading Rorty: Critical Responses to "Philosophy and the Mirror of Nature" (and Beyond)*, ed. Alan R. Malachowski (Oxford: Basil Blackwell, 1990), 257–75.

52. Rorty, *Contingency, Irony, and Solidarity*, 45.

53. The quote is from Friedrich Nietzsche, *Thus Spake Zarathustra*, trans. R. J. Hollingdale (New York: Penguin, 1969), 178. The Nietzschean character of Rorty's thought is pervasive. Rorty uses Nietzsche to argue that the ideal individual has complete ownership of her identity because she constructs her life out of the raw materials of lived existence, not the ephemeral ideals of metaphysical philosophies. The ideal life is an artistic exercise in self-invention, the courage to say "once more!" to the imaginary invitation to live one's life over again.

the "true self" or the "real world"—the realities that Platonists, Christians, and traditional liberal philosophers have used as the fiber and substance of moral and social order. But implicit in the process of inventing a private vocabulary as one's own is the recognition of the value of free and democratic public space for the realization of opportunities for self-creation. My private vocabulary is "none of your business," as Rorty says, but together we share the need for common space for making our vocabularies workable—we share a "common selfish hope, the hope that one's world—the little things around which one has woven into one's final vocabulary—will not be destroyed."[54]

This communal need and shared hope for moral-aesthetic "space" for creating one's private worldview provide Rorty with a negative ethic for answering the public question, What provides the social bonds for maintaining human community? His answer is not the positive ethic of normative philosophy and theology, which upheld the universal ideal that insofar as all people possess an inner light or are bearers of God's image, social organization has a sure foundation upon which to reconcile differences and build community. Rather, his answer is the negative ethic of bourgeois individualism: the acquisition of a private vocabulary implies the importance of public institutions and spaces for making this acquisition possible and fruitful. "[W]ithout the protection of something like the institutions of bourgeois liberal society, people will be less able to work out their private salvations."[55] There can be no nonrhetorical argument for the necessity of Western liberal institutions and structures, but if, as Rorty argues, the proper desideratum is the right to invent one's private sense of selfhood independent of previous assumptions, then such public institutions will be necessary for the working out of the "self" one has chosen.

A FALSE ALTERNATIVE?

In the story Rorty tells, no so-called experiences of transcendence or epiphanies of the Other have any "truth value" because such experiences are a private extension of a person's "in here" perspective, not the royal road to an "out there" reality. Rorty's therapeutic prescription for curing the metaphysical hunger for noncontingent truth, the nostalgia for pure presence, is the medicine of deconstruction; the cure is found in the unrestricted, dionysian practice of transforming the social space we all share into an environment for

54. Rorty, *Contingency, Irony, and Solidarity*, 91–92.
55. Ibid., 84–85.

poetic self-creation and democratic dialogue.[56] The remedy is to come of age and recognize that truth is made, not found; that reality is constructed, not discovered; and that language is the house (or prison) we live in, not the window through which we catch glimpses of another world. Anything less for Rorty is misguided because it is bound to an old inner-outer vocabulary that is no longer useful for a model of rationality that is right for our time—a model that champions contingency and irony rather than universality and metaphysics.

The problem with this approach is that it collapses possible discernments of divine presence into the quest for universal certainty characteristic of foundationalist philosophies.[57] This opposition is supported by Rorty's disjunction between truth as found (the old vocabulary) and truth as made (the new historicist mode). But while religious traditions do offer potentially healing resources for encounters with life's ambiguities on the basis of belief in transcendence, these traditions need not (and often do not) ground these beliefs in any metaphysical system. A life of faith can be a healing balm and source of meaning in times of trouble, but such a faith does not claim a direct purchase on reality as such. As we saw earlier in this chapter, faith in a rhetorical mode is the *wager of belief* on a set of possibilities, rather than the *assurance of knowledge* grounded on a philosophical foundation. From this perspective, Rorty's old–new and inner–outer distinctions between poetic-imaginary discourse and literal-descriptive language offer a false alternative. All fiction, religious or otherwise, both discovers *and* creates. Insofar as the one who wagers religious hope *discovers* novel possibilities for existence within the imaginative discourses of a religious tradition, she is also empowered to *invent* a life that is a recovery of those very values and possibilities. A religious tradition's powers of description-invention are linked to its capacity to reveal something "other"—what William James called the "more"—that can support and undergird one's journey to wholeness and selfhood. Belief is a fragile act of trust that cannot be secured by appeals to rational formulas or empirical proofs, rendering Rorty's insistence that such presumptions of alterity are rearguard metaphysical quests for ahistorical foundations and certainties a specious criticism.

Rorty's charge betrays, I believe, his vestigial attachment to the canons of positivist philosophy that he purports to have disavowed. Rorty's nominalism

---

56. See Rorty, "Philosophy as a Kind of Writing: An Essay on Derrida," in *Consequences of Pragmatism*, 90–109.

57. See Rorty, *Contingency, Irony, and Solidarity*, 73–95.

has its roots in analytic-empiricist thought, and I suspect his inability to accommodate the possibility of transcendence is a remnant of this intellectual provenance. Rortian postmodernism and the empiricism he claims to have rejected part company at a number of places, but on this issue there is committed agreement: the gods are dead and human experience is devoid of any epiphanic moments where something More or Novel can be manifested to the interpreter. The legitimacy of a life lived as a wager on this possibility is the fundamental disagreement between Rorty and the person who makes the religious wager.

In vintage Enlightenment form, Rorty champions the exigency of throwing off the shackles of authority and convention. But his appeals to self-construction exercise a certain tone-deafness to the rootedness of these appeals in a historical tradition, namely, the empirical and Enlightenment ideal of the human subject and its reason as the supreme arbiter of meaning and truth. "*Sapere Aude!* Have the courage to use your own intelligence! is therefore the motto of the enlightenment."[58] Kant's Enlightenment dictum is Rorty's epithet as well. In the Enlightenment spirit of determining one's own identity apart from the authority of tradition, Rorty postures as an inventor of new worlds and new vocabularies. In fact, however, his strident constructivist orientation is of a piece with the longstanding Western emphasis on the authority of the *rational self* as the final tribunal for all claims to truth.[59] Moreover, Rorty's implicit presumption that *only* the self that has cut the lead-strings to belief in transcendence can be a member of the "postphilosophical" conversation seems strangely akin to the "old" philosophical antipathy toward a genuine plurality of viewpoints.[60]

58. Immanuel Kant, "What is Enlightenment?" in *The Philosophy of Kant: Immanuel Kant's Moral and Political Writings*, ed. Carl J. Friedrich (New York: Random House, Modern Library, 1949), 132.

59. In this sense Rortian deconstruction is best understood not as postmodernist but, as I have learned in conversations with Stephen Dunning, as a variation on unhappy modernism. Rorty's ascription of supreme value to the task of forming personhood continues the modernist turn to the subject (albeit the subject now understood as the strong poet of Nietzsche rather than the empirical *tabula rasa* of Locke).

60. On this point, William C. Placher argues that Rorty has hoisted himself with his own petard. He writes that "Rorty's rhetoric is different from that of Rawls or Habermas, but he too is, as he says, very much one of the 'heirs of the Enlightenment.' . . . One aspect of the Enlightenment vision Rorty seems to share with [others], however, is an intolerance of points of view that consciously grow out of particular communities . . . to that extent, he seems the enemy of real pluralism" (*Unapologetic Theology*, 101).

We should ask, therefore, whether the Rortian decree against a religious tradition's referential intentions, its vision of the real, is a form of hermeneutical violence that disallows the very plurality of understanding that it purports to serve. True to his empiricist and Enlightenment pedigree, Rorty emphasizes the self-enclosed immanence of figurative (religious) discourse. But this stress is false to the experience of many who feel addressed by certain claims to attention that come to them from a source beyond and anterior to themselves. It is false for those who struggle to enact the "root-impulse of the human spirit to explore possibilities of meaning and of truth that lie outside empirical seizure or proof."[61] Rorty's historicism echoes a familiar refrain: his so-called plurality at the expense of openness to possible transcendence is as old as Western philosophy's turn to the privileged subject as the source for truth. The difference, however, is that whereas most philosophers of the Enlightenment still assumed that human beings had some tenuous contact with a reality beyond the empirical world, Rorty dismisses such an assumption as a transcendental illusion.[62]

For the person who has taken the religious wager, all life is charged with intimations of possibilities that cannot be accounted for by a thoroughgoing historicism. To disallow such possibilities under the banner of Nietzschean self-creation is to slide into self-referential incoherence: after asserting that all knowledge is contingent and perspectival the absolute claim is smuggled in that certain basic beliefs and experiences cannot possibly be true. This tacit intolerance of genuine plurality is specific to the orienting philosophical "gestures" that govern the differences between the religious person and Rorty. Beyond Rorty's Enlightenment dedivinization of the world for the sake of human flourishing, we must ask, therefore, whether an apprenticeship to the new modes of being projected by the divine Other might not be a more authentic mode of liberation than Rortian self-creation. We must ask whether one might profit from wagering her existence on a web of beliefs and values that have proven to be fertile and transformative for many, even though thinkers like Rorty can only regard such wagers as beyond the pale of conversation within his postmodern salon.

61. George Steiner, *Real Presences* (Chicago: University of Chicago Press, 1989), 225.

62. On the religious dimensions of the Enlightenment, see Mark I. Wallace, "The European Enlightenment: Religious Liberalism in the Age of Reason," in *Spirituality and the Secular Quest*, ed. Peter H. Van Ness (New York: Crossroad, forthcoming).

CONCLUSION

Rorty argues that there is no ur-reality at the base of human experience that can guarantee the process of becoming a self in a world of flux and impermanence. Holding onto the belief in such a reality is an exercise in cultural infantilism. The burden of the postmodern age, according to Rorty, is to abandon the search for moral and religious absolutes and own the fact that all descriptions of the world are essentially reinscriptions of the values and priorities held by particular communities. Since there is no way to "get it right," philosophy should abandon its craving for transcendental certainty and instead encourage persons to become artisans of their own lives. All life, therefore, is an exercise in interpretation, and perspectivism holds absolute sway.

The predictable theological response to this type of radical historicism has been to try to reanchor religious discourse with the moorings of metaphysics. In the normative tradition, we have seen that God is the supreme Being who is the ground of all relative beings. The experience of contingent selfhood leads one back to the primary affirmation of the ultimate worth of existence founded on the reality of God. I have suggested, however, that this type of theistic metaphysics is neither intellectually coherent nor religiously satisfying, Ogden's claims to the contrary notwithstanding. In the first instance, this approach frontloads its interpretation of experience with the highly contestable assertion that all persons, *whether they realize it or not*, presuppose God as the ground of their common experience. In the second case, the metaphysical approach is so governed by universal truth criteria that is unable to account for the eruption of radical alterity and novelty within experience.

On the one hand, then, my question is whether there might be a less stable and more flexible approach to the integrity of belief than that offered by liberal mediating theologies. On the other hand, my concern is whether it is possible to script one's life in response to "something more" that can press beyond the nominalist decree against ultimate reality claims. By avoiding the temptation of subscribing to a thought system that makes sense out of experience as such, we need not abide by the Rortian axiom that to be a narrator of one's own life means to abandon faith and hope in a transcendent Other. Faith is not knowledge, and hope is not certainty. Thus, in the impasse between metaphysics and neoempiricism, my case is that it is possible, though never certain, that the person who takes the risk of faith will win a construal of experience that is deeply satisfying and transformative—even though this wager must always operate in a world devoid of final answers, metaphysics notwithstanding.

CHAPTER THREE

Performative Truth
and the Witness of the Spirit

At the foundation of well-founded belief lies belief that is not founded.[1]

This, then, is the ultimate paradox of thought: to want to discover something that thought itself cannot think.[2]

Rather than a value, spirit seems to designate, beyond a deconstruction, the very resource for any deconstruction and the possibility of any evaluation.[3]

One of the more troubling legacies of the debate between metaphysics and constructivism has been a sterile opposition concerning questions of truth in matters religious. While some analysts like Ogden seek to secure religious beliefs through transcendental investigations into the conditions of universal experience, others like Rorty appeal to the ideal of private self-construction and label all religious claims as exercises in extrahistorical bad faith. The one writes that truth consists of "the most universal principles that are the strictly necessary conditions of the possibility of anything whatever,"[4] while the other avers that truth is "obedience to our own convictions . . . with no links to

1. Ludwig Wittgenstein, *On Certainty*, trans. Denis Paul and G. E. M. Anscombe (New York: Harper & Row, 1969), 33e.
2. Søren Kierkegaard, *Philosophical Fragments/Johannes Climacus*, ed. and trans. Howard V. Hong and Edna H. Hong (Princeton: Princeton University Press, 1985), 37.
3. Jacques Derrida, *Of Spirit: Heidegger and the Question*, trans. Geoffrey Bennington and Rachel Bowlby (Chicago: University of Chicago Press, 1989), 14–15.
4. Schubert Ogden, *Faith and Freedom: Toward a Theology of Liberation* (Nashville: Abingdon, 1979), 73.

63

something Beyond."[5] This polarity between metaphysical realism and inter-tribal skepticism travels the ground mapped out by contemporary conflicts concerning the nature of truth. But questions such as, Is reality objective and determinate, or is it constructed on the basis of human judgment? offer false disjunctions and little hope for resolution under the terms of these alternative philosophical vocabularies.

Though each faction regards the status of religious beliefs differently, they both operate on the same topography marked out by the history of meta-physics. Both factions tacitly presume that religious beliefs are predicated on philosophical assumptions about the essential nature of God, the universe, and humankind. At opposite ends of a common playing field, both perspectives beg the same question: Is God the *ens realissimum* who guarantees the search for truth and the value of existence? Metaphysicians respond, "Of course! What else could God be?" while antimetaphysicians grouse "See what we mean? They still crave for something transcendent to assuage their fini-tude!" And so the answer to the question at issue is assumed by both dis-putants to be the same, even though each faction then argues to opposite conclusions from this common starting point.

Both camps are right and both are wrong. The question of metaphysics in theology has left Christianity with a philosopher's god, a god frozen between the philosophical optimism of normative religious thought and the nominal-ism of neoempiricism and its variants. Such a god remains tethered between the metaphysical craving for universals and the deep-seated historicism of pragmatically minded philosophy. But such a god is not imperious enough to worship or hate, and has little relation to the often compassionate but also capricious God of the biblical witness. As highest existent, *ens a se*, pure actu-ality, being-itself, and *prima causa*, this deity is "the god of philosophy. Man can neither pray nor sacrifice to this god. Before the *causa sui*, man can nei-ther fall to his knees in awe nor can he play music and dance before this god."[6] Captive to the categories of Being, such a god can neither be loved nor struggled against, nor defended on evidential grounds as an object available to the knower.

My contention is that the god of philosophy must be overcome if the free-dom and alterity of the God of faith are to be preserved. But to "step back

5. Richard Rorty, *Consequences of Pragmatism* (Madison: University of Wisconsin Press, 1982), xlii–xliii.

6. Martin Heidegger, "The Onto-theo-logical Constitution of Metaphysics," in *Identity and Difference*, trans. Joan Stambaugh (New York: Harper & Row, 1969), 72.

out" of metaphysics, as Heidegger said, is easier said than done; the task cannot be accomplished with assertions. Even those thinkers, like Heidegger, who sought to free thought about God from being reinscribed with metaphysical categories have been read as once again rendering the concept "God" captive to the question of being.[7] Is it possible, then, to free thought about God from the domain of metaphysics? It is possible, I believe, when theology can thematize the *instability of faith* in a world of radical flux and abandon the foundationalist determination of God as the fundamental *ground of being*. In the economy of faith, it is possible to envisage God as beyond philosophy—that is, it is possible to imagine God without being. The overcoming of metaphysics in theology, therefore, must be crafted with language and praxis attuned to the indeterminacy and alterity of the Other who is not captive to the discourse of being. Of course, whenever "we open our mouths we find ourselves in the province of philosophy,"[8] but unless one tries to unsay what has been said, and unthink what has been thought, the liberty of God for *standing-over* one's projects of *under-standing* God will be precluded, and the freedom of God *to be* without *be-ing* will be denied.

Operating on the same terrain about what God is and is not, both the metaphysical and neoempiricist camps are *right* in their assumption that the metaphysical concept of God has been used to ensure the perdurance of all relative beings. They are right that this thesis has been the linchpin of Western metadiscourse about the nature of things since the Pre-Socratics. They are right that the idea of God as self-subsistent ground and final cause has provided a reassuring *fundamentum* in the time-honored search for permanence and certitude. But while this idea of God is the received viewpoint for both philosophical apologists of Christianity and their opponents, this idea has little to do with the always unpredictable (and sometimes despotic) God of biblical faith. The God witnessed to in the main and along the margins of the scriptures provides no foundational certainty, metaphysical or otherwise, for those who wager their lives on what they take to be the will and desires of this God.

Thus, both camps are *wrong* in their shared understanding of God under the question of Being because such an orientation is not able to account for the arbitrary nature of the Other whose reality cannot be grasped, objectified,

---

7. So Jean-Luc Marion, *God Without Being: Hors-Texte,* trans. Thomas A. Carlson (Chicago: University of Chicago Press, 1991), 37–73.

8. Karl Barth, *Credo*, trans. Strathearn McNab (New York: Charles Scribner's Sons, 1962), 184.

calculated, or categorized. These (un)related approaches cannot account for the "absolute freedom of God with regard to all determinations, including, first of all, the basic condition that renders all other conditions possible and even necessary—for us, humans—the fact of Being."[9] These approaches cannot account for the reality of God as unsayable, unthinkable otherness—the vanishing point toward which many persons struggle to gain access, but whose residence is beyond and outside the horizon of Being and beings. As I will suggest here, God as *Spirit* is the wind who blows where she wills; and *as* such, God as Spirit can no more be understood within the confines of a philosophical thought system than the wind can be explained by reference to a weathervane.

THE SPIRIT IS THE LAMP OF THE TRUTH: I

If the metaphysics–antimetaphysics disagreement has reached a stalemate, is it possible that a reevaluation of God as Spirit might be able to address the problem of truth in religious discourse? My initial answer to this question is that insofar as the Spirit is the power who enables the individual to discern the truth in particular circumstances, then one can profitably attune oneself to the Spirit's inner persuasions in order to realize an effectual relation to the truth. The Spirit is the *viva vox* of the truth whose interior witness enables one to figure the world in broad and generous terms.[10] But the role of the Spirit as the inner testimony to the truth has little place in recent theology. Much of contemporary religious thought ignores or assimilates the Spirit's work by specifying Spirit-indifferent methodological requirements that all questions about truth in religion must satisfy; such requirements allow little room for the subversive tutelage of the Spirit to disrupt and displace the criteria founded by the normative methods. In particular, the privileged accord assigned to metaphysical categories in religious thought has meant that debates about truth in philosophy have defined the terms for adjudicating questions about truth in religious studies. The perennial question in these debates is whether truth is composed relative to particular conceptual

9. Marion, *God Without Being*, xx.

10. The idea of the *testimonium internum Spiritus Sancti* is borrowed from Calvin and other Reformed thinkers and confessions. See John Calvin, *Institutes of the Christian Religion*, ed. John T. McNeill and trans. Ford Lewis Battles, 2 vols. (Philadelphia: Westminster Press, 1960), 1:78–81, 537–53. More on this point below.

schemes, or whether it can be assayed by forming a representation of reality that fits with the facts and is independent of human judgment. Some religious thinkers have followed the first tack by maintaining that all knowledge, including theological knowledge, reflects the contingent norms and worldviews of one's culture, while others hold out for a "God's eye" perspective on reality in which theory-independent statements about God and world are both possible *and* necessary for ensuring the objectivity, even the scientific character, of theological judgments. As in philosophy, let us call each party of theologians "antirealist" and "realist," respectively.[11]

My suggestion, however, is that the debate between realism and antirealism offers a false alternative to theology, and that a more adequate theory than that suggested by either of the standard options is what I will call a "performative" notion of truth. Against the sterile juxtaposition of truth as correspondence to a reality independent of perspectival bias (realism), or as intersubjective agreement about what a community takes to be the case under particular circumstances (antirealism), *a performative model maintains that a theological judgment is true whenever it enables compassionate engagement with the world in a manner that is enriching and transformative for self and other.*[12]

---

11. Theological antirealists include, among others, George A. Lindbeck, Mark C. Taylor, and Jeffrey Stout, while realists comprise such otherwise disparate theorists as Wolfhart Pannenberg, T. F. Torrance, and Franklin Gamwell. In this vein, cf. Lindbeck's claim that the Nicene Creed, for example, is not propositionally true in correspondence terms because it functions as a "communal doctrine [that] does not make first-order truth claims" (*The Nature of Doctrine: Religion and Theology in a Postliberal Age* [Philadelphia: Westminster Press, 1984], 19), with Torrance's statement to the contrary: "To be truthful theological statements must correspond in form and content to that divine Object, and they must be enunciated in a material mode appropriate to that correspondence" ("The Problem of Theological Statement Today," in *Theology in Reconstruction* [Grand Rapids, Mich.: Eerdmans, 1965], 61).

12. The fundamental criterion for this model of truth is practical, not hermeneutical. My presumption is that some degree of *fidelity* to the biblical texts and the Christian tradition should always be aimed at in any theological claim, but that the standard for *justifying* any such claim should be a positive answer to the question, Does this claim empower forms of life that are liberating and transformative? The primary source, then, for theology is the fund of biblical and historical imagery peculiar to the Christian tradition, but the justification for the different uses of this multifaceted source proceeds from the capacity of the interpretation in question successfully to guide and structure healthy praxis. Many liberation and feminist theologians make this point. From a performative perspective, for example, a Pelagian and semi-Pelagian reading of the Bible and the tradition could both be "true" depending on the practical uses to which the alternative readings are put, not on whether one of the two debated positions singularly corresponds to the propositional content of the Bible and the tradition on the question of human freedom and divine necessity. For an illuminating discussion of the role of praxis crite-

This model puts the stress on truth as the basis of action, as Wittgenstein puts it, not as a fit between mind and world, or as the result of communal agreement.[13] Of course, what does and does not count as "compassionate engagement" is a difficult problem for the performative approach, and how exactly this approach differs from its close counterpart, the antirealist position, also needs to be sorted out. These questions notwithstanding, my proposal is driven by a conviction that in theology, at least, a belief is true just insofar as it fosters a life of benevolent regard toward the "other." In this approach my hope is that the purpose of theology will again be regarded (as it was for Augustine) as the art of scripting one's life in fidelity to the Spirit's promptings to love and serve the neighbor.[14] I will argue, then, that the goal of theological truth-making will be to actualize in persons an *inspir(it)ed* openness to the neighbor.

WITTGENSTEIN AND BASIC BELIEFS

The question of truth is a thorny problem in theological reflection. The traditions of realism and antirealism in analytic philosophy have offered theologians resources for arbitrating the truth question in religious discourse, but the legacy of analytic philosophy in contemporary theology has been contested by theologians who question the value of importing philosophical approaches to truth into theological inquiry.[15] Nevertheless, the conceptualities expressed by the realist/antirealist debate are well represented in contemporary religious thought, even if the analytic labels are frowned upon, or not used at all. For many religious thinkers, the advantage to the realist approach is the isomorphism it announces between theological affirmations and the object of these affirmations. Persons can have context-independent and

---

ria in settling theological truth-claims, see Francis Schüssler Fiorenza, *Foundational Theology: Jesus and the Church* (New York: Crossroad, 1984), 265–323.

13. See Ludwig Wittgenstein, *On Certainty*, ed. G. E. M. Anscombe and G. H. von Wright; trans. Denis Paul and G. E. M. Anscombe (New York: Harper & Row, 1969), 52–73.

14. Augustine argued that love of God and charity toward the neighbor is the fulfillment and end of theology and biblical exegesis. A construal of the truth that does not serve this twofold goal is invalid. See Augustine *On Christian Doctrine*, esp. bk. 1.

15. Hans W. Frei and George A. Lindbeck are well-known for defending the integrity of theological reflection independent of extratheological and extrabiblical models of truth—what they call "*ad hoc* apologetics." For this discussion and the relevant bibliography, see my *The Second Naiveté: Barth, Ricoeur, and the New Yale Theology* (Macon, Ga.: Mercer University Press, 1990), 87–110.

determinate knowledge of God *a se* as a being not reducible to any theoretical paradigm. Insofar as God witnesses to God's self in the vocabulary of the Bible, the Christian community can be confident that its language about God is adequate to the reality it signifies. Scripture is *deus dixit*—a transparent medium through which the divine identity and will are communicated without being fundamentally altered by human culture or bias.[16]

Nevertheless, many contemporary theologians are uneasy with realist understandings of truth claims as referring to external realities (such as God and the world) independent of particular conceptual schemes. The charge is that realism betrays an objectivist bias insensitive to the interdependence of subject and object in all modes of inquiry, theological or otherwise. Realism carries the freight of a notion of representation that posits the mind as a clean mirror transparent upon a world of determinate objects. Knowledge consists of a correspondence or "fit" between the mirroring mind and the objects outside of it. Realist epistemologies presume a sharp subject/object distinction in which the rational atomized subject is understood not as actively *constituting* the real, but as passively *receiving* "impressions" or "representations" of the real. While some theologians are attracted to realism because of the objectivity and exteriority assigned to God and world in this schema, they are nervous about the fundamental split between the disinterested, bias-free subject and the external object characteristic of this position.

From my perspective, realism is deficient on two counts. First of all, the preservation of the subject/object split highlights realism's inability to account for the perspectival and reflexive nature of experience—namely, that the subject only knows the world on the basis of its own prior participation in it. There is no knowledge of the "innocent eye" divorced from the web of beliefs that generates understanding in the first place. There is no extralinguistic "sky hook," as Richard Rorty puts it, that permits an escape from the meaning-saturated and culturally embedded representations of reality to which all provincial perspectives, including those in the Bible, are beholden.[17]

16. Glossing Anselm, Karl Barth is the best-known defender of theological realism in our time: true knowledge of God has as its presupposition and ground the fact of divine revelation. Thus the hermeneutical circle of Barth's (and Anselm's) thought: to thematize the truth is to explicate the always already reality of God's self-disclosure in the language of the scriptures. Insofar as theology is grounded on revelation, its claims to truth are relatively adequate expressions of the realities they signify. See Karl Barth, *Anselm: Fides Quaerens Intellectum*, trans. Ian W. Robertson (Pittsburgh: Pickwick Press, 1975).

17. See Richard Rorty, *Objectivity, Relativism, and Truth*, vol. 1 of *Philosophical Papers* (Cambridge: Cambridge University Press, 1991), 9–17.

But what is especially pernicious in most forms of *theological* realism is the tendency to reduce the reality of God to an entity knowable under the terms of this or that particular metaphysical vocabulary. This reduction stems from the assumption that the term "God" is assimilable to a determinate concept (such as "Being") or catalogue of attributes (such as "omnipotent," "immutable," "impartial," and so forth). Such a reduction results in the reality of God becoming captive to certain philosophical conditions (what Heidegger called "ontotheology") that determine what does or does not count as true theological knowledge.[18] My contention, on the other hand, is that in the absolute independence of the Spirit, God is inexpressible mystery, indeterminate and unbounded, and always free to reveal and conceal God's self according to the divine will. Thus, God is never an object knowable under the gaze of the independent subject's bounded vision; God is not an object subsumable under the horizon of a particular vocabulary. God is not a determinate reality exterior to the knowing subject, a fixed entity "on the other side" of the subject–object split as iterated by realism. God, rather, is the all-encompassing reality within which all knowledge is generated and sustained; the source and end of all determinations; the eternal one who dwells prior to and beyond Being and all beings. God, in sum, surpasses every representation of God.

Given the problems associated with realism, an antirealist approach to truth has distinct advantages. Antirealism holds that there is no mind-independent reality to which all relative judgments about meaning and truth are directed—or, more cautiously, that even if there *is* such a reality one cannot have access to it. The upshot is that since there is no (knowable) overarching object or field of objects for evaluating competing claims, it follows that all such claims are relative to different, even incommensurable, conceptual schemes. The advantage to this approach is its recognition of the *locatedness* of all forms of rational inquiry in the particular forms of life that constitute one's understanding of the world. As we saw earlier in relation to the rhetorical response to metaphysics, since all knowledge is situated within the operative theories specific to particular interpreters, the data and criteria for establishing truth-claims are equally situation-specific and theory-laden.

In spite of antirealism's advantage over realism by virtue of its contextual understanding of truth, antirealism does not, in the final analysis, provide the

---

18. See Heidegger, "The Onto-theo-logical Constitution of Metaphysics," 42–74. Also see Marion, *God Without Being*, 33–107; and Kevin Hart, *The Trespass of the Sign: Deconstruction, Theology and Philosophy* (Cambridge: Cambridge University Press, 1989), 71–104.

most adequate model for adjudicating *theological* truth-claims. The problem with antirealism is that it can too easily degenerate into self-referential incoherence by falling prey to its own charge that no theoretical system possesses a universal standard for determining the nature of the world. By making the claim that *no* conceptual scheme can represent reality as such (or even that there is no such reality), it too is trading on the currency of a totalizing theory, its protestations to the contrary notwithstanding. As an exercise in philosophical hygiene antirealism is a necessary antidote to realism's quest for universals, but as a philosophical theory it violates its own prescription against constructing all-encompassing theories of knowledge by virtue of its assertion that the subject has no evaluative framework by which to judge the adequacy of particular perspectives on the world.

In asserting that different viewpoints are incommensurate, Donald Davidson argues that antirealism renders false its claim that there is no evaluative standard by which to judge conceptual schemes. "The dominant metaphor of conceptual relativism, that of differing points of view, seems to betray an underlying paradox. Different points of view make sense, but only if there is a common co-ordinate system on which to plot them; yet the existence of a common system belies the claim of dramatic incomparability."[19] In short, consistent antirealism is self-refuting. If, as antirealists argue, there is no meta-theory for adjudicating competing claims to truth, then antirealism can at best be a guess as to the contextual nature of knowledge and the constructed character of reality—not a final statement about the incommensurability of different conceptual schemes and the indeterminate nature of reality. Thus while realism is not adequate to the situational character of knowledge, antirealism as an overarching theory is inconsistent with its own relativist criteria.

The mediation of the realism/antirealism conflict is not a pressing task for contemporary theology, but an engagement with the issues raised by this debate is important for establishing the rationality that is characteristic of theological discourse. Wittgenstein's notion of everyday beliefs (including religious beliefs) as practically useful "*pictures*" of the world provides a way beyond the stalemate of the debate, and toward an understanding of the nature of truth in theological reflection. Consider, for example, his discussion of the everyday belief that the earth is a globular body suspended in space. "The picture of the earth as a ball is a *good* picture, it proves itself everywhere,

---

19. Donald Davidson, "On the Very Idea of a Conceptual Scheme," in *Inquiries into Truth and Interpretation* (Oxford: Clarendon Press, 1985), 184.

it is also a simple picture—in short, we work with it without doubting it."[20]
Commonsense cosmology consists of a pictorial representation of the earth as
a ball; this representation "proves itself" by providing the terms for certain
calculations in physics that would be impossible apart from this assumption.
This picture consists of a ball rotating on an axis in a steady orbit around the
sun. As such this is a *useful* picture for predicting and controlling events, but
it is by no means *certain* insofar as there is no guarantee that the earth is forever fixed on its axis, or that it could not alter its spherical shape or its helio-
centric orbit, on the basis of some future change of events. The point is that
for now the picture works even if, at some future date, the reality the picture
seeks to approximate could change as well as the picture itself. The picture of
the world as a ball, in the language of antirealism, is a *construct* of physics specific to the current cosmological paradigm, but from a realist perspective, it is
a *successful* construct because it is useful as a reference point for making pre-
dictions and for adjudicating between alternative models for understanding
the universe. In this framework, therefore, "truth" is an honorific assignable
to emergent and revisable belief systems that enable one productively to
engage the world in a manner specific to one's basic theoretical orientation.

Theological claims function analogously to cosmological propositions: as
basic beliefs that found, rather than being founded upon, one's fundamental
outlook on life, they offer a compelling "picture" of reality that "proves itself"
by rendering more meaningful and intelligible one's experience of the world
and others.[21] Such beliefs are an exercise in trust, not proof; they are always
fallible and function as ready candidates for revision. Their force lies in their
ability fruitfully to enlarge and deepen one's understanding of what one takes
to be reality, not in their susceptibility to canons of evidence independent of
these judgments in the first place. A person who believes that the Spirit
empowers her to love the neighbor, or that the earth is a ball, does not base
this belief on a set of supporting arguments independent of this original
assumption; rather, she uses this assumption as the working hypothesis for
understanding all reality and discovers that her experience of the world is elu-
cidated and expanded as a result.

As with other baseline beliefs, the logic of religious beliefs is circular. The
circle is not vicious, however, because it is always in tandem with the broad

20. Wittgenstein, *On Certainty*, 22e.
21. For a thoughtful use of Wittgenstein as a way beyond the realism/antirealism controversy, and with special reference to the controversy's purchase on theological reflection, see
Fergus Kerr, *Theology After Wittgenstein* (Oxford: Basil Blackwell, 1986), esp. 101–41.

plane of everyday experience that provides the confirming evidence (but never the final proof) for the daily usefulness of these beliefs. The person who remains committed to some form of realism or positivism will not, understandably, find this valorization of theological circularity persuasive.[22] Wittgenstein, however, writes that "[a]t the foundation of well-founded belief lies belief that is not founded," meaning that the criterion for the adequacy of a belief is not that it be *founded* on the basis of an apodictic warrant (for example, that it be self-evident to the mind or incorrigible to the senses), but that it be *generative* of a full and integrated understanding of experience.[23] For the later Wittgenstein, truth is a matter of performance and utility: a basic worldview proposition is true just insofar as it forms the basis for one's competent action in the world. The question of what constitutes "competent action" is of course contestable and, according to Wittgenstein, can only be adjudicated by paying close attention to the conduct codes and rational standards operative in particular communities of inquiry. But appeals to extracommunal values and norms for establishing the truth of a particular worldview or action are not valid. *The thrust of Wittgenstein's whole philosophy is that truth (religious, scientific, or otherwise) is a matter of empowering human agents to accomplish with integrity the difficult task of becoming thoughtful and successful persons in a world of conflicting loyalties and claims to attention.* Similar to other basic beliefs, founding religious beliefs appear baseless as candidates for rational demonstration in a manner convincing to the realist, but as useful leadstrings for making sense of one's experience they are extraordinarily fecund and useful.

Wayne Proudfoot maintains that the refusal to allow external criteria to adjudicate religious truth-claims wrongly insulates such claims from rigorous analysis and possible refutation. He argues against Wittgenstein-like appeals to intracommunal norms, because such appeals ensure that "the autonomy of religious life is defended in order to preclude inquiry and to stave off demands for justification from some perspective outside of that life."[24] While Proudfoot is right to criticize theologians and others for developing protective strategies that preclude disconfirmations of their beliefs from external sources, it seems that thoroughgoing natural explanations for religious phenomena are not adequate either. Such explanatory schemes cannot account

22. See Anthony Flew, *The Presumption of Atheism* (London: Pemberton, 1976).

23. Wittgenstein, *On Certainty*, 33e.

24. Wayne Proudfoot, *Religious Experience* (Berkeley: University of California Press, 1985), xv.

for the integrity of beliefs that presuppose a divine reality. The reduction of some religious beliefs to nonreligious explanations can be a helpful therapeutic in checking the excesses of religious credulity, but to argue that *all* such beliefs are so reducible is a hegemonistic gesture that serves neither the interests of intellectual inquiry nor religious understanding.

Returning to Wittgenstein, my point is that what is distinctive about truth *in religion* is that theological beliefs are both originary to one's fundamental worldview *and* oriented toward moral growth and renewal. In the performative approach a belief in *general* is true insofar as it unleashes expansive and productive encounters with the world, whereas the *particular* beliefs fostered by religious commitments are true whenever they engender ever-widening encounters with the world that aim to further the welfare of all parties in question. It is in this sense that truth in theological discourse is performative truth: the pragmatic power of certain beliefs and actions to set free engagements with others that are liberating and transformative.

Since truth-claims in religion are not available to rational proof or empirical confirmation, there are no easily available referents that can verify or disconfirm such claims. "An honest religious thinker is like a tightrope walker. He almost looks as though he were walking on nothing but air. His support is the slenderest imaginable. And yet it really is possible to walk on it."[25] While claims in other modes of discourse (in applied physics or calculus, for example) can sometimes be validated on the basis of logical relations or physical evidence, religious claims have no such bars of appeal. Instead the truth warrants in religion must be looked for elsewhere; my suggestion is that these warrants are intracommunal and practical in nature. As in literature and the arts the truth question in religion should be, Does this way of viewing the world enable the critical engagements and transformed relationships among the subscribers to the worldview that the perspective in question purports to offer? If positive answers to this sort of question are forthcoming, then such ways of construing reality are candidates for truth.

Influenced by Wittgenstein, a performative model of truth has distinctive advantages. Appropriate to the criteriological concerns of realism, this model posits "successful praxis" or "moral transformation" as the standards by which to judge the adequacy of particular formulations of a theological vision of the world. And in the manner of antirealism, the performative approach celebrates the diversity of such formulations as perspectival attempts to better

---

25. Ludwig Wittgenstein, *Culture and Value*, trans. Peter Winch, ed. G. H. Von Wright (Chicago: University of Chicago Press, 1980), 73e.

understand experience, which are themselves not in need of further philosophical justification. This approach preserves the values of contextuality *and* objectivity, for while there is no purely universal reality that can provide a fixed reference point for judging all truth-claims, such claims must nevertheless demonstrate their *agapic utility*, so to speak, as trustworthy guides for compassionate and intelligible engagement with the world. Theological claims that meet the performance criterion by serving as relatively adequate bases for such benevolent action and understanding cut through the false alternatives projected by the realism/antirealism debate, and lay the foundation for a deliberative making of truth-claims in religious life and discourse.

"I have arrived at the rock bottom of my convictions. And one might say that these foundations-walls are carried by the whole house."[26] My thesis that truth pertaining to religion is a matter of ethical performance is a baseline conviction that I use to elucidate the whole range of Christian beliefs and practices. Orienting field-encompassing theses such as this are what Charles Peirce called "abductive hypotheses" or Michael Polanyi labeled "tacit beliefs": heuristic presuppositions that explain a wide body of experiences, but which themselves admit of no external confirmations.[27] Such presumptions are the working idioms one uses to construct the world one inhabits. Similarly, Alvin Plantinga refers to abductive or heuristic beliefs as "basic beliefs," that is, beliefs fundamental to one's overall worldview, but beliefs that cannot be argued for or against on the basis of other beliefs even more basic than the first beliefs themselves.[28] Some convictions are so fundamental to one's experience of the world that they form the basis of all other experiences and are not in need of any other convictions for their support. Oftentimes beliefs in matters religious and ethical are of this sort as well; they are the first planks in one's fundamental noetic structure. That such presumptions are original to the way one thinks, and not derivative from other thoughts, does not mean that they are beyond the pale of rational discussion, but it does mean that such discussion minimally will have to grant the integrity, if not the truth, of these first-order presumptions in the first place if there is to be any understanding of the nature of the fundamental convictions

26. Wittgenstein, *On Certainty*, 33e.

27. See Charles S. Peirce, "Abduction and Induction," in *Philosophical Writings of Peirce*, ed. Justus Buchler (New York: Dover, 1955), 150–56; and Michael Polanyi, *Personal Knowledge: Towards a Post-Critical Philosophy* (Chicago: University of Chicago Press, 1958).

28. Alvin Plantinga, "Reason and Belief in God," in *Faith and Rationality*, ed. Alvin Plantinga and Nicholas Wolterstorff (Notre Dame: University of Notre Dame Press, 1983), 16–93.

that are central to the experience in question. "There is no mind-set in respect of consciousness and of 'reality' which does not make at least one leap into the dark (the *a priori*) of the unprovable."[29] Every argument assumes something, every argument begins somewhere—one can only argue *from* a fundamental presupposition, not *to* it. To those predisposed to taking the wager that truth is a question of performance, the risk is worth it, and to those who have decided against this gesture, no amount of argument can convince them otherwise.

THE FACE IN LEVINAS

Emmanuel Levinas's ethical philosophy is one of the most powerful articulations of performative truth in our time. For Levinas, truth consists in the drama of the face-to-face relation with the other person. Through the neighbor, God summons the subject to be responsible for the neighbor's welfare; in the presence of the neighbor's face (*visage*), an absolute demand is made on the subject to exercise justice and compassion toward the neighbor. For Levinas, truth is nurtured by my hospitality to the other; it follows my positive response to the other's query whether I am willing to be my brother's or sister's keeper. In grammatical terms, the face of the other directly *addresses* me in the vocative case and enjoins me to be *for* its interests in the register of the interrelational dative.[30] Truth, therefore, is not found in the Cartesian return of the self to the inner certainties of its interior life; instead, it is born in the self's going outside of itself toward the other.

Truth begins with the biblical Abraham's (and Isaiah's) open responses to the divine Other, "Here I am, Lord."[31] "God, the Infinite, is properly neither designated by words nor even indicated or named, but borne witness to in the peculiar character of the 'Here I am.' . . . The Infinite is there in the order that orders me to my neighbor."[32] Standing in openness to the mystery and call of the other (be it the human or divine other) enables one's readiness to follow a

29. George Steiner, *Real Presences* (Chicago: University of Chicago Press, 1989), 214.

30. Emmanuel Levinas, "God and Philosophy," in *The Levinas Reader*, ed. Seán Hand (Oxford: Basil Blackwell, 1989), 182.

31. Emmanuel Levinas, *Otherwise Than Being or Beyond Essence*, trans. Alphonso Lingis (Dordrecht: Kluwer Academic Publishers, 1974), 149–52.

32. Alphonso Lingis in the introduction to Levinas, *Otherwise Than Being or Beyond Essence*, xxxiv.

path (in the manner of Abraham) into an entirely unknown and foreign place that is not one's own—the place where the inviolability and integrity of the other are protected at all costs.

Truth, then, is not a matter of knowing but of doing. It is not arrived at either through the disclosure of universal structures (*pace* realism) or the usefulness of various vocabularies (*pace* antirealism), but rather with taking responsibility for one's obligations toward the other. In this sense truth is not an epistemological problem in the classical sense of correct knowledge about an object exterior to the mind. Truth is not the active acquisition of knowledge about the other as an "object" that is subject to the knower's calculations and control. It is not knowledge in the sense of *Auffassen* (understanding) which is also a *Fassen* (gripping).[33] In the classical scheme, the light of the mind brings into presence whatever is and grasps the "other" as an immediately available object for the knowing subject. Under the gaze of the mind's eye, the novelty and alterity of the other are stripped away so that the other can be categorized according to the subject's conceptual activity. But for Levinas, "[a] face confounds the intentionality that aims at it."[34] Truth, therefore, does not follow the sovereign subject's conceptual grasping, but originates in the openness and solicitude exercised by the subject toward the other *as an other*, and in the subject's renunciation of all claims to own or possess the other in the process. Practicing the truth is not a re-presentation of the other as a categorizable object, but risking a relationship with a being that is always different from me. Thus truth is categorically nonviolent: it begins in openness to the other's face and concomitant refusal to set upon and seize the other as a thing, an object, under the subject's disposal.

The face of the other is not the aggregate of physical features that makes up a person's appearance (though it includes this), but is rather the vulnerable site of my neighbor's appeal to me to take responsibility for his or her welfare. "The Other becomes my neighbor precisely through the way the face summons me, calls for me, begs for me, and in so doing recalls my responsibility, and calls me into question."[35] The countenance of the other person is the site of a kerygma that addresses me about my obligation for that person's wellbeing.

---

33. Levinas, "Ethics as First Philosophy," in *The Levinas Reader*, ed. Hand, 76.

34. Emmanuel Levinas, "Meaning and Sense," in *Collected Philosophical Papers*, trans. Alphonso Lingis (The Hague: Martinus Nijhoff, 1987), 97.

35. Levinas, "Ethics as First Philosophy," 83.

The face is not the mere assemblage of a nose, forehead, eyes, etc.; it is all that, of course . . . [but] the face, for its part, is inviolable; those eyes, which are absolutely without protection, the most naked part of the human body, none the less offer an absolute resistance to possession, an absolute resistance in which the temptation to murder is inscribed: the temptation of absolute negation. . . . To see a face is already to hear "You shall not kill," and to hear "You shall not kill" is to hear "Social justice."[36]

The resistance to murder is generated by one's encounter with the defenseless and unprotected eyes of one's neighbor. To look into another's eyes is to be caught short by the supreme ethical maxim "You shall not kill"; it is to refuse the temptation to violently impose one's will on the other. In their nakedness and openness, the eyes call the subject to responsibility; they summon the subject to respect the other's right to a full and productive existence.

The potential for violence against the other results from championing the interests of the "system" over and against the particular needs of the individual other. In Levinas, the "system" or the "totality" stands for any all-inclusive understanding of experience that would take away the alterity and novelty of the other by denying its transcendence to the system. All forms of totalitarian thinking destroy the individual identity of the other by flattening out its differences from the system. Here to know the other is to press the other into the service of the subject's totalizing consciousness, where self and other are brought together by a common luminous essence ("Being") that both share. Thus, the freedom and spontaneity of the other to stand in a heterogenous and asymmetric relation to the system are subordinated to the demands of the totality for sameness, commonality, synthesis, order, predictability, and control.

Levinas takes issue with Western philosophers' quest for a neutral third term—for example, Hegel's "*Geist,*" Husserl's "horizon," or Heidegger's "Being"—that would reduce the other to an intelligible and common sameness. "Western philosophy has most often been . . . a reduction of the other to the same by interposition of a middle and neutral term that ensures the comprehension of being."[37] Consider in this regard Levinas's criticism of Hegel's notion of Spirit. For Hegel, the Spirit achieves self-fulfillment by becoming its other in a double movement of self-discovery in history. First the Spirit

36. Emmanuel Levinas, "Ethics and Spirit," in *Difficult Freedom: Essays on Judaism,* ed. Seán Hand (Baltimore: Johns Hopkins University Press, 1990), 8.
37. Emmanuel Levinas, *Totality and Infinity,* trans. Alphonso Lingis (Pittsburgh: Duquesne University Press, 1969), 43.

becomes an object to itself by passing over into that which it is not; then the Spirit sublates its other in order to return to itself in a new synthesis between the Spirit in-itself and the Spirit other-than-itself. The problem with this movement, however, is that the Spirit requires all that it is not—including the lives of particular historical individuals—to be subsumed into the final totality that the Spirit seeks to become. Indeed, the Spirit requires the sacrifice of individuals' passions and interests on the altar of its own progress by using all that is "other" for a final reconciliation into the "same." Personal happiness and individual welfare must often be sacrificed on the "slaughterbench" of universal history so that the higher purpose of the Spirit's self-realization can be realized; in this regard, the hopes and dreams of individual persons are but the raw material for the Spirit's coming to itself through its (ab)use of historical persons and events.[38] "This may be called the *cunning of Reason*—that [Reason] sets the passions to work for itself, while that through which it develops itself pays the penalty and suffers the loss. . . . The particular in most cases is too trifling as compared with the universal; the individuals are sacrificed and abandoned."[39] In this schema true human freedom consists in the individual's conformity to the dictates of the Spirit's higher Reason or Plan. Persons who are adept at discerning such master plans within the vagaries of daily life are "world-historical individuals"—the ones who become means to the end of universal Reason's realization of its own interests.[40] Such persons successfully unify the concrete and the universal, the particular and the always necessary, and are thus accorded the high honor of becoming the "tools and means of the World Spirit for attaining its purpose."[41]

For Levinas, the epiphany of the other's face constitutes the most fundamental challenge to relating to the other as a tool within the master plan of universal Reason or the Hegelian Spirit. Inscribed in the face is a power that resists the totalizing subject's violent desires to subordinate the other to the dictates of an all-encompassing absolute. "The face is present in its refusal to be contained. In this sense it cannot be comprehended, that is, encompassed."[42] The epiphany of the face embodies a "surplus always exterior to the totality" which threatens the other's concrete specificity.[43] This surplus resists

38. See G. W. F. Hegel, *Reason in History: A General Introduction to the Philosophy of History*, trans. Robert S. Hartman (Indianapolis: Bobbs-Merrill, 1953), 27.

39. Ibid., 43–44.

40. Ibid., 25–49 passim.

41. Ibid., 31.

42. Levinas, *Totality and Infinity*, 194.

43. Ibid., 22. Also see Levinas, *Otherwise Than Being or Beyond Essence*, 99–109.

conformity to any predetermined order, including the order prescribed for it by universal Reason. The face therefore occupies a space that is disturbingly unstable and transcendent in relation to the space inhabited by the subject; it refuses to be subsumed under a uniform and harmonious system that denies the other's integrity in the name of balance, order, and the commonweal. Thus, the face signifies the breakup of totality and a threat to the impulse to dominate the other person's alterity and control the other's individuality.

In this refusal the face is alternately and at the same time both exterior and proximate to me: it is both a trace of absence and distance and the announcement of a demand on my loyalties which I am enjoined to obey. It is infinitely transcendent and foreign to me because it refuses to join me and be integrated into a core "being" or "nature" that we share, yet it is also the face-to-face force of a direct moral summons that obligates me to care for the one standing next to me, my neighbor. The face is the trace of the other's irrepressible capacity to call me to my responsibilities toward the other, but in a manner that resists all forms of domination and absolutism.

THE SPIRIT IS THE LAMP OF THE TRUTH: II

Up to this point I have suggested that a performative approach to truth in religion mediates the realism/antirealism debate, and that this approach is of the order of a framework belief not susceptible to demands for justification outside community-embedded norms and ideals. I have further sought to develop this model through an analysis of Levinas's defense of the integrity of the face which resists the assimilative powers of the system. *Truth, then, is born in nonviolent responsibility for the other; it is enacted in the praxis of compassion for another's well-being.* Nevertheless, while this approach may prove attractive as a *via media* in relation to the regnant accounts of truth in the current discussion, as a *practical* matter it seems to lack applicability and specificity. Jesus said that one can distinguish between true and false prophets on the basis of the fruit they bear (Matthew 7:15–20). Yet what are these fruits and how does one recognize them? If the performative approach works, then what precisely counts as a successful performance, a truth-claim, for religious life and belief? Moreover, how can a revival of discourse about the Spirit illuminate the problem of ethical truth-making in our own time?

In response, let us consider again the biblical image of the Spirit as the divine force for love and communion within the cosmos (the *vinculum caritatis*). From this perspective, to enact the truth is to respond to the prompt-

Kierkegaard was a virtuoso at describing the character of faith animated by the paradoxical and unpredictable influence of the Spirit. Kierkegaard writes that the movement of authentic faith is always grounded, humanely speaking, in the belief in the impossible, the hope in the unknown. Faith exists "by virtue of the absurd, by virtue of the fact that for God all things are possible."[46] Since the person who wagers faith "can be saved only by the absurd," the person of faith inhabits the world of spirit where the unexpected and impossible take the place of necessity and finitude.[47] To inhabit the world of spirit—a world made possible by the original movement of the divine Spirit toward the individual—is to inhabit a place that appears to be chaotically abnormal and irrational to the outside observer. "There is little belief in spirit, and yet the essential thing in making this movement is spirit. It is essential that it not be a unilateral result of a *dira necessitas* [cruel constraint of necessity], and the more this is present, the more doubtful it always is that the movement is normal."[48]

Kierkegaard's *locus classicus* for this abnormal movement of faith is the story of the divine command to Abraham to offer Isaac as a sacrifice in Genesis 22. In one sense Kierkegaard's whole philosophy can be read as a struggle to come to terms with the horrific implications of this story for Christian faith. His philosophy reads as a running *haggadah* on how this text of biblical terror and abandonment—what the rabbis called the *Akedah*, or "the binding"—shatters the innocence of the person of faith who (naïvely) trusts in God's benevolence and compassion. In *Fear and Trembling* Kierkegaard writes under the control of a pseudonymous literary personality, one Johannes de Silentio, who is revolted by God's command (demand?) that Abraham incinerate his son as a burnt offering on one of the nearby mountainsides God has chosen for this purpose. In the moment of irrevocable decision Abraham is brought face to face with the dark side of God's will. *In this moment, God becomes anti-God.* To violate one's intuitive moral sensibilities by following a God who could command such a thing—even if the command serves the putative higher purpose of testing the validity of one's faith—is to exercise an absurd pseudo-faith outside the boundaries of humane moral behavior and discourse.

46. Søren Kierkegaard, *Fear and Trembling/Repetition*, ed. and trans. Howard V. Hong and Edna H. Hong (Princeton: Princeton University Press, 1983), 46.

47. Ibid., 47. See also the discussion of necessity and existence in Søren Kierkegaard, *Philosophical Fragments/Johannes Climacus*, ed. and trans. Howard V. Hong and Edna H. Hong (Princeton: Princeton University Press, 1985), 72–88.

48. Kierkegaard, *Fear and Trembling/Repetition*, 46.

From Silentio's perspective, Abraham's faith is a license to kill: it transvalues all ethical norms and risks destroying what is most valuable by submitting to the divine appetite for blood and sacrifice. In the quick succession of three small verbs in verse 2—*take, go, offer*—the theological and ethical artifice constructed by the Hebrews—that their God is above the God of the nations because he forbids the barbarism of human sacrifice—is forever torn apart. As Silentio says, he can describe at some remove the movements of Abraham's faith, but he cannot make those moves himself; he is repelled by the logic of such moves that demand the immolation of Isaac as proof of Abraham's faith. The heroic obedience of Abraham's faith to the divine command is admirable, but the ethical implications of his faith are terrifying and repulsive to the extreme. Silentio finally approves of Abraham's obedience as a supreme, if offensive, exemplification of the highest faith, but his admiration of Abraham is only "in a certain demented sense" because he knows that the logic of such faith could lead to moral anarchy and monstrous psychopathology.[49]

It is to Silentio's credit that he does not gloss over God's order to Abraham to commit child-murder by trying to assimilate this repugnant command to normative standards of religious belief and practice. It is to his credit that he resists the temptation to relativize or categorize the *Akedah* as an event accountable to normative theological categories. It is to his credit that he refuses to sanitize or domesticate this extraordinary divine violence by harmonizing it with accepted standards of right and wrong. And it is this refusal that provides a warning against attempts to define too carefully the practical consequences of performative truth-making. If, as I have argued in this chapter, theological truth is a product of the Spirit's empowerment to love and heal the other, then it must be underscored that those who follow the Spirit's promptings might be led to a discipleship that few, if any, will recognize as "religious" or "Christian." The Spirit is a wind that blows where she wills, a fire that alights where she chooses, and no one can control her method or predict who her recipients will be.

If to make a belief true is to live this belief in compassion toward the other, then what will this living look like? The answer, in short, is that it is difficult to say. Such a life-style might appear similar to Abraham's odyssey: one may be called to exercise a faith, to live a truth, in an absurd manner that confounds reason and assaults conventional moral and social sensibilities. But if this is the case, then how will one recognize whether a particular belief or action is true or not? One will know if a conviction is true—if it is of God or

49. Ibid., 57.

not—on the basis of the Spirit's interior witness to this truth in the heart of the individual. The inner teacher seeks to guide the student into all truth, even if the final destination is a place difficult, if not impossible, to recognize as destined by God for those who seek to follow the divine mandate.

The alternative understandings of the divine summons both brings together and finally separates Levinas's notion of the face and Kierkegaard's hermeneutic of the *Akedah*. Both thinkers agree that responding to the call of the other (understood as both the other person and the divine Other) is best construed not as obedience to an anonymous moral norm but as a concrete response to individual persons under particular circumstances. To heed this call is to enter into a living relationship with the other that has no need of being justified by a universal philosophical ethics. Both thinkers privilege a relationship of spontaneity and freedom with the other that needs no general maxim or rational principle to justify its deployment. And they agree that subordinating the other to an overarching system of thought is to reconstitute the other as a thematized object (Levinas) or a species of the universal (Kierkegaard). They concur that the other, as Levinas writes, "is not what I comprehend: *he is not under a category.*"[50]

Still, Kierkegaard and Levinas part company at a critical juncture in their thought, respectively. Consider their different readings of the meaning of Abraham's faith/obedience. For Levinas, Abraham's exemplary importance rests on his obedience to the overtures of the Infinite to enter into an ethical relationship with the other. In saying "Here I am" to the divine call, Abraham follows the road prescribed for him in his journey toward responsibility for the neighbor. But the divine summons to Kierkegaard's Abraham follows a different path. This path borders on madness and the absurd—a path where the dividing line between faith and sacrifice, between religious obedience and ritual murder, is virtually impossible to distinguish. While Levinas and Kierkegaard agree that truth consists in the outer-directed movement toward, and in response to, the other, they disagree as to the final object of that movement. For Levinas, the absolute command not to kill the other cannot be set aside—no matter what the reason. For Kierkegaard, on the other hand, even this command is a candidate for "teleological suspension," as he puts it, if the divine Other summons the disciple to wager ultimate (dis)obedience and risk causing injury to the other person.[51]

Both authors write that the true self is the *summoned* self. But the question

50. Levinas, *Totality and Infinity*, 69.
51. Kierkegaard, *Fear and Trembling/Repetition*, 54–67.

remains, Summoned to what? It is clear, I believe, that God's command to love and serve the neighbor is a categorical imperative for all times, but it is also clear that *what* this mandate practically *means* in particular moments of decision remains vertiginously indeterminate (as the *Akedah* lucidly, painfully demonstrates). If one decides to follow Kierkegaard's formulation of faith on this question, then even the security of Levinas's exegesis of the face must be held in abeyance. There are no assurances when one places oneself within the auditory reach of the Other. There are no assurances for the followers of Abraham—indeed, not even the supreme command by God to Abraham to stop the sacrifice can be relied upon. Should Abraham seek to write God's will into the flesh of Isaac with a knife, or not? The person of faith, the one who seeks to emulate Abraham's mad obedience, is the person who leaps with abandon into the void without knowing what she will find: the bosom of a loving God, or the maw of the divine abyss. The person of faith trusts that she will discover the former on the other side of the chasm, but she cannot be confident of such an outcome. Indeed, if she could be sure of the result, she would no longer be performing the truth in the biblical register of hopeless hope, but in the standard key of everyday knowledge and certainty.

CONCLUSION

In this chapter, I have maintained that to perform the truth is to risk everything (at the Spirit's behest) for the welfare of the other, with no certainty of the outcome—or even of the "rightness" of the performance in question. It is to act, even as Abraham acted, without the assurance of *metaphysics* that one can understand the *being* of the one who calls me to obedience, or the security of *ethics* that I can ground my action on a definition of the *good* that is theologically justified or rationally self-evident. Cut free of any "rational" moorings, to live the truth is to enact a transformative concern for the neighbor in response to the divine mandate. We have seen that, beyond the contest between metaphysics and nominalism, Wittgenstein's reflections on framework beliefs mean that such transformative acts, and the beliefs that sustain them, need no extracommunal justification. Nevertheless, it is Kierkegaard who shows us that truth-making may *so* fly in the face of conventional wisdom that not even the community's intramural norms can sanction the acts or beliefs in question. Only the innermost witness of the Spirit can provide such a sanction. Only the power of the interior call to compassion in the moment of decision can provide an unstable guide for renewed relations with the other. Of course, such a broad ethical rule for theology permits a wide variety of disparate interpretations, some of which are incommensurable, but such polyphonic and asymmetrical discernments of the Spirit's promptings to love and service should be celebrated, not censored as too flexible and indeterminate. As Kierkegaard's consideration of Abraham makes clear, a life that hews close to the interior voice of the Spirit may often find its readings of God's will to be paradoxically at odds with the normative understandings of the same. Only the freedom of an *inspir(it)ed* cultivation of the truth can support such interpretations—so that if the interpreter is confronted in the moment with the divine mandate, she will be willing, albeit with fear and trembling, to sacrifice even what she considers to be "ethical" in fidelity to this summons.

PART TWO

*Toward a Life-Centered
Theology of the Spirit*

CHAPTER FOUR

The Spirit and Desire: Sacrificial Violence and Moral Insurgency

The Paraclete is called on behalf of the prisoner, the victim, to speak in his place and in his name, to act in his defense. The Paraclete is the universal advocate, the chief defender of all innocent victims, *the destroyer of every representation of persecution.*[1]

The Spirit is the strength of those who have no strength. It leads the struggle for the emancipation and fulfillment of the people of the oppressed. The Spirit acts in history and through history. It does not take the place of history, but enters into history through men and women who carry the Spirit in themselves.[2]

Attuning oneself to the Spirit's promptings to care for the other is the beginning of religious life and thought. Levinas writes that the Abrahamic response to the neighbor's request for justice and compassion is the central message of biblical religion. For Levinas and many others, religion *is* ethics— which is to say, a religious tradition is worthy of fidelity and respect insofar as it bears moral resources for attending to the needs of the other. In the last chapter, however, I suggested that this ethical approach to religious truth is problematized by the twofold demand on the self to respond not only to the needs of the human other (so Levinas) but also to the interior voice of the divine Spirit (so Kierkegaard). The resulting aporia is that attention to the neighbor's welfare and cultivation of the Spirit's inner promptings might lead to incommensurable responses. As Kierkegaard's reading of the *Akedah*

---

1. René Girard, *The Scapegoat*, trans. Yvonne Freccero (Baltimore: Johns Hopkins University Press, 1986), 207.

2. José Comblin, *The Holy Spirit and Liberation*, trans. Paul Burns (Maryknoll, N.Y.: Orbis Books, 1989), 185.

shows, Abraham's care of his son runs counter to his fidelity to the divine mandate. Whatever Abraham decides to do, he is trapped into breaking God's law: he can either kill his son and violate the basic requirement of the divine legislation to preserve innocent life, or he can refuse to sacrifice Isaac, but here again he also disobeys the Divine's express commandment that Abraham obey God at all costs.

Abraham's labors under the burden of this "twofold imperative"—the obligation both to seek the other's welfare and to follow the divine summons—are instructive of the dangers of a facile connection between religion and ethics. Thinking of religion on a continuum with ethical practice is, I have argued, a way beyond the realist/antirealist impasse on questions of religious truth, but I think we should be wary of pressing this way of thinking into applications for which it is ill-suited. The Abraham story has long served as a cautionary tale against cashing out the meaning of religion in exclusively ethical terms, since the reader is unclear what the ethical ideal stands for after an encounter with the story. But there is still another problem with the religion-and-ethics equation—the problem of noncoincident desire—and it is to this problem that I turn my attention in this chapter.

THE SERVILE WILL

What if the *ideal* of religion is to foster healthy engagements with the other, but the *reality* of human existence is that the realization of this ideal is impossible? That is, what if in spite of the religious imperative to love the other, human beings are structurally unable to respond to this imperative because of some basic flaw in human nature, some basic incapacity to live in co-relation with another human being? (Now this is not Abraham's problem, for while Abraham suffers from the burden of the "twofold imperative," he appears not to be constitutionally *unable* to exercise compassion toward Isaac; he is simply *commanded* not to do so.) But the question remains whether human beings are fundamentally incapacitated to love and serve the other, even though the generic ideal of all religious traditions is to do just that. Indeed, many religious traditions (and especially Christianity) teach not only the ideal of neighbor love but also the radical incapacity of human beings to realize this ideal. (Like Abraham's dilemma, this also is a theological Catch-22, though the terms are different.) Christian thought has long maintained belief in the faulted nature of human volition, namely, that the will must be healed if one is to exercise true compassion toward the other. Without this healing the will is hopelessly captive to self-centered desires that can never, fully, allow for other-directed concerns. Christian anthropology, then, is an exercise in mixed discourse about the ideal of neighbor love, on the one hand, and the reality of the servile will which finds itself unwilling and unable to comport itself to this ethical ideal, on the other. This mixed discourse renders the religion/ethics equation very problematic, if not impossible to maintain: the desideratum of neighbor love is at best a limit concept always in tension with the fact of the will at odds with its own best impulses.

The history of Christian thought is characterized by different attempts to solve the antinomy between the bad will and the moral ideal. The antinomy turns on the paradox that human beings are enjoined to do something that they cannot perform. The force of the moral ideal would seem to imply that persons are *able* to do that which is incumbent upon them, but in fact the burden of the divided will *prevents* them from doing just that. Augustine was the first theologian to formulate a systematic response to this anthropological paradox by arguing that human beings, as a result of Adam's first sin, are tragically faulted to being not able not to sin (*non posse non peccare*). Augustine's articulation of the dark side of the paradox has long held the imagination of the Christian West. In this schema the ideal of undivided love for the other— here defined as the human *and* divine "other"—functions not as an impulse to virtue but as a reminder of one's inability to perform the good required by God of all persons. Humans are endowed with free will (*liberum arbitrium*), but this endowment is hardwired to a limited range of ultimately fruitless options, none of which is able to serve the final interests of undivided love for God and neighbor. "Free choice alone, if the way of truth is hidden, avails for nothing but sin."[3] Because all humankind is implicated in Adam's originary sin, human beings are morally impotent truly to love and serve the other.

Augustine mediates the opposition between the broken will and the moral ideal with the promise of undeserved grace. God unilaterally grants to certain individuals the supernatural power to live out the demands of the religious life. This power is God's gift, not our right. Thus, the beginning, development, and final realization of human growth toward love of God and neighbor are not natural extensions of an innate ability but the results of an infused capacity for good, a renewed free will, that was originally lost to humankind through Adam's fall. Thomas Aquinas and the Protestant Reformers offer a similar analysis against the background of the myth of the fall. Thomas writes

---

3. Augustine, "The Spirit and the Letter," in *Augustine: Later Works*, trans. and ed. John Burnaby, Library of Christian Classics (Philadelphia: Westminster Press, 1955), 197.

that human beings can act ethically in proportion to the limits of their fallen nature, but that they need the medicine of grace to heal the will in order for persons to love their neighbors as themselves and love God above all else.[4] Calvin and Luther agree that the will is free only within a space of delimited opportunities. Instead of the so-called *free* will, which is limited to the exercise of only certain virtues, they privilege the *freed* will, which is a result of God's grace imputed to those who are undeserving of this gift. Their point is that the will apart from grace is not really free at all but is a bondslave to a "power" (the power of sin inherited from Adam) that disposes human beings to live contrary to their own (and others') best interests.[5]

The question of the alienated will divided against itself is a theme in contemporary philosophy as well. Paul Ricoeur's thought begins with deconstructing the substantialist thesis that the self is a stable entity with the ability to transcend itself and obtain ultimate fulfillment. As a philosopher rather than a theologian, Ricoeur does not analyze the idea of infused grace as a solution to the aporia between the moral ideal and the incapacity to realize the ideal. But his philosophical anthropology does resonate to the historic theological notion of the servile will. According to Ricoeur, human beings enter consciousness already alienated from themselves and disposed to their own enslavement; they suffer from a fundamental disproportion between volitional autonomy, on the one hand, and a restricted capacity for self-transcendence, on the other. The common burden of being noncoincident with oneself is borne out by persons who perform self-destructive actions that they barely understand, if at all. Since the paradox of the servile will cannot be directly apprehended by conscious reflection, Ricoeur argues that this dynamic is best thought and understood through a study of the mythic and symbolic literatures of Western culture. "The riddle of the slave-will, that is, of a *free will that is bound and always finds itself already bound*, is the ultimate theme that the symbol gives to thought."[6] In Kantian jargon, this paradox can only be posited as likely, never proven as necessary. The paradox can be *thought* indirectly as a possibility implied by the contradictory experience of being bound and free, but it cannot be *known* directly as an object of rational inquiry or empirical experience.

4. Thomas Aquinas *Summa Theologica* p.I–II, q.109.

5. John Calvin, *Institutes of the Christian Religion*, ed. John T. McNeill, trans. Ford Lewis Battles, 2 vols. (Philadelphia: Westminster Press, 1960), 1:289–340; and Martin Luther, *The Bondage of the Will*, trans. Henry Cole (Grand Rapids: Baker Books, 1976), 126–74, 324–93.

6. Paul Ricoeur, *Fallible Man*, rev. trans. Charles A. Kelbley (New York: Fordham University Press, 1986), xlv.

Ricoeur contends, therefore, that human beings are tethered between free-dom and nature, between the self-transcending powers of the imagination and the always limiting character of perspectival, fragmented experience. The always already noncoincidence between *freedom* and *finitude* is the constitu-tional weakness that makes one's captivity to negation possible. Though des-tined for fulfillment, humans are inevitably captive to an "adversary" greater than themselves. The bitter irony of this predicament is most effectively sym-bolized in the myth of Adam's fall. Though the story is putatively about his-torical origins, it functions as an etiological myth about a cosmic battle between good and evil already anterior to Adam's decision. Adam is figured as alternately *responsible* for his own free decision and yet in *bondage* to an evil power outside of himself. Thus as both free and determined, human beings, like Adam, are "responsible *and* captive, or rather . . . responsible for being captive."[7]

MIMESIS, DIFFERENCE, VIOLENCE: RENÉ GIRARD'S ANALYSIS OF DESIRE

René Girard offers a further analysis of the bad will in a manner that deep-ens and expands the approaches we have considered here. Girard posits the innate capacity to imitate the needs and desires of others—what he calls *acquisitive mimesis*—as the clue to understanding the structure of human volition. Mimesis is the basic human drive to copy what the other person finds valuable; it is the ambition to acquire as one's own what is deemed desir-able by the other. Girard maintains that nothing has value in and of itself; rather, objects only become valuable insofar as they are charged with desir-ability on the basis of another's attachments to the same. "The value of the article consumed is based solely on how it is regarded by the Other. Only Another's desire can produce desire."[8] Desire, then, is always mediated by another and is sustained by the other's possession of that which is deemed worthy of admiration. At this general and abstract stage Girard's analysis of mimesis as basic to human being appears relatively uncontroversial; it is not difficult to document the power of imitation in personality formation,

7. Paul Ricoeur, *The Symbolism of Evil*, trans. Emerson Buchanan (Boston: Beacon Press, 1967), 101.
8. René Girard, *Deceit, Desire, and the Novel: Self and Other in Literary Structure*, trans. Yvonne Freccero (Baltimore: Johns Hopkins University Press, 1965), 223.

including the formation of infants and children. Developmental psychologists, for example, have shown that an infant's earliest learning is mimetic and intracommunal in nature. Children learn by mimicking the behavior around them, and they grow to appreciate what is valued by others. Beyond childhood mimesis, all persons evolve into "desiring machines,"[9] where they learn subconsciously to value whatever is valued by the communities of desire they inhabit.

While acquisitive mimesis is a natural feature of the subject, it inevitably leads to tragic results. In this vein let us consider Girard's analysis of human being in four stages.

Mediated Desire

The first stage consists of the subject's misunderstanding of itself as a being with innate desires. The initial problem is that because the subject misinterprets its desires as "natural" and "self-evident," it inevitably finds itself bound to a system of values and preferences that it neither understands nor from which it is able to extricate itself. Since the subject considers as self-generated what is actually produced by another, it suffers an existence in which it is fundamentally self-deceived. At the wellspring of its existence the self is opaque to the motives of its own actions. Consider on this question Marcel Proust's *Remembrance of Things Past*, which painstakingly chronicles the derivative character of desire in the grip of the other's desire. The novel narrates Charles Swann's captivity to the preferences of an anonymous "old friend" and the Verdurins, a couple who oversee a fashionable salon with considerable pretensions. The unnamed friend introduces Swann to a courtesan named Odette, whom the friend speaks of as a "ravishing creature," but about whom Swann initially feels "no desire [and] which gave him, indeed, a sort of physical repulsion.´ . . ."[10] Yet on account of the quiet and persistent praising of Odette's beauty both by his "old friend" and the Verdurins, Swann quickly becomes completely besotted with Odette to the general exclusion of his other activities and relationships. In spite of this sudden change of heart,

---

9. The phrase belongs to Giles Deleuze and Felix Guattari in *Anti-Oedipus: Capitalism and Schizophrenia*, trans. Robert Hurley, Mark Seem, and Helen R. Lane (New York: Viking Press, 1977). The differences between Girard and Deleuze/Guattari are many, but they agree that contemporary culture functions to inculcate value preferences on a subconscious level.

10. Marcel Proust, *Remembrance of Things Past*, trans. C. K. Scott Moncrieff and Terence Kilmartin, 3 vols. (New York: Random House, Vintage Books, 1982), 1:213.

however, Swann fancies himself a master of independent taste and judgment regarding Odette (as well as regarding all his other attachments). What he does not—and cannot—realize is that his desire for Odette was subtly smuggled into his subconscious appetites by the crafty machinations of his supposed friends. When he finally wakes up to his bondage to Odette, it is too late, and he can only play a tragic part—the part of the sponsor of a kept woman—according to the dictates of the part as it has been scripted for him by his friends and associates.

What the reader of *Remembrance of Things Past* discovers is that whenever the origins and mechanisms of desire are occluded by the skillful obfuscations of the mediator, the subject of desire is no longer in control of its own destiny and instead becomes a slave to the other's tastes and preferences. If we transpose the theological idea of the servile will to a literary key, we now discover a similar insight but in a new register. As before, we are confronted with the basic anthropological insight that the self is radically noncoincident with itself because it cannot escape its own bondage—a bondage outside of itself to which it is continually *responding*, and a self-imposed bondage for which it is *responsible*. But the Girardian hermeneutic provides, I believe, an analysis of the *mechanism* of this enslavement that is lacking in the anthropologies we considered in the first part of this chapter. Girard shows that because the self formed by the other's desires can neither understand nor control the direction of its own appetites and infatuations, the mediated self is fated to an existence within a nightmare-world of culturally constructed needs and desires that it cannot comprehend. Everything that generates the culture of a particular social group—from tastes in food and fashion to codes of behavior and divisions of labor—operates within the same gravitational space of mimetic desire. Generally, however, this gravitational activity exists just beneath the threshold of conscious choices and activities. Thus mediated desire is the source of all acquisitive and addictive cravings, the foundation upon which the hierarchy of cultural values is established, and the criterion by which most interpersonal decisions are made in social groups. All this, and yet desire is rarely recognized to play such a role because its influence is so subtle and pervasive.

Loss of Differences

The next stage concerns the power of acquisitive mimesis to blur distinctions and merge identities whenever the subject becomes mimetically successful in obtaining the object of desire. As long as the other's desires remain a

distant and unreachable goal, there is no conflict between mediator and subject, but once the desired object is in the grasp of the subject, the potential for
bitter conflict arises. Now the *mediator* who had *modeled* a craving and
attachment to the object becomes the *rival* who *guards* the subject from
obtaining the object. This mimetic conflict is carefully played out in Swann's
internalization of his friend's and the Verdurins' valorization of Odette. After
implanting within Swann their high estimation of Odette, the Verdurins
grow increasingly uneasy with the fruition of their early labors in Swann's
gradual possession of Odette. Odette operates as "bait" in the Verdurins'
salon to attract articulate and powerful men to join the circle of the "faithful."
But her function as a sort of lure is threatened by Swann's increasing demands
on her time and affections. The Verdurins are particularly upset that Swann's
obsession with Odette might blunt her ability to secure the membership in
their "circle" of the titled aristocrat, the Comte de Forcheville, who is also
attracted to the courtesan. Like all mediators, the Verdurins want Swann to
imitate *their* likes and dislikes (in order to keep his allegiance to their group),
but they do not want Swann to become too *successful* at imitation (lest he
obtain the object of his, and others', mutual desires, namely, Odette, and
thereby take her out of circulation). Girard calls this the double bind of trian-
gular desire: the mediator contradictorily enjoins the imitator to "Imitate
me!" and "Do not imitate me!" alternately and at the same time. This leaves
the imitator twisted into a lose-lose relationship with itself, the mediator, and
the object between them.[11]

The mediator is comfortable with creating unobtainable desire in the
other, but if the other is successful at acquiring the object, then the "have"
and "have not" distinction, among others, that had separated subject and
mediator is eclipsed, as well as the ability of the mediator to control the new
rival. The result is that both parties now occupy the same playing field with a
common objective and shared influence over the other. "So the rivals come to
resemble each other more and more as the differences between them are pro-
gressively erased. What started as a one-way imitation becomes a two-way
imitation, each copying the desire of the other until they are identical."[12]
Now both parties see themselves in the other, imitating each other in a merging of their separate identities and a loss of the distinctions between self and
other, model and disciple, that had once defined their relationship.

    11. Girard, *Deceit, Desire, and the Novel*, 1–52.
    12. Robert G. Hamerton-Kelly, *Sacred Violence: Paul's Hermeneutic of the Cross* (Min-
neapolis: Fortress Press, 1992), 23.

Let us take a very simple example, if you like—that of the master and his disciples. The master is delighted to see more and more disciples around him, and delighted to see that he is being taken as a model. Yet if the imitation is too perfect, and the imitator threatens to surpass the model, the master will completely change his attitude and begin to display jealousy, mistrust and hostility. He will be tempted to do everything he can to discredit and discourage his disciple.[13]

Nietzsche often spoke to the rivalrous envy (*ressentiment*) that defines the master–disciple relationship. The disciple both *hates* its master's interior will to power and *desires* the master's inner-directed sense of morality and selfhood. Because the disciple cannot generate within itself its own sense of values and orientation, it must live a disgruntled life as a subscriber to the other's strong-willed choices and preferences rather than as an inventor of its own values and beliefs.[14] Girard adds to the Nietzschean analysis, however, by demonstrating that *both* master and disciple are locked in mimetic *ressentiment* with each other since neither is individually strong enough to "own" its own values, but must instead look to the other for support and confirmation. With the intense rivalry comes the breakdown of differences between the two competitors—and the Frankenstein horror of the apprentice taking the place of the master as the apprentice successfully learns to mimic, and then acquire, the object of the master's desires.

Scapegoats, Racism, and AIDS

The merging of the student's and master's once-separate identities into a single desire for a common object generates a loss of differences; this loss inevitably provokes a violent reassertion of the previous order in the interest of stable personal and communal identity-formation. This is the third stage in Girard's analysis: mimetic frenzy leads to a collapse of distinctions, which provokes reciprocal violence in order to shore up the threatened social structure. If everyone were allowed to carry out their mimetic desires unchecked, the system of differences, the hierarchy of values, the scaffold of distinctions

13. René Girard, *Things Hidden Since the Foundation of the World*, with Jean-Michel Oughourlian and Guy Lefort, trans. Stephen Bann and Michael Metteer (Stanford: Stanford University Press, 1987), 290.

14. See Nietzsche, "The Antichrist," in *The Portable Nietzsche*, ed. and trans. Walter Kaufmann (New York: Viking Press, 1980), 592–95; idem, *On the Genealogy of Morals*, trans. Walter Kaufmann and R. J. Hollingdale (New York: Random House, Vintage Press, 1967), 120–28.

that support and organize social identity would break down. When this happens the result is total chaos. "Order, peace, and fecundity depend on cultural distinctions; it is not these distinctions but the loss of them that gives birth to fierce rivalries and sets members of the same family or social group at one another's throats."[15]

Historically, the gut-level response to the debilitating threat of unregulated desire is to turn a blind eye to the real cause of the problem—the raw compulsion to acquire the desired object—and impute to an unprotected "other" the cause of the community's dissolution into an undifferentiated and disordered state. This renders the other a target of the community's rage over its loss of identity and cultural order. The other now becomes the victim, the scapegoat, of the group's disintegration insofar as the other functions to divert collective violence *to* itself and *away* from the mimetic crisis. *The solution to mimetic crises, therefore, is the prophylactic of scapegoating violence.* In order to save itself from the inevitable corrosion of mimetic disorder, the community must periodically plunge itself into a paroxysm of violence toward a "guilty" scapegoat. "If *acquisitive mimesis* divides by leading two or more individuals to converge on one and the same object with a view to appropriating it, *conflictual mimesis* will inevitably unify by leading two or more individuals to converge on one and the same adversary that all wish to strike down."[16] Imitative rivalry threatens to tear apart a society's order of differences and values unless it is regulated by a common agreement that it is some marginal member of the community, not everyone's unconscious and insatiable drive to imitate the other and possess what the other values, that caused the violent breakdown in the first place. This agreement generates a temporary unity in the community of persecutors and temporarily resolves the mimetic crisis until the next rivalrous relationship gathers steam.

The persecution of the outsider as the insidious cause of the community's problems is aptly set forth in Proust's novel. As the story progresses, Swann and Forcheville emerge as bitter rivals with the Verdurins playing the role of mediators of, and adjudicators over, their common object of desire, Odette. The Verdurins grow weary of Swann's jealousy and possessiveness regarding Odette and are likely nervous that he will frustrate their efforts to establish Forcheville's membership in their circle. So in a fit of rage Mme. Verdurin ritually expels Swann from the salon lest he permanently disrupt the fragile rela-

15. René Girard, *Violence and the Sacred*, trans. Patrick Gregory (Baltimore: Johns Hopkins University Press, 1977), 49.

16. Girard, *Things Hidden Since the Foundation of the World*, 26.

tions with the group. I say "ritually expel" because the Verdurins often banish members of the "faithful" from their home whenever tensions arise that can only be resolved through paroxysms of scapegoating expulsion. With the expulsion of Swann, the circle's unanimity and equilibrium are restored, and the purity of the group is preserved against the contagious influence of Swann's dangerous and unbounded infatuation.

This chain of events follows a narrative line not unlike the drama of Sophocles' *Oedipus Rex*. The play opens with Thebes in the grip of a plague brought on by the virulent presence of a parricide and perpetrator of incest, namely, Oedipus. This unbearable tragedy can only be resolved by destroying the original carrier of the disease. Oedipus's unpardonable sins make him the bearer of a lethal social virus; he has infected the city-state with his presence, and the result is that violence and chaos have replaced the rule of order and hierarchy. "Violence is the ultimate confuser, the chaos maker, the overturner of differences, the upsetter of systems."[17] Plagues always strike at the heart of social order, and someone must be held responsible for the chaos. "We must return once again to the so-called crimes of the son of Laius. The act of regicide is the exact equivalent, vis-à-vis the polis, of the act of patricide vis-à-vis the family. In both cases the criminal strikes at the most fundamental, essential, and inviolable distinctions within the group. He becomes, literally, the slayer of distinctions."[18]

The plague has its origins in the mimetic rivalry between Oedipus and his father, Laius, whom Oedipus murders in order to gain the advantage of passing ahead of Laius as they both struggle to be first on the road to Thebes. He compounds this original sin of rivalry by unknowingly cohabiting with his mother, Iocasta; he thereby unleashes the epidemic, which only further obliterates the distinctions, critical to social order, that Oedipus had initially violated. Oedipus is the "slayer of distinctions," as Girard says, because he is an alien in his own country, a beggar who comes into great wealth, a blind man who sees his errors—and, most tragically, a brother and father of his own children, son and husband of his mother, and killer of the man who gave him life.

American public life is no stranger to the creation of scapegoats as a response to the disintegration of time-honored cultural mores and values. As in the case of Sophocles' Oedipus, whose violation of customs and taboos threatened to destroy all of Thebes, we are not so far from ancient Greece in

---

17. James G. Williams, *The Bible, Violence, and the Sacred: Liberation from the Myth of Sanctioned Violence* (San Francisco: HarperCollins, 1991), 24.

18. Girard, *Violence and the Sacred*, 74.

our response to those who are accused of muddying differences and creating disorder. Consider the mimetic tensions between privileged Anglos and poor nonwhite communities in the United States. The rationale of capitalism—to maximize profits among the economic elite—functions to create wants and needs in persons for market goods and services whether or not the desires mediated by the need-making system can be fulfilled. For some people of color mired in poverty, however, this inequity leaves them increasingly frustrated because they cannot acquire the resources that white society enjoys as its seeming "birthright." The insidious racial overtones of this mimetic tension result from the white community, which controls most of the capital, barring nonwhites from accessing the opportunities (educational, professional, financial, and so forth) that the white community has taken for granted for generations.[19] The mimetic conflict is further exacerbated by some white persons' insistence that the full inclusion of nonwhites into the mainstream of American public life (whether through fair housing laws, desegregated schooling, or racially inclusive hiring practices) would be a mortal blow to many whites' sense of separate identity and privileged status.[20] Such inclusion would challenge many white Americans' self-understanding of their "patrimony of superiority," as Andrew Hacker puts it.[21] From this vantage point, everything from integrated neighborhoods and interracial relationships to multicultural school curricula and nonsectarian holiday celebrations is held up as an instance of the breakdown in the social order— which is to say, a breakdown in the special rights and advantages many whites feel are naturally theirs. Many whites feel threatened by these changes, and they often respond with hostility to minority voices that challenge all Americans to live in community, if not solidarity, with one another.

As a way of protecting its privileges and preventing the dissolution of its identity, the traditional mainline response to the challenge of racial inclusion has been to ignore the challenge and instead *blame* a vulnerable member (or members) of the "other" group for the country's grave social ills, and hold that person (or persons) responsible for the problems that characterize modern life. The response has been to shift attention away from the entrenched

19. See the analysis of the economic and racial dimensions of American political conflict in Cornel West, *Prophecy Deliverance! An Afro-American Revolutionary Christianity* (Philadelphia: Westminster Press, 1982), esp. 95–127.

20. See Andrew Hacker, *Two Nations: Black and White, Separate, Hostile, Unequal* (New York: Charles Scribner's Sons, 1992); and J. Anthony Lukas, *Common Ground* (New York: Knopf, 1985).

21. Hacker, *Two Nations*, 217.

structural problems that give rise to minority cries for justice by "blaming the victims" for destabilizing the social order—and thereby frustrating their own opportunities for advancement and success. *This strategy both protects the advantages of the power elite and scapegoats the outsider(s) as the instigator(s) of disorder.* During his lifetime, for example, Martin Luther King, Jr., was vilified as a Communist sympathizer, an inciter of riots and violence, and a criminal threat to the whole "American way of life." King was essentialized by the conservative white majority as a threat to mainstream values and made into a scapegoat for the country's numerous racial and urban problems. In my mind, King was one of the last truly great public theologians in America to command the attention and allegiance of many Americans through his life and message of nonviolent, multiracial social change. It should come as no surprise, then, that King was assassinated at the height of the campaign against him. From a Girardian perspective, King symbolized the potent threat of a black minority to the white majority and its historic entitlements, and the response was both to demonize and to destroy him in the process. Like Oedipus in this respect, King was branded as a slayer of the (racial) distinctions that had long defined national identity, and his violent death was interpreted as a way of restoring the sense of order that had broken down in America during the turbulent 1960s.[22]

The sometimes hysterical response to persons with AIDS can also be read as a case-study of the scapegoat hypothesis. Here the problem has less to do with so-called "race mixing" than with "gender bending," but in both cases the problem has its origins in the muddying of so-called essential cultural differences. Many religious fundamentalists (and others who share their convictions) have essentialized persons who suffer from AIDS, or are HIV-positive, as willing victims of a "moral" disease. Some fundamentalists and others argue that the victims of this new epidemic are suffering (some even say rightly) from the natural consequences of their ethical and religious transgressions of the laws of God and nature. They go so far as to argue that AIDS patients, even HIV-positive foreigners who seek entry permits into this country, should be quarantined lest they spread their viral *and* moral contagion to the straight population. Since many people define AIDS as a "homosexual disease," persons with AIDs are judged to be sexually deviant, that is, gay. For many fundamentalists and their ilk, "alternative" sexual orientations are

22. See the Girardian reading of King's ministry in Theophus H. Smith, "King and the Black Religious Quest to Cure Racism," in *Curing Violence,* ed. Mark I. Wallace and Theophus H. Smith (Sonoma, Calif.: Polibridge Press, 1994), 230–51.

regarded as frontal assaults on the innate differences between male and female commanded by God in creation.

> Thus, the fact that AIDS is predominantly a heterosexually transmitted illness in the countries where it first emerged in epidemic form has not prevented such guardians of public morals as Jesse Helms and Norman Podhoretz from depicting it as a visitation specially aimed at (and deservedly incurred by) Western homosexuals, while another Reagan-era celebrity, Pat Buchanan, orates about "AIDS and Moral Bankruptcy," and Jerry Falwell offers the generic diagnosis that "AIDS is God's judgment on a society that does not live by His rules."[23]

In right-wing theologies that rail against any gender confusion and the practice of alternative life-styles, the violation of sexual boundaries and taboos is vigorously punished by God/nature. Thus, the AIDS virus is interpreted as just deserts for those who challenge the putative biological order of creation by engaging in non-heterosexual behavior. In this framework, AIDS is construed as a lethal "visitation" of mythological proportions—like the plagues of biblical and Greek antiquity—because it is God's judgment against Westerners for their moral degeneracy and sexual deviance. The eerie parallels between the Theban response to the Oedipus plague and the American response to AIDS seem obvious: as the Greek city-state hurled invective at Oedipus as the diabolical origin of the epidemic, so many Americans attack gay and lesbian citizens as purveyors of a dangerous immorality that has provoked a national scourge. Further, as in the one case Oedipus's self-mutilation and internalization of his city's hatred of him are a fitting coda to his evils, so in the other case the public pillorying of AIDS patients, as objects of shame and humiliation, is regarded by many as an appropriate response to their "gender transgressions." AIDS is the plague of our time and we blame its victims for the disease's pernicious effects on all of us.

Double Valence of the Victim

The fourth stage in the Girardian analysis concerns the double valence of the victim. As the creation of the scapegoat becomes effective at diverting mimetic violence to the other, the scapegoat is constructed not only as the *cause* of the community's disintegration but also as the *source* of its new found unity. This unity provides the basis and justification for the institutions, pro-

23. Susan Sontag, *Illness as Metaphor and AIDS and Its Metaphors* (New York: Doubleday, Anchor Books, 1988), 149.

hibitions, myths, and rituals that constitute the culture of a particular group. All social groups intuitively realize that they will self-destruct into internecine warfare as long as they are unable or unwilling to control the mimetic frenzies in their midst. But since the conflicts' mimetic doubles are rarely if ever willing to back away from their rivalry, an indirect approach to ameliorating the tension must be employed. Enter the scapegoat. Almost instinctively, groups and individuals at war with themselves learn to channel their mimetic fury toward a substitute who, by absorbing their mutual hostility, functions temporarily to bring together the warring parties by allowing them to agree on at least one issue: it is the marginal other, not themselves, that is the catalyst of the disorder. "The return to peace and order is ascribed to the same cause as the earlier troubles—to the victim himself."[24]

With the success of the sacrificial expulsion or murder in stemming the mimetic fury, the victim is doubly reconstituted at the level of a communal foundation myth as the source of, and antidote to, the community's systemic problems.

> There is only room for a single cause in their field of vision, and its triumph is absolute, it absorbs all other causality: it is the scapegoat. Thus nothing happens to the persecutors that is not immediately related to him, and if they happen to become reconciled, the scapegoat benefits. There is only one person responsible for everything, one who is absolutely responsible, and he will be responsible for the cure because he is already responsible for the sickness.[25]

As a *pharmakon*, the victim is interpreted as the origin of the violent poison that destroys a society and the antidote that heals the society of its illness.[26]

Girard's general theory about the origins of culture and religion in the victimage mechanism has been succinctly narrated by Robert-Hamerton Kelly in the form of a "likely story":

> Once upon a time there was a group of hominids that found itself unable to do anything in concert because of rivalry among them. Each one found [it]self inwardly compelled to imitate some other. As the imitation became more successful [one member of the group] found [it]self a rival of [its] model, and the more like the model [it] became the more violent became the rivalry. Cooperation was impossible until one day, the greatest day in the history of human cul-

24. Girard, *The Scapegoat*, 55.
25. Ibid., 43.
26. Also see Jacques Derrida, "Plato's Pharmacy," in *Dissemination*, trans. Barbara Johnson (Chicago: University of Chicago Press, 1981), 61–171.

ture, the two of them discovered that it was possible to agree on one thing, to agree to kill someone else. This was such a compelling possibility that the whole group imitated them, and so the first moment of human solidarity happened as the fellowship of the lynch mob.

The victim, as the source of the sudden unity and order, was regarded as a savior; and [the victim] was blamed for causing the previous disorder. Thus [the victim] acquired the double valency of the sacred: attraction and revulsion. From the victim came the building blocks of social order: prohibition to control the course of rivalry; ritual sacrifice to reenact and so represent to the group the unifying energy of the founding moment; myth to explain and obscure the violence by covering it up with transformations. The victim became the god, at the stage of the emergence of the gods. Thus society formed in the crucible of religion.[27]

Culture has its origins, therefore, in the founding mechanism of the creation and destruction of the scapegoat. *Myths* serve to sacralize, and also mask, the founding violent mechanism usually by depicting human origins in relation to a cosmic battle between good and evil that is resolved by the gods' violent victory over their rivals. Most cosmogonies make the case for an originary violent event as necessary for bringing order out of chaos. *Rituals* also commemorate the originary event, but now through the lens of the myths they represent. The performance of rituals generally demonstrates the therapeutic benefits of symbolic actions; they show how the founding victimage brought unity and structure to the community. *Prohibitions* and *taboos* function similarly, but as potent reminders of the dangers of the original undifferentiated and chaotic state when the prohibitions were not in place or were being violated, rather than as commemorations of the triumph of order over chaos *in illo tempore* as is the case of myths and rituals. Likewise, all major cultural *institutions* function as reminders and inculcators of the myths, rituals, and prohibitions that undergird society. Political and legal institutions provide the routinized legitimation structures that reward and punish group members for obeying or disobeying the customs and laws that regulate the social order. And religious institutions similarly operate to provide the curative sacrificial rites that recall the "good" violence that formed the community in the first place and prevented its descent into the "bad" violence of confusion and chaos. "*Religion* in its broadest sense, then, must be

27. Quoted from James G. Williams, "Myth, Aphorism, and the Christ as Sign," unpublished paper presented to the Bible, Narrative, and American Culture Seminar of the Westar Institute, Sonoma, Calif., April 1988, 9–10.

another term for that obscurity that surrounds man's efforts to defend himself by curative or preventative means against his own violence."[28] In the Girardian framework, therefore, religion, along with most other cultural practices and institutions, operates to render opaque and legitimate the generative violence that founded the community; as well, religion functions to control further outbreaks of violence by deflecting the danger toward the "guilty other" who stands in the place of the community's intractable intramural problems.

What are the data and methodology Girard uses to yield these insights? Like Michel Foucault, whose archaeology of historical documents seeks to recover the subjugated knowledge of oppression submerged within these texts by their creators,[29] Girard digs beneath the surface narratives of persecution texts—such as Guillaume de Machaut's fourteenth-century account of the black death, Aztec myths of self-sacrifice to the sun-god, Greek mythology, and biblical stories of vengeance and sacrifice—in order to uncover the scapegoat mechanism as the mainspring of cultural formation and religious ritual. All of these accounts of victimage are narrated from the perspective of the persecutors, not the victims, in an effort (albeit sometimes unconsciously) to sacralize the logic and practice of that by which the society is held together: sacrificial violence.

Girard's reading of persecution texts constitutes an antisacrificial ideology critique of the founding violent mechanisms of culture.[30] His critique cuts against the grain of the persecutors' intended message, a message that offers a subtle apology for occasional paroxysms of vengeance as both necessary for regulating more widespread outbreaks of violence and for sustaining the community's fragile sense of order. Architects and defenders of the established order agree that violence, under the control of appropriate safeguards, applies the brakes to further violence. But Girard disagrees. For Girard, the moral demand directed to all readers of texts is to pull back the veil of self-justifying violence that conceals the plight of the oppressed and voiceless buried deep within the pages of many of the "great books" within the Western canon. "We cannot read the text of persecution correctly unless we become able to rehabilitate the victims, to realize that the accusations against them are

28. Girard, *Violence and the Sacred*, 23.

29. See, inter alia, Michel Foucault, *The Archaeology of Knowledge* (New York: Pantheon Books, 1972).

30. On the helpful insight that Girard's theory is a species of ideology critique, see William Schweiker, "Sacrifice, Interpretation, and the Sacred: The Import of Gadamer and Girard for Religious Studies," *Journal of the American Academy of Religion* 55 (1987): 791–810.

groundless."[31] Girard's "ethical reading" is really, then, a transformative mis-reading—an intentional, but liberating, misconstrual of the text's *prima facie* message insofar as that message is a justification for the destruction of the marginal scapegoat. The demand to "misread" consciously and programmatically the text is a demand incumbent upon all readers, because "one must either do violence to the text or let the text forever do violence to innocent victims."[32]

QUESTIONS CONCERNING THE VICTIMAGE HYPOTHESIS

Girard argues that religion has its origins in sacrificial violence which later myths, rituals, and prohibitions serve to camouflage and justify. The founding unanimity against the victim is the mainspring of cultural formation, and virtually all cultural classics in the West operate according to the code of the victimage mechanism—a mechanism that is rooted in past events of mimetic conflict and that engenders new rationalizations for more violence today. Nevertheless, Girard's indictment of textually mediated violence is not a generic indictment of all *prima facie* persecution texts as such. In fact, it is precisely at the point where his antisacrificial hermeneutic appears to be most universal and comprehensive in its scope that he isolates one cultural classic as immune from the unity of all religious rites in the creation and destruction of scapegoats.

This special text is the four versions of the Jesus story recorded in the Gospels. Girard maintains that the Gospels present a singular repudiation of sacrificial violence by uncovering the scapegoat mechanism at the base of culture, and by promoting an ethic of love that allows the reader to expose the lie that scapegoating is inevitable and necessary. The uniqueness of the Gospels rests in their refusal to narrate history from the perspective of persecutors, to provide an indirect vindication of the executioners through an uncritical recounting of events of sacrifice and vengeance. While other biblical writings accomplish this task as well (for example, the prophets' judgments against cultic infanticide), the Gospels consistently avoid succumbing to the myth of the eternal return of violence by exposing and repudiating the structures of

31. René Girard, "Violence and Representation in the Mythical Text," in *"To Double Business Bound": Essays on Literature, Mimesis, and Anthropology* (Baltimore: Johns Hopkins University Press, 1978), 192.

32. Girard, *The Scapegoat*, 8.

sacrificial religion through an ethic of reconciling love for the whole human community. "Jesus invites all men to devote themselves to the project of getting rid of violence, taking into account the illusions it fosters, the methods by which it gains ground, and all the laws that we have verified over the course of these discussions. . . . This is the Kingdom of love, which is also the domain of the true God, the Father of Jesus, of whom the prisoners of violence cannot even conceive."[33]

The kingdom of love is the environment where a complete renunciation of all so-called legitimate violence (violence as reprisal for being wronged or even for self-defense) is unconditionally repudiated. Such a renunciation places Girard's analysis at odds with a Niebuhrian ethic between-the-times— an ethic that requires a this-worldly compromise between the ideal of love and the demands of justice.[34] Similar to Levinas's ethic of the face, Girard's approach eschews attempts to balance strategically the ultimate value of altruism and the *lex talionis* of retributive justice. His nonsacrificial reading of the Gospel text gives no quarter to a philosophical or religious hermeneutic that is an apologetic for the dissemination of violence, legal or otherwise. Instead, his project is to expose the historic fallacy of the belief in the curative benefits of reciprocal violence—a belief that undergirds the legitimation structures of ancient and modern societies.

> Once the basic mechanism is revealed, the scapegoat mechanism, the expulsion of violence by violence, is rendered useless by the revelation. It is no longer of interest. The interest of the Gospels lies in the future offered mankind by this revelation, the end of Satan's mechanism. The good news is that scapegoats can no longer save men, the persecutors' accounts of their persecutions are no longer valid, and truth shines into dark places. God is not violent, the true God has nothing to do with violence. . . .[35]

In spite of the liberating potential and innovative appeal of this approach, some troubling questions arise for the interpreter of Girard. One problem concerns his limitation of the power of antisacrificial revelation to the biblical environment. Girard does not claim that his cultural metatheory is an extrapolation from the New Testament, but he does argue that his antisacrificial ethic of universal love is uniquely and definitively derived from the Gospels. One must wonder, however, what he thinks about other unveilings of the scapegoat

33. See Girard, *Things Hidden Since the Foundation of the World*, 197.

34. See Reinhold Niebuhr, *Moral Man and Immoral Society* (New York: Charles Scribner's Sons, 1932), esp. 257–77.

35. Girard, *The Scapegoat*, 189.

mechanism, about other lives and teachings of nonviolent love that make up the harvest of the world's varied cultures and forms of religious expression. Many examples come to mind in this respect: Socrates' exemplary refusal to the death to betray his own sense of mission and integrity; the Buddha's life of, and teaching about, universal compassion for all sentient beings; or Gandhi's distinctively Indian recapitulation of the Vedic maxim that all natural and human life is a breath of the eternal Thou. In the light of these other embodiments of the kingdom of love, Girard's vision appears restrictive and totalizing. It is too narrow to insist that the biography and message of Jesus are singularly revelatory, to insist that "[t]here is no common ground between what happens in the Gospels and what happens in myths, particularly the more developed myths,"[36] or that the "Gospels, in fact, are not only superior to all the texts placed in the category of magical [and mythical] thought but are also superior to all the modern interpretations of human relationships."[37] As one of Girard's most trenchant critics puts it, Girard's argument for the uniquely revelatory character of the Gospels "presupposes the same monism that it attacks; one can enter into a Manichaean combat only if one assumes that one's own position is grounded in absolute truth."[38] As noted in the previous chapter, any religious tradition that engenders compassion for the other is an exercise in truth-as-performance. From this perspective, therefore, Girard's delimitation of hard boundaries between biblical revelation and other belief systems betrays an absolutism unable to account for the capacity for truth-making outside the Christian scheme of salvation.

Girard's myopia on this point refracts another problem in his hermeneutic, namely, his unwillingness to acknowledge that the whole Bible, including the Gospels, is suffused with the rhetoric of sacrificial violence. On the margins of Girard's construal of the biblical texts, another face of God appears to the reader: an arbitrary and sometimes malign divinity who authorizes nationalistic holy wars against Israel's enemies (Joshua), relinquishes his care of his servant Job in a wager with Satan (Job), threatens torture and a fiery hell against the hardhearted in the final judgment (the Gospels), and destroys a family because of a lie about tithing (Ananias and Sapphira in Acts). Girard maintains that the Bible, culminating in the Gospels, presses toward a nonviolent vision of God, and that it is the reader's unwillingness or inability to

36. Ibid., 166.
37. Ibid., 195.
38. Hayden White, "Ethnological 'Lie' and Mythical 'Truth,'" review of *Violence and the Sacred*, by René Girard, *Diacritics* 8 (1978): 7.

track this trajectory that results in the concealment of the scripture's liberating message. *But no text, even the biblical text, is self-interpreting.* The burden of trying to make sense of the violent and nonviolent mixed discourse, the pathologically frozen distortions, at the base of the biblical witness is an onus all readers must shoulder. This burden cannot be sloughed off by a sublimation of the "original scenes" of violence within the text as somehow tangential or irrelevant to the Bible's overall sense.

Even Girard's *locus classicus*, the Jesus story, is caught up in the Priestly christology of the scapegoat cultus. The Markan refrain that the Son of Man came not to be served but to serve and give his life as a ransom for the many is indicative of a theology of blood atonement, woven into the fabric of the Synoptic picture of Jesus, that militates against Girard's antisacrificial hermeneutic. "At no point in the Gospels," he writes, "is the death of Jesus defined as a sacrifice."[39] But such a claim does not sit well with the Gospel texts themselves (not to speak of Paul and Hebrews) which often stress the significance of Jesus' redemptive death (symbolized by his spilled blood and broken body) as the new propitiatory reality in the relationship between God and humanity. While Girard is right to dispute the reliability of the history of Christian interpretations of the Gospels as promoting reciprocal violence, his claim that the Gospel accounts do not in any way warrant these appropriations is forced.

These criticisms do not nullify the power of Girard's approach, but they do suggest that his approach should be more careful to guard against an inflated appreciation of the Bible that divorces it from other cultural incarnations of nonviolent praxis, on the one hand, and an ignorance of the Bible's collusion with the violence it purports to disavow, on the other.

ALTERNATIVE THEORIES OF INTERPRETATION: PAUL RICOEUR AND JACQUES DERRIDA

Paul Ricoeur's literary theory offers an expansive corrective to Girard's biblical hermeneutic. Ricoeur suggests that any text can potentially occasion a positive "revelation" to the degree that it discloses new aspects of reality, novel possibilities for existence.[40] Girard avers that the Bible alone is uniquely revelatory because of its disclosure and repudiation of the scapegoat mechanism,

---

39. See Girard, *Things Hidden Since the Foundation of the World*, 180.
40. Paul Ricoeur, "Toward a Hermeneutic of the Idea of Revelation," in *Essays on Biblical Interpretation*, ed. Lewis S. Mudge (Philadelphia: Fortress Press, 1980), 73–118.

while Ricoeur maintains that any imaginative text, including but not limited to the Bible, that can metamorphize the world of the reader by opening up new possibilities of being-in-the-world is a candidate for revelation. Potentially, any literary work of art can be both "revealing and transforming. Revealing, in the sense that it brings features to light that were concealed and yet already sketched out at the heart of our experience, our praxis. Transforming, in the sense that a life examined in this way is a changed life, another life."[41]

Texts are revelatory not because they are *deposits* of divinely inspired truths but because they faithfully *enact* a productive clash, and sometimes a fusion, between their world and the world of the reader. Since Ricoeur understands revelation in interactive, rather than propositional terms, he uses the category of an "areligious sense of revelation" to refer to the disclosive power of figurative (including sacred) texts. In a manner similar to Heidegger's thesis concerning the truth of art and Gadamer's notion of a "fusion of horizons," revelation for Ricoeur occurs in the to-and-fro dialogue between text and interpreter whenever the interpreter is willing to be put into question by the text and risk openness to the world of possibilities the text projects. Thus Ricoeur is wary of assigning final priority to any one particular textual construal of reality because all forms of literary discourse (and not only biblical discourse) can potentially refigure one's experience and offer new possibilities for understanding. While the biblical stories are a medium of revelation, they are a species of a wider revelatory function which any text (biblical or otherwise) can participate in that unleashes novel and emancipatory alternatives for the reader.

For Ricoeur, textual revelation is moderated by the play of literary genres. In the case of the Bible, the Bible's different modes of signification—narratives, hymns, wisdom sayings, laws, poems, gospels, apocalyptic writings, and so forth—generate a surplus of meaning outside the control of any one genre or particular theme. These various forms of articulation are not simply taxonomic devices for categorizing discourse but rather the means by which theological meaning is produced. "The literary genres of the Bible do not constitute a rhetorical facade which it would be possible to pull down in order to reveal some thought content that is indifferent to its literary vehicle."[42] The Bible's different registers of discourse are more than just classificatory codes or

41. Paul Ricoeur, *Time and Narrative*, trans. Kathleen Blamey and David Pellauer, vol. 3 (Chicago: University of Chicago Press, 1988), 158.
42. Ricoeur, "Toward a Hermeneutic of the Idea of Revelation," in *Essays on Biblical Interpretation*, ed. Mudge, 91.

decorative literary trappings because the *content* of religious discourse is generated and determined by the literary *forms* employed to mediate particular theological understandings.

Ricoeur's discourse analysis of the Bible seeks to show how the stories and sayings of the Bible are not one-dimensional exercises in coherence but rather multivalent points of intersection for a variety of discourses and their contrasting theological itineraries. From this perspective, the scriptural figuration of the divine life is radically problematized by attention to the mixed genres employed by the biblical writers. "Throughout these discourses, God appears differently each time: sometimes as the hero of the saving act, sometimes as wrathful and compassionate, sometimes as he to whom one can speak in a relation of an I-Thou type, or sometimes as he whom I meet only in a cosmic order that ignores me."[43] In this approach the Bible emerges as a heterogeneous intertext of oppositional genres—genres that alternately complement and conflict with one another—rather than a stable book unified by a particular discourse or singular perspective.

Ricoeur's openness to the revelatory power of poetic language per se calls into question Girard's circumscription of revelation to the Gospel texts' unveiling of the scapegoat mechanism. From a Ricoeurian perspective, the strength of Girard's hermeneutic—its disclosure of a sometimes nonviolent deity—is also its weakness. While Girard rightly recognizes the principles of mimesis and scapegoating at work in culture and religion, he fails to situate these principles within the play of genres that make up the polyphony of biblical revelation. His homophonic reading of the Bible as an antipersecution text ignores the surplus of meaning that spills over from the Bible's dynamic intertextuality—its crisscrossing modes of discourse, fractured surfaces, zones of indeterminacy, occult story lines, and conflicting theological itineraries. Girard's hermeneutic precludes dimensions of meaning that count against his metatheory by too narrowly construing the biblical witness as the definitive expression of the victimage principle.

A more balanced—and more biblical—handling of the issue of the Bible's own complicity with polarizing, sacrificial violence would be to read the biblical texts against themselves, to develop a hermeneutical criterion of antisacrificial violence and inclusive love as the key to decoding and appropriating the biblical witness. "Perhaps Girard's own principle of interpretation

---

43. Paul Ricoeur, "Philosophy and Religious Language," in *Figuring the Sacred: Religion, Narrative, and Imagination,* ed. Mark I. Wallace, trans. David Pellauer (Minneapolis: Fortress Press, 1995), 41.

may be used against his own specific readings: the disclosure of the innocent victim and the meaning of divine love is a criterion always to be applied, even to the sources that give witness to this very criterion."[44] The point is to read the Bible against the Bible in the light of its own announced antiviolent message, even if that message is frequently garbled by the texts cutting back on the very principle they gave rise to in the first place. Such a criterion for an antiviolent "working canon" provides a more honest acknowledgment of the mixed discourse at work in the Bible's conflicted avoidance of, and occasional capitulation to, the sacrificial language and mores it often condemns.

We have seen that Girard maintains that the whole Bible, culminating in the New Testament and the Gospels, follows an evolutionary trajectory toward a categorical rejection of all forms of sacrificial violence. I have suggested, however, that the Bible is an irreducible mixture of antiviolent *and* violent teachings, even in the Christian scriptures. Nevertheless, this fact should not discourage the reader from deploying an antisacrificial hermeneutic of the Bible, as long as the reader recognizes that this hermeneutic is just that—an act of interpretation—and not a discovery of the Bible's "original meaning." The problem with Girard is that he proceeds *as if* his biblical reading is an *uncovering* of the Bible's hidden sense, rather than a *construal* of its more liberating possibilities. If Ricoeur is right, however, meaning is not given in the words of the biblical texts themselves but instead is produced on the basis of the reader's active engagement with the texts' projection of new possibilities for existence. Meaning is generated in the to-and-fro, give-and-take interaction between text and interpreter; it is not a timeless property of the text that awaits discovery by the passive reader. In this sense, the burden of making sense of the Bible can only be handled by the reader who self-consciously takes a particular interpretive stance toward the Bible in the light of her own "working canon" or "hermeneutical template."

Of course, Girard is not unaware of the Bible's betrayal of its own best insights concerning nonviolence. He is not unaware, in the language of Derrida's philosophy, of the *supplemental* character of written discourse—namely, that writing always tries to make up for a lack of "presence" in the text itself.[45] He recognizes that there is always some slippage and spacing between the text's ultimate referent (the God of victims) and its various signifiers (the language

44. James G. Williams, "The Innocent Victim: René Girard on Violence, Sacrifice, and the Sacred," *Religious Studies Review* 14 (1988): 325.

45. See Jacques Derrida, *Of Grammatology*, trans. Gayatri Chakravorty Spivak (Baltimore: Johns Hopkins University Press, 1974), 141–64.

employed to make present this subject matter). He acknowledges that "minor defects have managed to creep into the text" and have reinscribed even in the gospel stories a discourse of divine violence and vengeance.[46] But no sooner does Girard make this concession to the failure of writing, even biblical writing, to render transparent the presence of the God of the victims, than he redoubles his efforts to arrest the play of signifiers by securing the biblical texts on the firm ground of the scapegoat mechanism. Having already determined the texts' centering referent, he resists any reading strategies that might deconstruct this center by implicating it in the endless freeplay of the signifier.

"For some twenty years the referent has been considered more or less inaccessible. It is unimportant, we hear, whether we are capable or not of reaching it; this naive notion of the referent would seem only to hamper the latest study of textuality. Now the only thing that matters is the ambiguous and unreliable relationships of language."[47] In this quotation and elsewhere, Girard takes issue with Derridean poetics and similar theories of interpretation because he regards their celebration of the play of figurative discourse as an attempt to suspend the text's referential capacities and claims to truth. But Girard misreads Derrida on this point. Derrida's criticism of referential theories of meaning stems from his recognition that textual signifiers are never free from the play of signification and ambiguity that marks all forms of discourse, including written discourse. In spite of its claims to the contrary, no text can signify, or refer to, an extratextual realm of pure meaning or pure presence that is somehow prior to and removed from the complications and obscurities of language itself. Derrida questions the philosophical quest for "a region or layer of pure meaning or a pure signified [that] is allegedly rigorously delineated or isolated" from cultural bias and semantic obliquity.[48] For Derrida, the master illusion of Western thought has been the claim that it is possible to uncover a pure, unmediated "transcendental signified" within texts through philosophical analysis. He criticizes the quixotic hope in a transcendental signified that can be secured by attending to a particular mode of discourse or type of text supposedly undetermined by the plurality of unstable and contradictory meanings characteristic of all other discourses and texts.

From this perspective, Derrida would most likely regard Girard's attempt to recover the christological referent of a fully present, nonviolent God within

46. Girard, *Things Hidden Since the Foundation of the World*, 188.
47. Girard, *The Scapegoat*, 9.
48. Jacques Derrida, *Positions*, trans. Alan Bass (Chicago: University of Chicago Press, 1981), 32.

the biblical texts as a longing for a "lost native country of thought" where the ambiguities and obscurities of human culture and language have not taken residence.[49] The Girardian hope of recovering such a "lost country" of pure, christological presence untouched by the indeterminacies and slippages of discourse presumably would be regarded by Derrida as a failed attempt to erect a once-and-for-all barrier between signified and signifier, theology and rhetoric, God and violence. For Derrida, however, the meaning of *all* textual signifiers, including the Girardian referents "God" or "Christ" or "innocent victim," is already *embedded* in the endless play of textual dissemination and contradiction where no purely determinate and self-present referent is available to the reader.

Girard, on the other hand, regards Derrida and other poststructuralists as tendentiously overemphasizing the immanence of figurative discourse (including biblical discourse) at the expense of its referential powers. In particular, he argues that the biblical texts are not self-enclosed aesthetic preserves but reliable indices to an extratextual reality, namely, the reality of the God of victims who reveals the hidden mimetic desires at the base of cultural victimage. Girard concedes the logic of the Derridean supplement, but consistently leads his analysis back to the hidden signifiers of the biblical witness and away from the play of differences that blunt the text's powers of reference to the victim. Girard's fear is that the ludic celebration of language for its own sake will obscure either the text's complicity with, or revelation of, the creation of scapegoats as the structural principle of the victimage mechanism.

It may appear, then, that only Girard is interested in the dialectic of violence and textuality, but a more sustained inquiry shows that this dialectic is a driving concern of Derrida's as well. As early as 1964 in "Violence et métaphysique: essai sur la pensée d'Emmanuel Levinas," Derrida argued that the totalizing goal of Western metaphysics has been the violent neutralization of the integrity and uncanniness of the other by subsuming and enclosing the other within a universal thought-system.[50] But until recently Derrida has not concretely analyzed the structures of cultural victimage in the light of his theory concerning the role of violence at the origins of philosophy in the West.[51]

49. Jacques Derrida, "Différance," in *Margins of Philosophy*, trans. Alan Bass (Chicago: University of Chicago Press, 1982), 27.

50. See Derrida, "Violence and Metaphysics," in *Writing and Difference*, ed. and trans. Alan Bass (Chicago: University of Chicago Press, 1978), 79–153.

51. By the mid-1980s, however, Derrida had made an explicit turn to integrating social analysis into his general understanding of philosophy and violence. See "Racism's Last Word,"

In this sense, Girard offers both an immanent critique of and extension beyond Derridean deconstruction insofar as he seeks to ground a model for understanding the mechanism of sacrificial violence in a general theory of culture and religion. On this reading, Girard makes explicit what remains implicit in Derrida's thought: the generative character of violence at the foundations of culture. As Andrew J. McKenna puts it, "Whereas Girard advances a theory of violence, Derrida is concerned with the violence of theory."[52] McKenna continues: "What Girard does is thematize the moral impulse of deconstruction in its ever more subtle detections of unconscious violence. This is an impulse all too often ignored by both advocates and adversaries of deconstruction, which uncovers violence in texts only to concern itself thereafter with textuality and not with violence."[53] Girard's attempt to thematize in concrete and universal terms what remains generally inchoate in Derrida's project—the understanding of the foundational role of violence in culture— spells out from the Girardian perspective the critical difference between his metatheory and the poetics of *différance* in poststructuralists such as Derrida. At the other end of the spectrum, Derrida would presumably see matters differently. While acknowledging the debilitating effects of philosophies that efface the integrity of the other, Derrida would remain suspicious of Girardian attempts to anchor the play of signifiers in a theological referent outside the endless dissemination of textual meaning. For Derrideans, then, the difference between Girard and Derrida is the difference between the Girardian longing for the full and original meaning of the biblical message of nonviolence beyond the play and uncertainty of language, and the Derridean suspicion of such longing as a failed nostalgia for plenitude and origins.[54]

Derrida is right, I believe, to criticize thinkers like Girard who claim to have unveiled a stable center in literary texts, such as the Bible, that does not dissolve into the endless dissemination of meaning, even as Ricoeur is right to argue against Girardian positions that fail to account for the irreducible plurality of written texts, including the biblical texts. But these criticisms do not,

---

Critical Inquiry 12 (1985): 291–99; "The Politics of Friendship," *Journal of Philosophy* 75 (1988): 632–45; and "Force de loi: le 'fondement mystique de l'autorite'"/"Force of Law: The 'Mystical Foundation of Authority,'" *Cordozo Law Review* 11 (1990): 920–1045.

52. Andrew J. McKenna, *Violence and Difference: Girard, Derrida, and Deconstruction* (Urbana: University of Illinois Press, 1992), 24.

53. Ibid., 34.

54. See Jacques Derrida, "Structure, Sign and Play in the Discourse of the Human Sciences," in *Writing and Difference*, ed. Bass, 278–93.

..ermine the extraordinary force of Girard's scapegoat hypothesis as a ..rmeneutic of the liberating potential of the Bible's message (though a con- flicted message) of forgiveness and nonviolence. Girard's critics rightly recog- nize in his thought (and in thinkers like him) a strained attempt to restore the loss of the center announced by hermeneutics and deconstruction—to arrest the play of differences and uncertainty that is the destiny of all textual dis- course. In my mind, however, these criticisms do not vitiate the range and power of Girard's project *as a transformative guide to biblical reading.* That is, while Girard's project fails as a *countertheory* to postmodernism in its longing for secure access to pure presence, the project still succeeds as a *hermeneutical strategy* by virtue of its extraordinarily fruitful exposures of the structures of victimage within Western culture and literature. In this sense, what thinkers like Ricoeur and Derrida help us to see in relation to Girard is that his project has as much to do with his own tacit (and generally unacknowledged) "work- ing canon" as it does with the clash of contrapuntal meanings occasioned by a sustained engagement with the full range of the biblical texts.

TRACES OF THE SPIRIT

Yes, Girard does eisegete the Bible and short-circuits its discontinuities. But, having said this, is it possible to evaluate the usefulness of his approach for understanding interhuman violence, even if this approach is insensitive to the heterogeneity characteristic of the texts used by Girard as warrants for his theory? Is it possible to move on to a further consideration of the utility of his theory, and not only with reference to biblical interpretation? In the context of the argument of this book, does Girard's theory provide sufficient analyti- cal power for explaining the nature of violence in contemporary culture, on the one hand, and the role of the Spirit in ameliorating such violence, on the other? Can the victimage hypothesis both account for the range of violence in human society and also offer a solution for checking its further deployment?

As a further test of the explanatory range of the theory, let us look at the strange story of Jesus' healing of the Gerasene demoniac as a case-study of Girard's hypothesis. The account, which appears in all three Synoptics, opens with the disturbing picture of a half-clad, demon-possessed man who period- ically gashes himself with stones as he runs wildly among the tombs outside of the town (Matthew 8:28–34; Mark 5:1–20; Luke 8:26–39). The towns- people, to no avail, try to restrain the man with chains, while Jesus comes to the man and exorcises his demons (who, when asked their name, utter the famous reply, "My name is Legion for we are many"). Jesus leaves the man in his right mind and then sends the demons into a herd of pigs, which run madly off a steep cliff. What makes the story so odd, however, is the reaction of the townspeople, who respond to the exorcism with fear and request Jesus to leave them, in spite of the healing of their fellow citizen. Oddly enough, the townspeople do not respond to the healing with gratitude, although gratitude would seem to be the likely response if the man's neighbors wanted to help him, which appears to be the case since they regularly bind him to prevent his self-mutilating madness.

Some commentators suggest that the Gerasenes' fear and demand to Jesus to leave them result either from their shock at seeing the man healed and fully clothed (but this is unlikely since the man's regular demonic appearance would be more terrifying than his restoration), or from their disappointment over losing their livestock (but if they really were concerned with their neighbor's welfare, is not his life worth more than a herd of pigs?). Girard, however, questions whether the townspeople really *did* desire the man's complete healing, and his interpretation of the anomalies in this passage makes sense of the townspeople's strange response to the exorcism. He suggests that in spite of the Gerasenes' "ritual" of restraining the man with chains in order to prevent his outbursts, the townspeople in reality are coparticipants with the man in a violent theater of cyclical suffering and partial deliverance—with the demoniac at center stage—because this sick drama meets some deep need on their part. The townspeople desperately want to protect their drama: they secretly enjoy and enable its recurrence by binding the man with chains that cannot secure him and by insisting that the only real healer the man has ever known, Jesus, leave the town.

> The Gerasenes are consternated at the idea of being deprived of their suffering. They must gain some enjoyment from this drama and even feel the need of it since they beg Jesus to leave immediately and stop interfering in their affairs. Their request is paradoxical, given that Jesus had just succeeded, without any violence, in obtaining the result that they had professed to be aiming at with their chains and fetters but which, in reality, they did not want at all: the complete cure of the possessed man. In this episode, as always, Jesus' presence reveals the truth of the hidden desires.[55]

If, as Girard argues, scapegoats are necessary for the preservation of a community's fragile economy, then the demoniac is the Gerasenes' scapegoat, a necessary support in their distorted social hierarchy, because he is the one

---

55. Girard, *The Scapegoat*, 169.

who mimetically embodies the community's distinctions between sickness and health, madness and sanity, violence and security, death and life. Psychosocially, the Gerasenes need their town demons, as it were, and they profit from a collective catharsis whenever the man is alternately plunged into, and then (temporarily) delivered from, his violent self-mutilations. "These unfortunate people fear that their precarious balance depends on the demoniac, on the activities they share periodically and on the kind of local celebrity their possessed citizen had become."[56]

For this need-meeting system to work, however, the man and his "friends" must tacitly agree that the man's delivery from the demons always be temporary if the town's rickety emotional structure is to be preserved. When the delivery becomes final in Jesus' complete exorcism, then the rules that governed the pathological game between victim and victimizers change forever, and, with this change, the threat of nondifferentiation, the most potent threat to any social organization, is now raised because the man, once a mad outcast, has become just like the "normal" Gerasenes. The townspeople are desperately afraid of the man's change from madman to one of them: "And they came to Jesus and saw the demoniac sitting there, clothed and in his right mind . . . and they were afraid" (Mark 5:15). With this change the disintegration of key distinctions in the town occurs—as embodied in the distinction between the sanity of the town and the madness of the tombs—and the Gerasenes can no longer vicariously work out their fears and desires and anxieties through the tortured existence of the demoniac/scapegoat. It is for this reason, as strange as it may seem on a first reading, that Jesus' therapeutic miracle is not greeted with joy and admiration but with fear and isolation—and, perhaps, outright hostility.

The story of the Gerasene demoniac is a story about power and control. It is a story about the contest between evil spirits who inspire the demoniac's self-destructive mutilations, and Jesus, under the power of the Holy Spirit, who seeks to release the man from his physical and spiritual anguish. The narrative's two protagonists, the possessed man and Jesus, embody the oppositional forces that consistently wage war against one another in the Gospels. These twin forces are often named Satan and the Spirit—the accuser and perpetrator of violence, and the advocate and defender of victims. "The Spirit is working in history to reveal what Jesus has already revealed, the mechanism of the scapegoat, the genesis of all mythology, the nonexistence of all gods of violence. In the language of the Gospel the Spirit achieves the defeat and condem-

56. Ibid., 181.

nation of Satan."⁵⁷ Satan is identified as the ruler of this world who inspires his subjects to hate and murder, while the Spirit is defined as the truthful witness who testifies to Satan's wiles against the victims of systemic evil.

Most of us, however, are distinctly uncomfortable with the Gospels' precritical portrayal of a cosmic conflict between Satan and the Spirit. Politically speaking, we are well aware of how quickly such a binary mythology of religious violence can be used to legitimize patriotic wars against the evil "other" (for example, medieval Christian pogroms against Jews, Cromwell's attacks on the "dregs of popery" in Protestant England, or America's Persian Gulf war of "liberation" against the "Butcher of Baghdad," Sa[d][t]a[m][n] Hussein). We are generally more comfortable with the modernist call to denude the Bible of its three-tiered universe, reliance on miracles, and belief in devils and evil spirits. Against Girard's remythologization of experience by understanding reality with primary reference to biblical narrative, many of us remain sympathetic with Rudolf Bultmann's now-quaint observation that "in this age of electric lights and the wireless the prescientific world of the Bible is obsolete."⁵⁸ Obsolete, indeed, and positively dangerous insofar as the Bible's primitive view of reality has often been used to sacralize violence against the dangerous outsider.

The problem with demythologization, however, is that it evacuates the Bible of much of its rhetorical and analytical power. The call in our time for a sanitized spirituality free of the corrosive influence of precritical mythology renders us tone deaf to the Bible's distinctive, albeit troubling, diagnosis of the human condition and prescription for individual and corporate renewal. The advantage, then, of a Girardian hermeneutic is its sensitivity to biblical analyses of psycho-social depth structures in human relations while eschewing the temptation to reify these structures by converting them into metaphysical absolutes.

A similarly nonreifying sensitivity to biblical mythology is evidenced by Walter Wink's study of the language of *power* in New Testament literature. Wink argues that the biblical "principalities and powers" in the Gospels and Paul—including archons, spirits, demons, angels and the like—are best understood not as descriptions of supernatural beings but as names for the interior forces at work in the lives of persons and institutions. "What I pro-

57. Ibid., 207.
58. Rudolf Bultmann, "New Testament and Mythology," in *Kerygma and Myth*, ed. Hans Werner Bartsch, trans. R. H. Fuller (New York: Harper & Row, 1961), 3.

pose is viewing the spiritual Powers not as separate heavenly or ethereal entities but as *the inner aspect of material or tangible manifestations of power.*"[59]
Wink understands the powers not with reference to transcendental entities
but in terms of their function within everyday social systems; this nonentita-
tive model of the powers allows the reader to conceive of the powers seriously,
though not literally, to borrow Reinhold Neibuhr's famous phrase concerning
biblical interpretation. If one thinks of the powers in *rhetorical* rather than
hypostatic terms, then the term "powers" can be used imaginatively to describe
or figure the inner spirituality, so to speak, that underlies the concrete relations that define any individual or group within society. In spite of many persons' understandable wariness about the usefulness of such language, Wink
argues that the biblical language about power speaks so profoundly to certain
dimensions of our experience that we should neither reduce this concept to
an outmoded figure of speech nor reify it as an invisible substance that controls human affairs.

> When we read the ancient accounts of encounters with these Powers, we can
> only regard them as hallucinations, since they have no real physical referent.
> Hence we *cannot* take seriously their own descriptions of these encounters—as
> long as our very categories of thought are dictated by the myth of materialism.
> ... For us the intermediate realm—what Henry Corbin has called the "imagi-
> nal" realm—is virtually unknown. We simply do not have categories for think-
> ing of such Powers as real yet unsubstantial, as actual spirits having no existence
> apart from their concretions in the world of things.[60]

The advantage to Girard's and Wink's approaches to biblical reading is that
they provide a vocabulary for figuring the identity of "real yet unsubstantial"
realities such as the Spirit. To think of the Spirit in rhetorical rather than substantialist terms means to think beyond the reductionist methods of
demythologization, on the one hand, and the metaphysics of normative theology, on the other. It means that the Spirit is best thought of as neither an
empty remainder concept left over from premodern times nor a being or substance reducible to a conceptual system. *To think the Spirit beyond the confines
of secularism or metaphysics is to put into play a rhetorical notion of the Spirit in
relation to the structures of lived existence.* Like Girard's scapegoat or Wink's
powers, this means that the Spirit exists in a transformative relationship with
the concrete social systems that alternately serve to block and enable human

59. Walter Wink, *Naming the Powers: The Language of Power in the New Testament*, vol. 1
of *The Powers* (Philadelphia: Fortress Press, 1984), 104.
60. Ibid., 4.

renewal. The Spirit is not a self-subsistent, static entity that exists apart from its coinherence with other living beings. Rather, the Spirit has its very life in communion with the liberative and healing relationships that various persons and groups share with one another. This approach desubstantializes the Spirit and understands the Spirit's work in adjectival rather than nominative terms, in spite of the way the word "Spirit" is conventionally used as the syntactic subject. Far from this model denying the reality of the Spirit, it rather posits this reality as a dynamic life-force that circulates among the transformative power relations that undergird aspects of postmodern culture.

On the basis of various portrayals of the Spirit within the Bible, three characteristics of the Spirit's work in the world come to the fore with the help of a rhetorical model of the Spirit indebted to Girard and Wink.

1. *First, in the Gospels the Spirit is portrayed as the divine agent of political and cultural subversion who inverts the normal power relations within society.* The heart of the Spirit's mission is the scandal of inclusivity, which challenged the fundamental social structures that defined persons and groups in the first century C.E. The Gospel of Luke, for example, is punctuated with numerous stories of social inclusion, inspired by the Spirit, in which Jesus and his followers express solidarity with marginalized individuals and groups. At the inauguration of Jesus' public ministry, Luke writes that Jesus "filled with the power of the Spirit" (4:14) stood to read to the synagogue congregation in Nazareth the following passage from the book of Isaiah:

> The Spirit of the Lord is upon me because he has anointed me to bring good news to the poor. He has sent me to proclaim release to the captives and recovery of sight to the blind, to let the oppressed go free, to proclaim the year of the Lord's favor. (Luke 4:18–19)

Jesus then announces that this proclamation, which he regards as a messianic prophecy concerning his own work, has been "fulfilled." In the Spirit, Jesus reads the Isaiah text in the manner of a perlocutionary speech act, to use J. L. Austin's terms, in which the very reading of this text produces a certain effect—namely, that in Jesus' own person the prophecy is fulfilled that the Messiah will liberate the forgotten and dispossessed. The content of this prophecy is that the Holy Spirit has anointed Jesus to *reverse* the established power relations within society by inspiring Jesus to offer good news to the poor, sight to the blind, and freedom to captives and the oppressed. Each of these groups identified as the object of the Spirit's work occupied the lower strata of first-century Palestinian society—those who had few material resources, or were physically challenged, or were oppressed by political and institutional structures.[61] By empowering Jesus to minister to these disenfranchised communities, the Spirit challenges the regnant social ordering of the time. Those who had suffered chronic social and economic dislocation by oppressive rulers, landlords, and proprietors are now the particular foci of the Spirit's emancipatory activity.

The Spirit is a master of irony, a virtuoso of change, a trickster who turns upside-down the normative patterns of political and social organization. Luke consistently figures the Spirit as a destabilizing and insurgent political force within the communities of Jesus' prophetic activity. We have considered the Spirit's subversive work in the Gerasene demoniac story (Mark 5:1–20; cf. Luke 8:26–39), but other accounts in Luke make the same point. Mary and Zechariah, filled with the Spirit, sound the theme of God's eschatological judgment against oppressors (1:46–55, 68–79). John the Baptist promises a baptism in the Holy Spirit in which religious and political power-mongers will be judged and set aside (3:1–17). Rejoicing in the Spirit, Jesus teaches that the meaning of the new kingdom of God will not be available to the wise and powerful but will only be understood by the powerless, even infants (10:21). He continues in this vein with the parable of the Good Samaritan, reminding his listeners that it was a lowly "half-breed" Samaritan, not the priestly aristocracy, that came to the aid of the traveler on the road to Jericho (10:29–37). Later, Jesus teaches that the Spirit is the *Paraclete*, an advocate for and defender of the victims of the ruling class; in times of trial, the Spirit will empower such victims to testify effectively on their own behalf (12:8–12). The underlying theme that ties these texts on the Spirit together is the rhetoric of sedition and reversal. The Spirit is an agent of moral subterfuge who works to dismantle the structures that keep oppressed persons under the heel of corrupt hierarchies. The Spirit is an instigator of constructive anarchy who prompts the victims of cultural oppression to rise up against their oppressors.

I believe we can describe the Spirit's insurgency in Luke in terms of the history of class conflict, as some Marxist-inspired exegetes have argued, or by using the language of the preferential option for the poor, as liberation theologians have suggested.[62] In biblical times, the Spirit challenged the illegitimacy of power wielded by political and social elites over the lives of peasants

61. See Richard A. Horsley with John S. Hanson, *Bandits, Prophets, and Messiahs: Popular Movements at the Time of Jesus* (San Francisco: Harper & Row, 1988), 48–87, 135–89.

62. See, for example, Leonardo Boff, *Trinity and Society*, trans. Paul Burns (Maryknoll, N.Y.: Orbis Books, 1988); and Comblin, *The Holy Spirit and Liberation*.

and others who lived on the margins of society. In our own time, against the privileges enjoyed by the upper class, the Spirit demands social and economic justice for the forgotten and oppressed. "The Holy Spirit lies at the root of the cry of the poor. The Spirit is the strength of those who have no strength. It leads the struggle for the emancipation and fulfillment of the people of the oppressed. The Spirit acts in history and through history. It does not take the place of history, but enters into history through men and women who carry the Spirit in themselves."[63]

One of the ways the Gospels specify the Spirit's agency as a role-reverser is in terms of the Spirit's power to set free liberating discourse. Lukan pneumatology figures the Spirit as the power of speech—from enabling Mary's and Zechariah's and Jesus' proclamations concerning God's compassion for the poor, to empowering the oppressed to speak out against their oppressors. Insofar as the Spirit is the power of transforming speech, the cry of the poor for justice is the cry of the Spirit for social transformation and spiritual renewal. "The more specific works of the Spirit in history are to bring freedom and give speech to the poor. With this gift of speech, the poor begin to act in the world. These same poor carry the hopes of new communities."[64] The Spirit actualizes in persons a willingness to enter the fray of history in order to wage peace and speak the truth on behalf of those who are persecuted and without hope.

2. *The threat of violence against the bearers of the Spirit's advocacy for victims is a second characteristic of the Spirit's work in the Gospels.* Girard understands this threat as the outworking of the "scapegoat mechanism," where the hierarchical distinctions that define a culture are challenged by those who have suffered the imposition of these distinctions. This challenge is met with force, usually lethal force, because the power elite know that unless they reassert their hegemony over the dispossessed they will lose their special entitlements, even their "identity" as the keepers of order within society. Girard argues that the unanimity of all against one is the result of challenges to the status quo, and that the Spirit, as the biblical *Paraclete* or comforter, suffers with and empowers those who advocate for radical social change.

> For an understanding of [the scapegoat] logic, we must consider the implications of violent unanimity when it occurs. In that fundamental moment for human culture, there are only persecutors and a victim confronting them. There is no third position, no way out. Where would the God of victims be, if

---

63. Comblin, *The Holy Spirit and Liberation*, 185.
64. Ibid., 76.

he were to find himself among men at that point in time? Obviously he would not be on the side of the persecutors, so he would have to be the victim. Rather than inflict violence, the Paraclete would prefer to suffer.[65]

The anger of the mob against the outsider is well illustrated in the account of Jesus' public proclamation in the synagogue at Nazareth. After Jesus castigates the congregation for not acknowledging his prophetic mission, Luke writes that the townspeople were "filled with rage, got up, drove [Jesus] out of the town, and led him to the brow of the hill on which their town was built, so that they might hurl him off the cliff" (Luke 4:28–29). It is significant that the townspeople attempt to murder Jesus by throwing him off the promontory around which their town is built. Could it be that the brow of the hillside is an identifying reference point for the town, and that it is therefore the appropriate place from which to ritually expel the outsider who is threatening the town's corporate identity? Ritual sacrifice often takes place in an area demarcated as the symbolic center of a people's common life: the middle of the town square, the inner sanctum of the temple, the top of the high altar. A sacrifice at the place where a community's identity is symbolically centered performs the ritual service of purifying the group from the bad influence of the troublemaker; it functions to reaffirm the imperative to exorcise the evil one who has caused the social and political upheaval that is undermining the community's basic sense of order. The destruction of the ritual victim reasserts the community's identifying structures of distinction because it permanently removes the threat to these structures posed by the scapegoat; this destruction brings together groups whose common identity was challenged by prophets critical of the prevailing social order. And with the destruction of the scapegoat, the group discovers a newfound sense of unity. Thus the unanimity of the mob/community is the pathological unity enjoyed by all cultures who single out in order to destroy the nonconformist as the poisonous instigator of debilitating social change.

From a Girardian perspective, an insurgency model of the Spirit based on the Gospels allows us to recognize that violence is never a completely random or inexplicable feature of social life. Outside the legalized violence of the state, the direction of lethal force against others often appears to be a spontaneous outbreaking of mysterious depth-drives within a society that defy explanation and understanding. But while violence of this sort may appear

---

65. René Girard, *Job: The Victim of His People*, trans. Yvonne Freccero (Stanford: Stanford University Press, 1987), 157.

unannounced and divorced from any rational explanation, in fact such violence is either a direct result, or an indirect by-product, of the ritual use of culturally-sanctioned violence as a means of checking the dangerous influence of insurgent groups and individuals. *Seemingly random violence operates according to the logic of the scapegoat mechanism, whether the practitioners of such violence are aware of this logic or not.* When social groups are threatened by the prospect of even healthy change and instability, they can either embrace the change as a constructive dynamic in a growth cycle, or suppress it as a danger to their regnant sense of social order. Few social groups, however, have the requisite flexibility and courage for entertaining the first option; most groups retreat within themselves and become hostile to the forces of change whenever their steady-state existence is challenged. Even so-called progressive groups and institutions in these circumstances become intractably conservative and treat with suspicion the cultural maverick who may or may not be responsible for the group's loss of control and identity.

From this perspective it should come as no surprise that in contemporary culture, where violence against the "other" is sanctioned by various legal and political and religious authorities, members of that culture learn (as if by osmosis) that violence is an effective check against the change and destabilization that are inevitable features of human growth and community. This dynamic is readily apparent in contemporary Western societies. Individual violence in domestic or workplace environments, or group violence in large urban areas, takes its cues from the wider cultural forces that legitimize and sacralize the destruction of victims in the name of the "war on drugs" at home, or "national security" abroad. The legitimation structures that support the excoriation of the "other" as a corrosive threat to the national welfare or global security are the same structures that engender smaller scale, but similarly lethal, acts of regular violence at home, at school, and in the neighborhoods where people live and work. Whenever a political leader or policy-maker, a father or mother, or a teacher or police officer feels that his or her status or person is threatened by a troublemaker, violence against the other is generally the almost unconscious reflex response to this threat. Likewise, anyone who sides with the other, in the name of the Spirit, in order to blunt the effects of reflexive violence now becomes as well a target for collateral recrimination.

3. *A third feature of the Spirit's work observable on the basis of a rhetorical method is the presence of Spirit-filled countercommunities forged by persons who respect difference and renounce the use of violence to suppress difference.* I say "countercommunities" in order to underscore the mission of social groups who labor against the temptation to impute guilt to a marginal other in order

to explain away their inner conflicts and tensions. Such countercommunities celebrate their members' heterogeneity even as they struggle to abandon the class structures that beset mainstream societies caught up in ritual victimage.

The book of Acts, the companion volume to Luke's Gospel, provides a blueprint for creating diversity and solidarity within just such a counter-community. Acts records that on the first day of Pentecost after the resurrection the Holy Spirit was poured out onto the disciples and their associates gathered together in Jerusalem (2:1–21). Tongues of fire rested on each person at the meeting; filled with the Spirit, the group began speaking in different languages. What is remarkable, however, is that the crowds that had gathered nearby heard and understood the disciples to be speaking in their own native languages. Some believed that this was a sign of God's presence in their midst, while others sneered at the company of speakers and suspected that they were all drunk on especially potent "new wine." Peter then proclaimed to the crowd that the prophecy in Joel, that "in the last days God will pour out the Spirit on all flesh," was now being fulfilled as evidenced by the phenomenon of many languages being spoken and understood without the need of translators.

The eruption of *heteroglossia* in Acts is a clue to the Spirit's special mission in our own time: to enable diverse, multicultural communities to celebrate their differences, while empowering members of such communities to understand their differences according to the integrity of each person's own cultural identity and traditions. The Spirit in Acts used the explosion of regional dialects as the vehicle for promoting both individual identity and corporate understanding. The Spirit is doing a similar work in our time as well. As at Pentecost, the panoply of cultural dissimilarities and personal traits that define persons and groups are celebrated today by the Spirit as the mediums through which the "new wine" of the Spirit's power is communicated.

> Therefore, the Spirit is the originator of differences, on the one hand, and, on the other, the instigator of communion. . . . People are not reduced to a single category, nor are their differences suppressed; on the contrary, these differences make up the riches of the community. At Pentecost, the Spirit did not make all those present speak the same language, but made them all hear the good news of salvation in their own language.[66]

The Spirit does not suppress difference but allows those who follow her promptings to exercise ownership over the process that brings together discrete individuals into common, yet asymmetrical, communities of integrity and hope.

66. Leonardo Boff, *Trinity and Society*, trans. Paul Burns (Maryknoll, N.Y.: Orbis, 1988), 195–96.

A COROLLARY NOTION OF DIFFERENCE:
MICHEL FOUCAULT'S ANALYSIS OF POWER

In the contemporary setting, Michel Foucault's writings express a similar concern with the formation of communities that respect difference and eschew the exclusion of nonconformists as threats to the established order. Similar to Girard's scapegoat hypothesis, Foucault's argument is that Western society has consistently marginalized persons who are labeled "unnatural" or "deviant" by the wider culture. In this vein consider his study of the origin of insane asylums in the modern West. In *Madness and Civilization*, Foucault analyzes the routinized exclusion of the mentally ill in relation to the decline in reported cases of leprosy in the late Middle Ages. He argues that the putative "leper" was a category of person invented by a culture afraid of a family of so-called "abnormal," even "subhuman" diseases that had to be vigorously guarded against lest they contaminate the health of the wider population. Lepers were housed in lepersariums so that they would not infect healthy members of society. But as leprosy waned, a new disease took its place, mental illness, and now another large group of persons—in particular, those who were rendered idle and indigent by bourgeois commercial activity, and later the Industrial Revolution—was labeled a threat to the social order and quarantined in various institutional "sites of confinement," such as poor houses, slums, and even insane asylums.

In the modern era the name of the "disease" changed from leprosy to madness, but the same structures of exclusion and scapegoating remained in place.

> The asylum was substituted for the lazar house, in the geography of haunted places as in the landscape of the moral universe. The old rites of excommunication were revived, but in the world of production and commerce. It was in these places of doomed and despised idleness, in this space invented by a society which had derived an ethical transcendence from the law of work, that madness would appear and soon expand until it had annexed them.[67]

In profit-driven economies where work is the supreme value, the only rational explanation for a *physically* healthy person not being a regular member of the labor force is that she or he must be suffering from a debilitating *mental* disease. By being unable or unwilling to enter the labor force, such persons pose a threat to the inner logic of the capitalist state, which privileges labor

---

67. Michel Foucault, *Madness and Civilization: A History of Insanity in the Age of Reason*, trans. Richard Howard (New York: Random House, Vintage Books, 1965), 57.

and production above all else. Like the lepers before them, the unemployed must then be removed from the "body" politic lest they "infect" it with their own peculiar "disease," namely, idleness—a sort of disease of the mind that reinscribes the previous prohibitions against persons who suffered from diseases of the skin.

Foucault's other books on hospitals, prisons, monasteries, and schools deploy similar analyses of persons and behaviors deemed threatening or perverse by the wider society and in need of structures of exclusion that prohibit them from undermining the society's basic values and institutions. His belief was that the study of these fundamentally oppressive attitudes and institutions in Western culture would enable critics and reformers to challenge the assumptions and structures that make such oppression possible. His wide social vision projects a transgressive "heterotopia" in which anomalous groups, by learning about the origins and influence of social systems that repress difference, are empowered to resist these systems of domination.

It is difficult, however, to apply the lessons of Foucault's analyses of these structures to the task of articulating specific political strategies for subverting them. Moreover, his analyses trade on an understanding of power that is so elastic and undifferentiated that at times he appears to argue that *all* forms of social control and authoritative knowledge are impediments to political change and should be correspondingly resisted. The problem is that Foucault does not discriminate between the tyranny of power networks that crush freedom and desire, on the one hand, and the social benefit of curbing individual freedoms in order to protect the common good, on the other.

> Foucault is certainly right to say that the conventional truths of morality, law, medicine and psychiatry are implicated in the exercise of power; that is a fact too easily forgotten by conventionally detached scientists, social scientists, and even philosophers. But those same truths also regulate the exercise of power. They set limits on what can rightly be done, and they give shape and conviction to the arguments the [social critics] make.[68]

There is a difference between the disciplinary structures that frustrate the realization of freedom and the cultural wisdom and conventions that strive strategically to balance the exercise of freedom and the responsibilities of each person to her or his neighbor.

The problem with Foucault's one-sided notion of power is illustrated by

68. Michael Walzer, "The Politics of Michel Foucault," in *Foucault: A Critical Reader*, ed. David Couzens Hoy (Oxford: Basil Blackwell, 1986), 65.

his interpretation of the relationship between an itinerant "farmhand" and a "little girl" in a French village in 1867.[69] In the story Foucault tells, the farmhand and the girl played surreptitious sexual games (one was called "curdled milk") until the man was arrested and charged by the authorities with moral turpitude against a minor. Eventually the farmhand was institutionalized for life because he was diagnosed as mentally ill and labeled sexually deviant, or so it appears from Foucault's account. While Foucault may well be right that the lifelong incarceration/hospitalization of the man was too severe a response to his behavior, his behavior, nevertheless, may not have been as innocent as Foucault assumes. What was the nature of the exchange between this man and the village girl? Depending on the girl's age, was she old enough to give her informed consent to the man's overtures? Is the story an example of all-too-familiar abuse of a child, or a case of "barely furtive pleasures between simple-minded adults and alert children," as Foucault argues?[70] Was the girl seduced or harassed into compliance with the older man? Was she raped under the guise of a harmless sexual sport? Foucault's story leaves the reader, then, with a series of troubling questions: Should children be protected from sexual encounters with adults? Or should they be liberated from the discourses and prohibitions that inhibit both the free play of their own budding sexuality and adults' sexual desire for them?

Foucault's inability to discern the possible sinister subtext to the man's behavior in this narrative reveals the blind spot in what is a generally impressive analysis of power. The pursuit of pleasure, while it may serve the immediate desires of the pursuer, may also so damage another person that it sometimes needs to be constrained by social convention, even a legal apparatus. Foucault rightly argues against the imposition of oppressive structures that crush individual autonomy by punishing nonconformists as dangerous threats to the commonweal. But his inability to isolate at least *some* social mechanisms as conducive to the realization of the common good is a serious shortcoming in an otherwise powerful critique of power and its abuses.

CONCLUSION

In this chapter I have examined the problem of violence against the outsider through the lens of the Girardian scapegoat mechanism. This mecha-

---

69. See Michel Foucault, *The History of Sexuality*, trans. Robert Hurley, 3 vols. (New York: Random House, Vintage Books, 1978–86), 1:31–32.
70. Ibid., 32.

nism sets in motion the rituals, prohibitions, and institutions that isolate the marginal other as the party responsible for larger social problems—and it then proceeds to sacrifice the other in order to reestablish unity and cohesion in the society. Advocates of racial inclusion and persons with AIDS represent for many Americans the "other" who must be marginalized, if not altogether destroyed, so that the health and stability of the larger whole can be preserved. From the perspective of a rhetorical notion of the Spirit in Luke-Acts, however, we have seen that the Spirit is an agent of social transformation who empowers persons and groups to challenge the structures of domination and oppression that make up modern-day sacrificial societies. Nevertheless, while sacrificial violence is inherently pernicious, not all forms of social constraint are debilitating (*pace* Foucault).

On the basis of this chapter, my hope has been that a broader and more detailed description of the identity of the Spirit, as a counterforce in the struggle for justice, can fill in my earlier formal claim that the Spirit is the inner voice who guides her listeners toward taking responsibility for the welfare of the other. Now, however, the question of the identity of the "other" toward whom the Spirit guides her followers needs further development as well. The widening of the category of the "other" to include the welfare and integrity of nonhuman species is the topic of the next chapter.

CHAPTER FIVE

The Spirit and Nature:
The Wild Bird Who Heals

I enter a swamp as a sacred place,—a sanctum sanctorum.[1]

Spirit of God in the clear running water,
blowing to greatness the trees on the hill,
Spirit of God in the finger of morning,
fill the earth, bring it to birth and blow where you will.[2]

The spirit of this compassionate God has been always with us from the time of creation. God gave birth to us and the whole universe with her life-giving breath (*Ruach*), the wind of life. . . . We also experience the life-giving Spirit of God in our people's struggle for liberation, their cry for life, and the beauty and gift of nature.[3]

I believe that man is at the top of the pecking order. I think that God gave us dominion over these creatures. . . . I just look at . . . a chicken . . . and I consider the human being on a higher scale. Maybe that's because a chicken doesn't talk.[4]

In the previous chapter, I articulated an understanding of the Holy Spirit as a healing power who enables resistance to the social forces that make scape-

---

1. Henry David Thoreau, "Walking," in *The Norton Book of Nature Writing*, ed. Robert Finch and John Elder (New York: W. W. Norton, 1990), 183.

2. East African Medical Missionary Sisters, "Invocation," in *Earth Prayers: From Around the World, 365 Prayers, Poems, and Invocations for Honoring the Earth*, ed. Elizabeth Roberts and Elias Amidon (San Francisco: HarperSanFrancisco, 1991), 177.

3. Chung Hyun-Kyung, "Welcome the Spirit; hear her cries: The Holy Spirit, creation, and the Culture of Life," *Christianity and Crisis* 51 (July 15, 1991): 221.

4. Manuel Lujan, Jr. [former Secretary of the Interior], "The Stealth Secretary," *Time*, 25 May 1992, 58.

goats out of persons blamed for the violence that permeates Western culture. This notion of the Spirit as the power of social transformation is a material application of the model of performative truth outlined in chapter 3—a model that served as a counterpoint to the metaphysical and neoempiricist paradigms for truth analyzed in chapter 2. My point was that the Spirit's work of overcoming structures of victimage enacts the truth of biblical faith that nonviolent compassion toward the other is the ideal of religious life. These two themes concerning the Spirit's subterfuge of the scapegoat mechanism (chapter 4), and the understanding of truth in religion as care for the neighbor (chapter 3), now need to be expanded to include a coherent model of the relations between human beings and *other* species within the purview of the Spirit's interanimation of all life-forms. This expanded focus points the way to an "ecological pneumatology" in which the boundaries that separate the human from the nonhuman order are blurred by the Spirit's challenge to our nature-indifferent (even nature-hostile) definitions of selfhood.

THE SPIRIT AS LIFE-FORM

Few observers of the contemporary situation doubt that we face today an ecological crisis of unimaginable proportions. Whether through slow and steady environmental degradation or the sudden exchange of nuclear weapons, the specter of ecocide haunts all human and nonhuman life that shares the resources of our planet home. Many of us have become numb to the various dimensions of the crisis: acid rain, ozone depletion, global warming, food-chain pesticides, soil erosion, mass consumption of nonrenewable fossil fuels, agricultural runoff, radioactive wastes, overpopulation, deforestation and desertification, carbon emissions, and loss of habitat.[5] In our time nature has been commodified and domesticated into a piece of real estate; it has become one more consumer item to be bought and sold in order to maximize profits. Nature has become a "resource" for corporate exploitation; its bounty has been harvested in order primarily to fuel the commercial and industrial complexes of developed nations in the northern hemisphere. Once a source of terror and awe, nature no longer functions as wild and sacred space for the eruption of the sublime or the manifestation of transcendence.

5. See Bill McKibben, *The End of Nature* (New York: Random House, 1989); and Jeremy Rifkin, *Biosphere Politics: A Cultural Odyssey from the Middle Ages to the New Age* (San Francisco: HarperSanFrancisco, 1991), 71–91.

We have exchanged the power and mystery of the earth for the invisible hand of the marketplace and we are all the poorer for it.

The prospect of slow environmental death is a direct result of human beings' consistent lack of identity with their natural habitat. Developed human societies generally have had little sense of their dependence on the web of biological interconnections that makes their existence, and the existence of other species, both possible and meaningful. In an era of processed food, air-controlled environments, and private modes of transportation, we are generally unaware of the ties that bind us to the web of life that sustains all creation. Part of the blame for our lack of identity with other living things lies with the ancient Western and biblical confusion about nature as alternately a creation of God's goodness, on the one hand, and a transitory mass of brute forces that is irrelevant to the process of spiritual transformation, on the other. Ecologically speaking, the normative tradition's mixed discourse on the topic of nature has generated two opposing understandings of the human–nature relationship: nature as God's *good creation* is to be enjoyed and nurtured by all living beings, human and nonhuman, or nature as *dumb matter* is to be lorded over by God's viceroy, humankind.[6]

This double vision has had debilitating consequences for the task of sustaining and renewing the earth. Historically, it has helped to sacralize humankind's exploitative treatment of nature, because if natural objects are dead matter and not imbued with the Spirit (or spirits) of divine presence, then such objects can be used and abused to serve human ends.[7] Today this ambivalence toward nature has resulted in a fruitless polarization of positions both within religious communities and in the national environmental debate, pitting "wise-use developers" against "the spotted owl crowd," "tree-killers" against "tree-huggers," "conservation managers" against "ecoterrorists," and so forth. For many, what is lost in the rancor is the recognition that all life-forms are codependent, that nature has intrinsic and not merely instrumental value, and that no one species should arrogate to itself the right to commandeer a disproportionate number of natural resources at the expense of other species' needs to flourish and survive. At this stage in my discussion, these claims are more assertions than arguments. The goal of this chapter will be to

---

6. See Clarence J. Glacken, *Traces on the Rhodian Shore: Nature and Culture in Western Thought from Ancient Times to the End of the Eighteenth Century* (Berkeley: University of California Press, 1967), esp. 35–79, 150–70, 288–354.

7. See Lynn White, Jr., "The Historic Roots of Our Ecologic Crisis," *Science* 155 (1967): 1203–7.

defend these claims concerning the inherent worth of living things from the perspective of an earth-centered theory of the Spirit.

I maintain that the most adequate response to the current crisis lies in a recovery of the Holy Spirit as a natural, living being who indwells and sustains all life-forms.[8] The point is not that the Spirit is simply *in* nature as its interanimating force, as important as that is, but that the Spirit *is* a natural being who leads all creation into a peaceable relationship with itself. Spirit and earth internally condition and permeate each other; both modes of being coinhere through and with each other without collapsing into undifferentiated sameness or equivalence. Insofar as the Spirit abides in and with all living things, Spirit and earth are *inseparable* and yet at the same time *distinguishable*. Spirit and earth are internally indivisible because both modes of being are living realities with the common goal of sustaining other life-forms. But Spirit and earth also possess their own distinctive identities insofar as the Spirit is the unseen power who vivifies and sustains all living things, while the earth is the visible agent of the life that pulsates throughout creation. The Spirit inhabits the earth as its invisible and life-giving breath (*rûah*), and the earth (*gaia*) is the outward manifestation of the Spirit's presence within, and maintenance of, all life-forms.[9]

The understanding of the Spirit as a life-form intrinsically related to nature emphasizes a generally neglected model of the Spirit in the history of Western theology. In theory, the Spirit has always been defined as both the Spirit *of God* and the Spirit *of creation*. As the Spirit of God, the Spirit is the power of

---

8. While my position is that an ecological recovery of the Spirit is the best theological hope for changing the attitudes that lead to violence against the earth, some ecological theologians have seen little hope in a pneumatological approach to ecotheology. In her earlier work, for example, Sallie McFague argued that the model of God as Spirit is not retrievable in an ecological age. She criticized traditional descriptions of the Spirit as ethereal and vacant, and concluded that Spirit-language is an inadequate resource for the task of earth-healing because such language is "amorphous, vague, and colorless." See *Models of God: Theology for an Ecological, Nuclear Age* (Philadelphia: Fortress, 1987), 169–72. In her recent writing, however, McFague performs the very retrieval of pneumatology she had earlier claimed to be impossible: a revisioning of God as Spirit in order to thematize the immanent and dynamic presence of the divine life within all creation. See *The Body of God: An Ecological Theology* (Minneapolis: Fortress Press, 1993), 141–50.

9. See Jürgen Moltmann's *The Spirit of Life: A Universal Affirmation,* trans. Margaret Kohl (Minneapolis: Fortress Press, 1992), 274–89, and his model of the Spirit as the *vita vivificans* who sustains all creation; and James E. Lovelock's *Gaia: A New Look at Life on Earth* (Oxford: Oxford University Press, 1979) in defense of the model of the earth as a single living organism that supports all life-forms within a common ecosystem.

reciprocity between the first two persons of the Trinity, on the one hand, and the interior power of redemption within human beings, on the other. And as the Spirit of creation, the Spirit has been defined as the breath of God who indwells and sustains the cosmos. In practice, however, the Spirit has been almost exclusively understood as the Spirit of God; the stress has fallen on its roles as the source of consubstantiality within the Godhead and the divine agent of human salvation. The result is that the *cosmic* role of the Spirit as the power of life-giving breath within creation, including nonhuman as well as human creation, has been consistently played down.[10]

This long-standing deemphasis on the Spirit's ecological identity is remarkable given the abundance of imagery about the Spirit drawn from the natural world within the Bible. Indeed, the body of symbolism that is arguably most central to the scriptural portraiture of the Spirit is suffused with nature imagery. Consider the following tropes for the Spirit within the Bible: the *vivifying breath* that animates all living things (Genesis 1:2; Psalm 104:29–30), the *healing wind* that brings power and salvation to those it indwells (Judges 6:34; John 3:6; Acts 2:1–4), the *living water* that quickens and refreshes all who drink from its eternal springs (John 4:14; 7:37–38), the *purgative fire* that alternately judges evildoers and ignites the prophetic mission of the early church (Acts 2:1–4; Matthew 3:11–12), and the *divine dove*, with an olive branch in its mouth, that brings peace and renewal to a broken and divided world (Genesis 8:11; Matthew 3:16; John 1:32). These nature-based descriptions of the Spirit are the basis of my attempt to shift the theological focus back to the Spirit as the Spirit *of creation*. Such a focus neither

---

10. Jürgen Moltmann's *God in Creation: A New Theology of Creation and the Spirit of God,* trans. Margaret Kohl (San Francisco: Harper & Row, 1985) and *The Spirit of Life* are notable exceptions to this general orientation, but most other contemporary theologies of the Holy Spirit generally deemphasize, or ignore altogether, the model of the Spirit as God's mode of ecological renewal and healing within the cosmos. This shortcoming applies to a number of otherwise invaluable books in pneumatology, including Hendrikus Berkhof, *Theologie des Heiligen Geistes,* 2d ed. (Neukirchen-Vluyn: Neukirchener Verlag, 1988); Yves M. J. Congar, *I Believe in the Holy Spirit,* trans. Geoffrey Chapman, 3 vols. (New York: Seabury Press, 1983); George S. Hendry, *The Holy Spirit in Christian Theology* (Philadelphia: Westminster Press, 1965); Alasdair I. C. Heron, *The Holy Spirit: The Holy Spirit in the Bible, the History of Christian Thought, and Recent Theology* (Philadelphia: Westminster Press, 1983); G. W. H. Lampe, *God as Spirit* (Oxford: Clarendon Press, 1977); and John V. Taylor, *The Go-Between God: The Holy Spirit and the Christian Mission* (London: SCM Press, 1972). In addition, the writings on the Spirit in the important systematic theologies of authors such as Karl Barth, Karl Rahner, and Paul Tillich reflect a similar lacuna, though this oversight is understandable given the general lack of cultural awareness of the ecocrisis at the time these authors were writing.

denigrates nor ignores the normative understanding of the Spirit's other roles as the power of relationship between the Father and the Son, or as the agent of human sanctification within the history of salvation. Rather, this emphasis on the Spirit's cosmic identity as the divine breath who interanimates all other life-forms readdresses our attention to the Spirit's work in *all* creation— which includes, but is not limited to, the inner life of God and salvation history. Part of the burden of this book, then, is to shift the weight of theological emphasis away from understanding the Spirit either *theocentrically* or *anthropocentrically* toward an explicitly *biocentric* model of the Spirit in nature.

Note that a Spirit-centered theology of nature is not equivalent to a natural theology. I do not claim that one can have positive, independent knowledge of God apart from revelation, but rather that through the work of the Spirit in creation one can receive disclosures of the divine presence in communion with the earth and its inhabitants. Historic Protestant thought, culminating in the theology of Karl Barth, has had considerable anxiety over the prospect of natural knowledge of God through the powers of unaided human reason. But *if* the Spirit indwells all life, including the life of the mind within the body, *then* there can be no "pure" natural theology because all knowledge of God is mediated by the Spirit's omnipresence. From this perspective, the neoorthodox criticism that theologies of nature are fundamentally flawed because they are categorically distinct from, and thereby inferior to, so-called revealed theology trades on a false alternative.[11]

To reconceive the Spirit as a natural entity—as a living, breathing organism like a dove or an inanimate life-form such as wind or fire—is to emphasize the coinherence of the Spirit and the natural world. This model, however, presents an extraordinary challenge to the traditional doctrine of God. One intriguing but troubling implication of an ecological pneumatology of internal relatedness is that it places the divine life at risk in a manner that an extrinsic doctrine of the Spirit vis-à-vis the earth does not. *If Spirit and earth mutually indwell each other, then God as Spirit is vulnerable to loss and destruction insofar as the earth is abused and despoiled.* While this association is beginning to be felt by many people today, most theologians are hesitant to postulate that ecologically toxic relationships with other life-forms places the presence of the Spirit in the world in fundamental jeopardy.

---

11. For this discussion, see Moltmann, *The Spirit of Life*, 1–14.

SALLIE MCFAGUE AND CHRISTIAN PAGANISM

The hesitancy to reenvision God as thoroughly immanent to the world is apparent in what is arguably the most searching reunderstanding of Christian theology from a biocentric perspective, namely, Sallie McFague's ecotheology. McFague's central thesis is that theology for our time must first and foremost be able to account for the environmental crisis through a restructured understanding of God's relation to the world. She argues that traditional theology has been dominated by a dualistic and monarchical model of God in which God was seen as both in control of, and unrelated to, the world in a manner similar to a medieval king's relationship to his feudal possessions. In tandem with this model there emerged a hierarchical understanding of human beings as God's special image-bearers who are given the responsibility to exercise lordship and dominion over the earth. In the Great Chain of Being, God, as the disembodied source of all life, places humankind in between the highest order of being, heaven, and the lowest order, earth, so that human beings can be God's viceregents over the created order. Since in the monarchical model neither God nor humankind is understood as intrinsically related to the world, it follows that the earth can be used—and sometimes abused—to serve human ends. Traditional Christian thought is indicted by McFague as partly responsible for the environmental crisis insofar as it has sacralized this monarchical model of God and humankind as standing over against the earth—which, in turn, is relegated to the status of a lower order of being that needs human control and oversight.

McFague offers an organic or bodily understanding of God as a counterpoint to the regnant monarchical model. God is the "inspirited body" or "embodied spirit" of the universe; as the radically immanent reality within which we "live and move and have our being" (Acts 17:28), God is the "body of the universe." In this model of the natural world as God's body, all forms of life, from the smallest microorganisms to the great whales of the ocean deep, are embodiments of God. All creation bodies forth the divine life in McFague's pan-*en*-theistic model of God: God is *in* every living thing and all living things are *interanimated* by the divine life-source. This model affords theology a new planetary agenda, because once the Christian community can learn to reconceive of the world as God's body, it will understand that the health and well-being of the earth and the health and well-being of God are coterminous values that are achievable only on the basis of earth-friendly lifestyles. But this model also appears to subject God to fundamental loss, perhaps even destruction, in a manner that an extrinsic and hierarchical theology does not, because while "God is not reduced to the world, the metaphor of the world as God's body puts God 'at risk.' If we follow out the implications of the metaphor, we see that God becomes dependent through being bodily, in a way that a totally invisible, distant God would never be."[12]

On an initial reading of McFague's work, therefore, God appears to be fundamentally immanent to the world: the world, as God's body, is the primary medium of God's presence, and God is "at risk" in a world suffering from acute environmental degradation. But on a further reading we find that God is not dependent on the world in the same way we are dependent on our bodies, in spite of what might appear to be the logical force of McFague's panentheistic model of God. "Everything that is is *in* God and God is *in* all things and yet God is not identical with the universe, for the universe is dependent on God in a way that God is not dependent on the universe."[13] God is *in* all life-forms, but the reality of God is not *identical* with nor *exhausted* by God's embodied participation in the well-being of the planet. McFague's organic notion of God signals a novel and promising direction for critically correlating Christian theology and our culture's well-founded concern for healing and renewing the earth. But her slipping and sliding on the question of the precise relationship between God and the earth is an index to a troubling incoherence at the heart of her theological vision. McFague appears to equivocate on the critical issue: if the world *is* God's body, and if "being embodied" (as opposed to simply "having a body") entails that an entity is fundamentally dependent on its body for its well-being, then in what sense is God *both* bodily and yet *not* dependent on God's body, the universe, for the divine life's health and maintenance? McFague seems to want to have it both ways. She wants to maintain both God's identity *with* and autonomy *from* the universe, God's body, without specifying the exact manner in which God both *is* and *is not* dependent on the earth.

McFague's equivocation on the God–world relationship is at odds with a consistent earth-centered model of God as Spirit. In spite of her nonhierarchical model of God, her approach betrays a residual dualism. In the final analysis, God remains up in heaven ultimately secure and insulated from the environmental squalor suffered on the earth here below. Ultimately, God is not vulnerable to loss and destruction in the event that God's earth-body is

12. Sallie McFague, *Models of God: Theology for an Ecological, Nuclear Age* (Philadelphia: Fortress Press, 1987), 72.
13. Sallie McFague, *The Body of God: An Ecological Theology* (Minneapolis: Fortress Press, 1993), 149.

destroyed—in spite of the fact that if we were to lose our bodies, meaningful personal identity as we know it would be lost as well. God is *seemingly* at risk in McFague's paradigm, but not in any terminal sense. The alternative to McFague's half-turn to a biocentric model of God is a full-turn to reimagining God as casting her lot with the earth to the degree that God's fate and the world's future are fundamentally bound up with one another. This is my own perspective. In a thoroughgoing earth-centered model of God, God is a no-holds-barred incarnational reality; by deciding in freedom, and not by any internal necessity, to indwell all things, God places God's self at risk insofar as the earth's biotic communities suffer environmental degradation. God, then, is so internally related to the universe that the specter of ecocide raises the risk of deicide: to wreak environmental havoc on the earth is to run the risk that we will do irreparable, even fatal harm to the Mystery we call God. The wager of this model is that while God and world are not identical to each other (so McFague), their basic unity and common destiny raise the possibility that continual degradation of the earth's biotic communities may result in the attenuation and eventual destruction of the divine life itself (*pace* McFague).

But does this new paradigm for the God–world relationship purchase a coherent environmental theology at too steep at price, namely, the conventional understanding of God's sovereign nature as self-subsistent and independent from the fate of the earth? Does the deprivileging of the monarchical doctrine of God in favor of a fundamentally immanent and vulnerable understanding of God push Christian theology in the direction of paganism and heresy? My response is that Christian thought will continue to suffer serious impoverishment unless it begins a conversation with earth-friendly spiritualities that offer correctives to the indifference, even antagonism, to nature within historic Christianity.

Listening to Indian and neo-Indian spiritualities is one beginning for this conversation. Consider in this regard the worldview of native peoples of the Northern Plains. These communities lived the belief that the earth is the Great Mother's sacred flesh, and that Euroamericans' gold hunting and bison killing did irreparable harm to God's body. It was inconceivable to indigenous peoples that foreigners could willingly assault the very being of their own divine birth parent in an effort to make financial gain by destroying native animals and hunting grounds.[14] "The Wasichus [white people] did not

14. The spiritual terror occasioned by such an ecological crisis is movingly expressed in John G. Neihardt, *Black Elk Speaks: Being the Life Story of a Holy Man of the Oglala Sioux* (Lincoln, Neb.: University of Nebraska Press, 1979). With reference to the *global* ecological crisis,

kill [the bison] to eat; they killed them for the metal [gold] that makes them crazy, and they took only the hides to sell. Sometimes they did not even take the hides, only the tongues. . . . You can see that the men who did this were crazy."[15] In Lakota culture, since all life-forms are spirit-filled members of a common earth-community, human beings can responsibly take the life of another animal, such as the bison, only if they can use the whole animal—hide for clothing, sinews for thread, bones for needles, flesh for food—for the health and sustenance of their own tribal needs.[16] Since every form of life needs other living things in order to survive, it is often necessary to use certain animals for food, such as the bison, but never for profit or sport.[17] But when the two-leggeds laid waste to large stretches of habitat for the four-leggeds and other life-forms, they evacuated the land of the spirits of the creatures that once lived there.[18] From the perspective of an earth-centered model of the Spirit in dialogue with Lakota religion, our habitual exploitation of the earth for profit violates the integrity of, and risks extinguishing altogether, the presence of the cosmic Spirit who indwells and sustains all living things.

A related sensibility is found in the writings of contemporary neopagan environmental activists. Many ecological radicals in our own time espouse a primal spirituality of biotic unity that is akin to so-called "pagan," including Amerindian, cosmologies.[19] One such radical group is Earth First!, which

---

a similar and yet distinctly Western Christian sentiment is expressed in McFague, *Models of God*, 69–78.

15. Neihardt, *Black Elk Speaks*, 213.

16. See Wallace H. Black Elk and William S. Lyon, *Black Elk: The Sacred Ways of a Lakota* (San Francisco: Harper & Row, 1990), 32-48. Also see William K. Powers, *Oglala Religion* (Lincoln, Neb.: University of Nebraska Press, 1977); and Ed McGaa, Eagle Man, *Mother Earth Spirituality: Native American Paths to Healing Ourselves and Our World* (San Francisco: Harper & Row, 1990).

17. We should understand the intense reverence for the powers of nature among native cultures not as an expression of a magical and superstitious "paganism," but as reflecting an astute sensitivity to what it takes to survive in an alternately harsh and awe-inspiring universe. Native peoples were not "benighted savages" with a primitive fear of nature, but practical people who understood that biotic interdependence with other living things is the key to collective survival. On this point, see Julian Rice, *Black Elk's Story: Distinguishing its Lakota Purpose* (Albuquerque: University of New Mexico Press, 1991), ix–47, 148–53.

18. Black Elk and Lyon, *Black Elk*, 138–70.

19. See, for example, Margot Adler, *Drawing Down the Moon: Witches, Druids, Goddess-Worshippers, and Other Pagans in America Today* (Boston: Beacon Press, 1986), esp. 399–417, and John Seed et al., *Thinking Like a Mountain: Towards a Council of All Beings* (Philadelphia: New Society Publishers, 1988). While the term "paganism" carries pejorative connotations, Adler notes that in the Middle Ages the word "pagan" was coined from the Latin *paganus* to

uses as its motto "No compromise in defense of Mother Earth." Many Earth First!ers and other direct-action environmentalists practice quasi-Indian nature rituals, what Bron Taylor calls "primal spirituality," in order to actualize their fundamental unity with other life-forms.

> At meetings held in or near wilderness, [Earth First!ers] sometimes engage in ritual war dances, sometimes howling like wolves. Indeed, wolves, grizzly bears, and other animals function as totems, symbolizing a mystical kinship between the tribe and other creature-peoples. This is another example of primal spirituality. Native Americans often conceive of non-human species as kindred "peoples" and through "rituals of inclusion" extend the community of moral concern beyond human beings.[20]

The ritual reenactment of native folkways gives modern (non-native) Americans some awareness of their belongingness to nature, as well as the corresponding sense that the *uni*-verse is charged with the presence of the sacred.[21] In this vision all species should be protected as members of a biosphere in which the Spirit is embodied within the plethora of living things. Practitioners of nature spirituality believe that the sacred is dynamically present within the cycles of the seasons and the rhythms of biological growth and change. From this perspective, mastery of nature is a direct assault on the integrity of the divine life within the ebb and flow of natural forces. As in Lakota spirituality, here the "death of God" is the crisis of mass environmental destruction suffered by all forms of life, not the loss of meaning experienced by secular intellectuals. To understand, then, that God is at risk in our time is to make a full turn to a biophilic earth spirituality that figures all life, including the divine life, as interdependent. If the Spirit is fundamentally interrelated with the biosphere, then we must confront the strong possibility that both ecocide *and* deicide are the results of chronic environmental abuse of our fragile planet-home.

This position may strike some as more pantheistic (God and world are equivalent) than pan*en*theistic (God and world are internally related), but Christian thought has always maintained that nature and grace, world and God, while not the same reality, are inseparably interrelated. The eucharistic doctrine, for example, that Christ's true body and blood are really present in

---

refer to the country people outside the city walls, whereas the word "heathen" emerged as a description of the "people of the heath" in the British Isles (*Drawing Down the Moon*, ix).

20. Bron Taylor, "Earth First!'s Religious Radicalism," unpublished paper, 1991.

21. See Bron Taylor, "The Religion and Politics of Earth First!" *The Ecologist* 21 (November–December 1991): 259–66.

the Lord's Supper underscores the mutual indwelling of the Divine in and with everyday foodstuffs. Put simply, then, if God can become a loaf of bread or cup of wine, then why can God not become a bird or a beast or a tree or a mountain or a river? Unless one believes that the biological order is nothing more than a cosmic megamachine with no inner spiritual life, then it follows that God in God's freedom can kenotically, vitally indwell and become any and all created beings through the power of the Spirit.

The charge of pantheism may be the understandable response to this approach, and to a degree the charge sticks. I am proposing a sort of *revisionary paganism* as the most viable biblical and theological response to the prospect of present and future environmental collapse. This ecological approach will seek to reverse centuries of Western Christian hostility toward nonhuman life by again revisioning all of creation as a virtual sacred grove—a living, breathing sacrament—that cries out for our codependent nurture and affection. The biophilic approach calls us beyond respect for nature or even reverence for nature toward love of nature, even worship of nature, insofar as all life, from people and pelicans to wetlands and wildlands, bodies forth the reality of the Creator Spirit. Correspondingly, this approach resists the human-centered assumptions that lie behind the *stewardship* model in religious environmentalism in favor of a *friendship* ideal for an earth ethic: our task has less to do with being wise custodians of the resources that are "ours" than with simple life-styles that register minimal impact on the rich ecosystems that belong to all of "us." Perhaps some readers would prefer not to label such a biophilic theology "Christian paganism," but I believe anything less radical is not adequate to the crisis. Only a thoroughgoing *green theology* that presses the limits of conventional church discourse and runs the risk of heterodoxy is sufficient to the moral and theological tasks before us.[22]

THE *VINCULUM CARITATIS* IN CREATION

In chapter 3, I took up the role of the Spirit as the inner teacher in reference to a performative model of truth. In chapter 4, I applied this model to

22. On the prospects of rapprochement between Christianity, environmentalism, and neo-pagan traditions, see Dolores LaChapelle, *Sacred Land, Sacred Sex: Rapture of the Deep* (Silverton, Colo.: Fine Hill Arts, 1988); Judith Plant, ed., *Healing the Wounds: The Promise of Ecofeminism* (Philadelphia: New Society Publishers, 1989); John Seed et al., *Thinking Like a Mountain;* Rosemary Radford Ruether, *Gaia and God: An Ecofeminist Theology of Earth Healing* (San Francisco: HarperSanFrancisco, 1992), 143–72, 229–53; and Starhawk, *Dreaming the Dark: Magic, Sex, and Politics* (Boston: Beacon Press, 1982).

the task of social transformation through antisacrificial praxis. In this chapter I continue to examine the Spirit's work in terms of her third defining characteristic, namely, the ministry of preserving and renewing the whole created order. In deference to a fuller examination of the Spirit's work in human community and ecological transformation, I have not developed in this book the Spirit's intratrinitarian role as the bond of charity between the other members of the Trinity. Nevertheless, I consider the Spirit's identity as the *vinculum caritatis* within the life of God *and* the life of the cosmos to be the most adequate model for describing the Spirit's work in our time.

In the history of Christian thought, the Spirit has been defined according to three distinct but related roles. According to the Western theological tradition, the Spirit is identified with reference to (a) the trinitarian economy of the Godhead, (b) the interior lives of human persons, and (c) the community of beings within creation. The Spirit is the bond of love between Father and Son in the doctrine of the Trinity (*vinculum caritatis*); the inner minister to the human heart who instructs and sanctifies the faithful to seek the welfare of the other (*interior magister*); and the power of dynamic union within creation who continually animates, integrates, and preserves all life in the cosmos (*continuata creatio*).[23] While these ministries characterize different aspects of the Spirit's work, what unites all three modes of activity is that each is characterized by the Spirit's promotion of unity, intimacy, and reciprocity. In the life of the Trinity, human transformation, and the renewal of creation, the Spirit is the power of healing and communion within all forms of life—divine, human, and nonhuman.

In the immanent Trinity, the Spirit is the love which unites the Father and the Son in consubstantial fellowship; the Spirit subsists in the loving relationship between the Creator and the Redeemer within the Godhead. "And if the love whereby the Father loves the Son and the Son loves the Father displays, beyond the power of words, the communion of both, it is most fitting that the Spirit who is common to both should have the special name of love."[24] In the bosom of the Trinity, the Spirit is the power of communion who ensures the coinherence of the divine persons with each other. "This togetherness or communion of the Father and the Son is the Holy Spirit. The specific element in the divine mode of being of the Holy Spirit thus consists, paradoxi-

---

23. For an excellent survey and interpretation of these different models for identifying the Spirit, see Thomas C. Oden, *Life in the Spirit*, vol. 3 of *Systematic Theology* (San Francisco: HarperSanFrancisco, 1992), 1–75.

24. Augustine *De Trinitate* bk. 15, 37 (xix).

cally enough, in the fact that he is the common factor in the mode of being of God the Father and that of God the Son."[25] The term "*perichoresis*" (coinherence) is generally used to describe the Spirit's eternal enactment of the reciprocal interrelations between the other two members of the Godhead. The Spirit is the bond of love who consummates the friendship and mutuality that characterize the inner relations of the divine life.

In the economic Trinity, the Spirit works to promote intimacy and heal divisions among God's creatures, human and nonhuman. As she forges perichoretic sociality between the divine persons within the Godhead, she likewise labors in creation to foster mutual respect and admiration among the many beings that coexist within the web of life. Beyond the initial act of creation itself, the Spirit continually empowers human persons and other beings to create life-affirming communities that support all members of the planet (*continuata creatio*). In the New Testament the Christian community is enjoined to "maintain the unity of the Spirit in the bond of peace," because there is "one Spirit . . . and one God . . . who is above all and through all and in all"; in this unity, the community is asked not to "grieve the Holy Spirit" by descending into "bitterness and wrath and anger and wrangling and slander" (Ephesians 4:3–6, 30–31). The mark of the Spirit's presence, therefore, is reciprocity and cohabitation, even as the sign of the Spirit's absence is the erection of false barriers that blunt the Spirit's power to be "through all and in all." *Thus my central point: at a time when the earth and its many inhabitants are at risk of extinction because of our habitual anthropocentrism, it follows that the special unity the Spirit seeks to engender today is the unity forged by the erasure of artificial boundaries between the human self and the nonhuman other.* If the Spirit is rightly understood as the guarantor of perichoretic mutuality within the divine life, on the one hand, and the bond of unity and love within creation, on the other, then compassion for all life-forms within the biosphere is the fundamental disposition that the Spirit seeks to engender in all of us.

In an ecological age, therefore, the Spirit works intentionally to muddy the time-honored distinctions between humanity and nature that support the assumption that human beings are superior to nature. She asks us to resist the temptation to essentialize and totalize the nonhuman other by subsuming the other under the categories of "inferior organism" and "nonrational species." She entreats us to realize that the human self is naturally dependent on the other-than-self for its total health and well-being. *The world's forests are*

25. Karl Barth, *Church Dogmatics*, vol. 1:1, 2d ed., trans. G. W. Bromiley (Edinburgh: T. & T. Clark, 1975), 469.

the lungs we breathe with; the ozone layer is the skin that protects us; and the earth's lakes and rivers are the veins and arteries that supply us with vital fluids. The human self, then, has its very being in the nonhuman other because both self and other are integral members of a biological system of interdependence. Thus, the survival of each member of the biosphere is dependent on the integrity of the physical environment that all members share.

Unfortunately, however, the regnant intellectual traditions in Western culture have taught us to view humankind and otherkind according to a set of debilitating binary oppositions: humans are dynamic, ensouled, intelligence-endowed, image-bearers of God, while nature consists of soulless, non-rational, inert elements and subhuman plants and animals. This polarity enables the continual separation of human beings from other beings and obscures the natural kinship both modes of being have with one another. The culturally approved preservation of these distinctions ensures the separate identities of both "opposites," and the Spirit's violation of these polarities in the interest of unleashing mutual cobelonging strikes at the very heart of individual and corporate definitions of the human self and nonhuman species. As long as my sense of self goes no farther than the limits of my own body, I can live comfortably insulated from other life-forms within the confines of my own "skin-encapsulated ego," as Joanna Macy puts it.[26] As long as I construct myself as a solid rock rather than a porous membrane who is sustained by, and through which passes, the variegated life-support systems that make up our common biosphere, I can live the Great Lie of Western technosociety that I am entitled to abuse the earth because I exist *a se* as a self-subsistent being who needs no one or no thing for my survival. It is only when I am forced to confront the fact that my general health—even my very existence—is co-dependent on the welfare of this particular aquifer or that particular food chain that I become sensitive to the Spirit's homogenizing activity.

Mary Midgley argues for human beings' fundamental kinship with the whole biosphere in spite of historic attempts to distinguish humans from otherkind. She debunks the familiar standards that grade humans as superior to other life-forms on the biological ladder; she rebuts the popular stereotype of the human being as a more evolved organism. Whether in terms of fitness for survival, proportionate brain size, capacity to speak, or ability to reason, Midgley notes that many animals share these attributes with humans (for example, chimpanzees can communicate their intentions in sign language),

---

26. Joanna Macy, "Faith and Ecology," in *The Green Fuse: The Schumacher Lectures 1983-8*, ed. John Button (London: Quartet Books, 1990), 102.

and in some instances other organisms are superior to humans in the exercise of certain abilities (for example, grasses, insects, and rats are extremely resilient and less vulnerable to habitat loss than humans). Even our much ballyhooed rationality, Midgley argues, is questionable: if true rationality consists in the recognition that one is dependent on other forms of life, a member of a common biological heritage and not the center of the universe, then many animals are "smarter" than we are.[27]

The Spirit's overcoming of the inculturated distinctions that separate humankind from other beings makes possible a healing of the systemic ecological abuse perpetrated in the contemporary setting. When nature remains "other" or "different" from human beings, and only marginal to human flourishing, it remains ripe for exploitation. Large-scale, energy-intensive programs and policies that wage war on fragile ecosystems make sense if the earth is simply an object or a resource to be used, and not the creative matrix out of which all life comes and is sustained. The Creator Spirit responds directly to this challenge by intentionally laboring to obliterate the attitudinal partitions that separate human beings from the rest of creation.

COMPOSTING RELIGION:
JULIA KRISTEVA AND MARY DOUGLAS

Personal identity is forged in the crucible of differences, and no individual or group takes well to attempts to blur the distinctions, the identity markers, against which the person or group has staked out its identity. In the last chapter we saw how Girard and Foucault offer distinct, but related, arguments that social order is dependent on rules and prohibitions for maintaining the cultural distinctions that define group identity. "Order, peace, and fecundity depend on cultural distinctions; it is not these distinctions but the loss of them that gives birth to fierce rivalries and sets members of the same family or social group at one another's throats."[28] As culture-bred distinctions serve to solidify the group's unity, they also function to check the nonconformist influence of the marginal "other" from undermining the larger group. Societies are threatened by the anomalous and irregular, and systematically perse-

27. See Mary Midgley, *Beast and Man: The Roots of Human Nature* (Ithaca, N.Y.: Cornell University Press, 1978), esp. 145–283.
28. René Girard, *Violence and the Sacred*, trans. Patrick Gregory (Baltimore: Johns Hopkins University Press, 1977), 49.

cute persons (such as Girard's Gerasene demoniac or Foucault's madperson) they hold responsible for purveying abnormal attitudes and behaviors. "Since cultural eclipse is above all a social crisis, there is a strong tendency to explain it by social and, especially, moral causes. . . . But, rather than blame themselves, people inevitably blame . . . other people who seem particularly harmful for easily identifiable reasons."[29] The suspects of social disorder are stereotypically identified according to peculiarities of behavior, dress, religion, ethnicity, gender, and so forth. Since the victim's guilt is easily identifiable according to the mainline group's standards for "normalcy," the destruction of the victim is an inevitable consequence of the group's maintenance of the systems of *difference* that define its corporate identity.

Other cultural theorists such as Julia Kristeva and Mary Douglas make a similar point. Kristeva maintains that culturally sanctioned moral codes and religious rituals keep the symbolic order of society intact by erecting impenetrable partitions between human and nonhuman, clean and unclean, permissible and taboo, sane and abnormal, natural and unnatural, holy and sinful. These codes and rituals establish a system of differentiation within which the community can develop a "strategy of identity."[30] In analyzing the rules for ritual purity in the biblical levitical codes, for example, Kristeva underscores the "biblical text's basic concern with separating, with constituting strict identities without intermixture."[31] The Bible's prohibitions against mixtures and category confusion serve to protect biblical religion from contamination with other rival religious traditions, especially fertility cults and nature paganism, where the violation of oppositional taboos is regularly practiced. "The pure/impure mechanism testifies to the harsh combat Judaism, in order to constitute itself, must wage against paganism and its maternal cults."[32] Here nature is a dangerous mass of muddy confusion where the fecund mother, menstrual flow, physical deformities, bowel movements, and bodily decay are forms of pollution that break the boundaries that separate the pure body from the defilements and impurities of the natural order.

According to Kristeva, the Bible erects an impenetrable partition between the "clean" and "natural" behaviors of levitical religion and the "abominable" practices of pagan religious traditions. Kristeva argues that while biblical reli-

---

29. René Girard, *The Scapegoat*, trans. Yvonne Freccero (Baltimore: Johns Hopkins University Press, 1986), 14.

30. Julia Kristeva, "Semiotics of Biblical Abomination," in *Powers of Horror: An Essay on Abjection*, trans. Leon S. Roudiez (New York: Columbia University Press, 1982), 92–95.

31. Ibid., 93.

32. Ibid., 94.

gion is an exercise in order making, nature-based spiritualities are regarded as heterogeneous economies of excreta and pollution. Men who seek to observe the Torah, for example, must avoid defilement from bodily wastes, seminal emissions, and sexual contact with menstruating women (Leviticus 15). Kristeva suggests that similar strategies for ordering social behavior are especially applicable to women since women are regarded as more body-identified and nature-bound than men; women and mothers are particularly vulnerable to defilement because of their roles in menstruation, sexuality, and reproduction. Their bodies are mediums of secretions (blood) and discharges (birth) that violate the sense of order and control required by God's law. In the biblical taxonomy of purity and prohibitions, female blood is dangerously charged with the valence of impurity, and it is the occasion for reprisals against those who allow it to pollute the community's religious observance. Kristeva maintains that it is the vigorous protection against ritual impurity, especially in regard to the female members of the covenant, that separates what the Bible regards as divinely legislated behavior from the pagan practices of nonbiblical societies.

Douglas also analyzes how bodily boundaries are vulnerable modes of existence that present potent threats to social and religious order. Many societies seek to discipline the body so that it will symbolically uphold the system of separations the culture relies on for its collective identity. Bodies are microcosms of the cultural macrocosm: as symbols of society, they serve to maintain the sharp distinctions between purity and impurity that undergird ritual order. Unfortunately, however, bodies have a tendency to break down at their margins and behave erratically. They leak and ooze at their orifices in sometimes embarrassing ways that cannot be controlled, and instead of structuring society they function to undermine established patterns and values. As societies are vulnerable at their margins to the incursions of foreign enemies, so also are bodily openings dangerous occasions for aberrations and impurities that threaten the established order.

> [A]ll margins are dangerous. If they are pulled this way or that the shape of fundamental experience is altered. Any structure of ideas is vulnerable at its margins. We should expect the orifices of the body to symbolize its specially vulnerable points. Matter issuing from them is marginal stuff of the most obvious kind. Spittle, blood, milk, urine, faeces, or tears by simply issuing forth have traversed the boundary of the body.[33]

---

33. Mary Douglas, *Purity and Danger: An Analysis of the Concepts of Pollution and Taboo* (London: Routledge, Ark Paperbacks, 1966), 121.

In the classification schemes of social order, nature and bodies are dangerous mediums for the novel and untameable. Natural forces and bodily discharges undermine the religious and cultural structures that keep formlessness and disorder at bay; thus they are potent testimonies both to the *constructed*, and the *unstable*, character of the social prohibitions and behavior codes that undergird all societies.

As does Kristeva, Douglas also examines the abominations of Leviticus in order to analyze the role of religious (especially biblical) taboos in forging social order and cultic purity. In the Bible, the command "Be holy" means "Be separate" (Leviticus 20:26). Douglas notes that the Hebrew words for "holiness" (*qōdeš* and *ḥērem*) mean "separateness": to be holy like God is to keep oneself pure by observing the precepts concerning the proper modes of eating, dressing, washing, defecating, socializing, lovemaking, curing, planting, birthing, and so forth. Observant followers of Torah prosper by conforming their lives to these complex legal systems, while those who deviate from the covenant by, for example, eating animals that are hybrids or not pure types of their class, are cursed to live outside the law in confusion and disorder. "God's work through the blessing is essentially to create order, through which men's affairs prosper. . . . Where the blessing is withdrawn and the power of the curse unleashed, there is barrenness, pestilence, confusion (Deuteronomy 28:1–14)."[34]

Kristeva and Douglas underscore the theme of *separation from bodies and nature* as the key to understanding biblical religion. While their analyses are generally accurate, there is a one-sidedness to their conclusions that needs some adjustment. The Jewish and Christian traditions have not only emphasized the distinctions but also valorized the connections between religious practice and bodily/ecological life. A recognition of the Bible's mixed discourse on this question renders problematic the overarching conclusion that biblical faith is a sustained exercise in the logic of separation from nature. On the contrary, a more inclusive emphasis on the goodness of bodies and nature can be found in a variety of scriptural registers: in the opening creation hymn, where humankind is fashioned by the cosmic artisan from the earth; in the historical literatures, where human fertility is privileged as the condition for the continuation of the covenant people; in the wisdom writings, where the intimacy of human love is interpreted as a symbol of God's fellowship with Israel; and in the Gospels, where the divine life itself takes on bodily flesh in order to bring salvation to the world. From this perspective, the Bible at times

---

34. Ibid., 50.

mixes up what it elsewhere strives to distinguish. It juxtaposes both body-affirming and earth-loving themes along with harsh antinature taxonomies that seek to keep the observant community pure and free from physical contamination. It both sacralizes the earth and bodily existence as expressions of the good creation God has made and inveighs against the failures of the covenant people to remain ritually clean by upholding the distinctions necessary for cultural order.

Douglas argues that "healthy" forms of spirituality (to borrow an adjective of William James) are always "mixings" of the categories and forms of experience that less flexible religious traditions try to distinguish and separate. While some system of distinctions remains in place for even broad-based religions, these traditions learn to reintegrate the anomalous and "dirty" back into the mainstream of the community's life. Using agricultural imagery, Douglas writes that open-minded religious traditions, including some forms of biblical spirituality, practice "composting" in which "weed-like" behaviors and life-forms that were once labeled unclean and forbidden are now regarded as life-giving and thereby reintegrated into the community's existence. "The special kind of treatment which some religions accord to anomalies and abominations to make them powerful for good is like turning weeds and lawn cuttings into compost."[35] Healthy spiritual communities are able to suspend their hierarchical systems of order and revalue again their dependence on all living creatures, even those previously deemed unclean or lowly, as necessary for a spiritually and biologically rich common life. This melding of distinctions between human and nonhuman, clean and unclean, normal and abnormal sets free, "to continue the gardening metaphor, a composting religion. That which is rejected is ploughed back for a renewal of life."[36]

In a world at risk, the Spirit as the *vinculum caritatis* confronts the religiously sanctioned distinctions between humankind and otherkind that undermine attempts to "compost" all living things into a "heap" of interconnected life-forms. Persons use conventional boundaries and definitions of what it means to be a "self" in order to secure their identity over and against the reality of the natural "other." The Spirit's blurring of such distinctions immediately threatens one's "strategy of identity," to use Kristeva's phrase, because of its challenge not to set oneself apart from the other by denying that one belongs to the other. The Spirit's work threatens to tear apart the nature-indifferent *imago Dei* self-concept many persons prize as their birthright and

35. Ibid., 163.
36. Ibid., 167.

replace it with an *imago mundi* anthropology instead.[37] Living on the borders of the postindustrial megamachine as a catalyst for disorienting change, the Spirit reminds us that as God's images we are earth creatures fashioned from the muck and mire of the soil. This ecological theme is consistent with the emphasis we saw in chapter 4, where the Spirit was understood as a revolutionary force who labors to invert the established social order. Pneumatologically, we have seen that the Bible is suffused with the rhetoric of reversal: in John the Spirit brings supernatural peace to a community bereft and divided over Jesus' departure (John 14–16); pentecostal Spiritfire in Acts establishes a multiethnic church where old nationalisms are sacrificed for a new order (Acts 2:1–21); and Paul writes that all believers drink of one Spirit through the grace received in baptism and the gifts of the Spirit (1 Corinthians 12:4–13). The Spirit upsets conventional mores and replaces them with the new fellowship of the pneumatic community. To borrow from Douglas, the Spirit is an agent of "creative formlessness" who dangerously foments "boundary transgression" and the dissolution of "order" into "formlessness."[38] Thus, in an ecological age the Spirit is working to subvert our privileged boundaries between human and nonhuman species. This subversion strips human beings of their sacrosanct self-understandings as God's hierarchs in the Chain of Being and renders us bereft of our taken-for-granted privileges and identities in opposition to other life-forms.

To dismantle the debilitating differences that separate humankind from otherkind—this is the Spirit's special work in a world teetering on the edge of ecological collapse. We can learn to understand the Spirit's ministry of biotic reconciliation by resensitizing ourselves to the double identity of the Spirit as *personal agent*, on the one hand, and *inanimate force*, on the other. The nature of the Spirit as both personal and inanimate is an index to the common destiny between human and nonhuman creatures the Spirit seeks to enable. In the Bible we have seen that the Spirit is figured as wind, breath, fire, light, power, and life—natural forces within creation that engender transformation and renewal. Yet the Spirit is also described in the Bible in the language of personal agency and is addressed in personal pronouns, as "you" or "she" or "he." Insofar as *every* member of creation, sentient and nonsentient, is interanimated by the breath of the divine life, *all* forms of life are knit together by the dynamic power of the cosmic Spirit. Both personal and impersonal entities have their common life in the Spirit. This means, first of

37. See Moltmann's *God in Creation*, 185-243, for a discussion of this dialectic.
38. Douglas, *Purity and Danger*, 161.

all, that even nonsentient life-forms such as mountains and rivers and trees possess their own *personalities*, so to speak, resulting from their special evolutionary trajectories by virtue of the particular manner in which the agential Spirit infuses and empowers them. By the same token, second, sentient beings such as humans and other animals are *embodiments* of the natural elements and forces that make up all life. The point is that as the Spirit can be addressed as both an "it" and a "thou," so also should we learn to understand every member of creation that the Spirit inhabits in both personal and impersonal terms. From this perspective, the *personhood* of the nonhuman order is signified by the Spirit's abiding presence in creation, and the *creatureliness* of the human order is reaffirmed on the basis of its always already partnership with the wider biotic community that the Spirit indwells. This dialectic points to the common kinship and destiny of both the human and nonhuman orders: the realization of each life-form's dual identity as both personal and impersonal, agential and creaturely, thou and it.

"SPIRIT IS BUT THINLY AND PLAINLY CLOTHED": JOHN MUIR'S WILDERNESS PNEUMATOLOGY

An excellent source for reenvisioning the work of the Holy Spirit in creation is John Muir's nature writings. For Muir, the Spirit is best understood in relation to wild places, where God's coinherence with the rhythms of nature is most obvious. Muir sought to craft a new earth-centered vocabulary for describing the intimacy between God and world; his writing speaks to an almost total loss of distinctions between God, humankind, and otherkind. Muir's richly suggestive rhetoric embodies the Christian paganist sensibility alluded to earlier in this chapter. The wager of my argument is that the theological demand of our time is to reimagine God as Spirit in a manner consistent with Muir's pneumatology of the wilderness.

In the latter third of the nineteenth century, John Muir wrote of the "interpersonal" kinship human beings can have with the natural world. "When we dwell with mountains, see them face to face, every day, they seem as creatures with a sort of life—friends subject to moods, now talking, now taciturn, with whom we converse. . . ."[39] Muir believed that friendship with one's sister and

39. John Muir, Yosemite Journals, 1872 (?); *John of the Mountains: The Unpublished Journals of John Muir*, ed. Linnie Marsh Wolfe (Boston: Houghton Mifflin Co., 1938), 98.

fellow earth creatures (be they sentient or nonsentient, including the great mountains of Yosemite) is made possible by the Spirit whose presence reverberates within all living things. Muir exulted in the brilliant displays of what he called "Spirit" or "Nature" in the High Sierra Mountains of Northern California. His sojourns in the canyons and peaks of Yosemite, among other places, signaled his conscious rejection of the Calvinist, book-bound religion of his youth in favor of discovering the mystery and substance of the Divine in the drama and splendor of natural processes. Substituting wilderness for the Bible, his preferred "text" for discerning the path to salvation became the Book of Nature. Muir evolved into a "fundamentalist of the wilderness . . . [in which] the mystery of Nature became a living truth and could be known by those who were willing to repeat the mystical experience of living *in* the wilderness, as a Christian would live *in* Christ."[40]

Taking his cues from John the Baptist, Muir became John of the Mountains: a voice crying in the wilderness for all to be baptized into the healing waters and holy mysteries therein. "Heaven knows that John Baptist was not more eager to get all his fellow creatures into the Jordan than I to baptize all of mine in the beauty of God's mountains."[41] Through his popular writings and published journals, Muir preached fiery mountain sermons that sought to reverse civilization's contempt for wild places. He was well aware of the irony of his message: what the theologians have regarded as at best ancillary to Christian existence—the natural world—is in fact the *only* place where spiritual wholeness and renewal can be found. "In God's wildness lies the hope of the world—the great fresh unblighted, unredeemed wilderness. The galling harness of civilization drops off, and the wounds ere we are aware."[42] Here the "unredeemed wilderness" is in reality the true medium for salvation, while the seeming freedoms and comforts of modern society are actually a "galling harness" that confines human beings to lives dependent on chemicals and machines. Moreover, the "wounds" that leave urban dwellers broken and confused can be better healed by the pure air and natural medicinals of "fresh, unblighted wilderness" than by orthodox medicine and establishment reli-

40. Michael P. Cohen, *The Pathless Way: John Muir and American Wilderness* (Madison: University of Wisconsin Press, 1984), 127.

41. John Muir, Yosemite Journals, October 1871; *John of the Mountains*, ed. Wolfe, 86. On Muir's self-styled identity as a new John the Baptist within the modern-day (as opposed to the biblical) wilderness, see Richard Cartwright Austin, *Baptized into Wilderness: A Christian Perspective on John Muir* (Atlanta: John Knox Press, 1987), esp. 85–92.

42. John Muir, Yosemite Journals, 11 July 1890; *John of the Mountains*, ed. Wolfe, 317.

gion. Muir practiced a sort of homeopathic spirituality in which he sought
for the curative possibilities *within* nature as an aid toward recovering from
the effects of our habitual abuse *of* nature. "Earth hath no sorrows that earth
cannot heal. . . ."[43] In this manner, Muir regarded life in the wilderness as a
natural prophylactic against the diseases of "civilized" existence.

Muir saw fragments and remnants of the Spirit's presence wherever he trav-
eled. In his writings he promulgates a *wilderness pneumatology* in which
flashes of divine presence are refracted through the multifaceted complexity
of all natural things—from microorganisms in the clefts of glacial-polished
stones to the shimmering, icy brilliance of the Tuolumne river in the dead of
winter.

> Now we observe that, in cold mountain altitudes, Spirit is but thinly and
> plainly clothed. . . . When a portion of Spirit clothes itself with a sheet of lichen
> tissue, colored simply red or yellow, or gray or black, we say that is a low form of
> life. Yet is it more or less radically Divine than another portion of Spirit that has
> gathered garments of leaf and fairy flower and adorned them with all the colors
> of Light, although we say that the latter creature is of a higher form of life? All
> of these varied forms, high and low, are simply portions of God, radiated from
> Him as a sun, and made terrestrial by the clothes they wear, and by the modifi-
> cations of a corresponding kind in the God essence itself.[44]

Spirit is "thinly clothed" with a variety of life-forms—from sheets of lichen
tissue to garments of leaves and fairy flowers. Sparks of the divine flicker
everywhere; the *vestigia Dei* are traceable within the natural world; portions
of Spirit are in all living things. Since all beings are both "modifications" of
God as well as "terrestrial" in their common earth identity, it is impossible to
adjudicate which forms of life are "higher" or "lower" than their fellow creatures, or what, if any, fundamental ontological differences finally separate one
life-form from another. In Muir's paean to the omnipresent Spirit, the
boundaries between God and nature blur, and the "pantheistic-vitalistic
strains" of his ecotheology clearly emerge.[45]

Muir's work is a captivating expression of a spirituality of nondifferentiation between humankind and otherkind that results from an all-consuming
earth love. This loss of distinctions reverberates again in a remarkable passage

43. John Muir, Yosemite Journals, 1872 (?); *John of the Mountains*, ed. Wolfe, 99.
44. John Muir, Yosemite Journals, 15 March 1873; *John of the Mountains*, ed. Wolfe, 138.
45. See Catherine L. Albanese, *Nature Religion in America: From the Algonkian Indians to the New Age* (Chicago: University of Chicago Press, 1990), 95, as well as the excellent section on Muir and New England Transcendentalism (pp. 80–105).

where Muir writes effusively of a eucharistic feast devoted to drinking the woodsy "blood" from a giant sequoia, the king tree of the Yosemite forests.

> But I'm in the woods woods woods, & they are in *me-ee-ee.* The King tree & me have sworn eternal love—sworn it without swearing & I've taken the sacrament with Douglass Squirrel drank Sequoia wine, Sequoia blood, & with its rosy purple drops I am writing this woody gospel letter. I never before knew the virtue of Sequoia juice. Seen with sunbeams in it, its color is the most royal of all royal purples. No wonder the Indians instinctively drink it for they know not what. I wish I was so drunk & Sequoical that I could preach the green brown woods to all the juiceless world, descending from this divine wilderness like a John Baptist eating Douglass Squirrels & wild honey or wild anything, crying, Repent for the Kingdom of Sequoia is at hand.
>
> There is a balm in these leafy Gileads; pungent burrs & living King-juice for all defrauded civilization; for sick grangers and politicians, no need of Salt rivers sick or successful. Come Suck Sequoia & be saved.[46]

Muir's orgiastic evangelical prose locates salvation in the tree sap and wild animals of his mountain church; redemption and healing for the "juiceless world" lie in an overthrow of the sanitized and civilized religion of books and creeds. The "King-juice" of the sequoia tree, indeed, the organic medicinals of "wild honey or wild anything," are the surest means for a restored relationship with nature and oneself beyond the destructive habits of "defrauded civilization." Only a total immersion in the wild world of God's natural beauty can heal the tired, broken body and the hungry, thirsty soul.

In the wild world of Muir's nature mysticism, the lines of division between humankind and otherkinds melt away because there are "no harsh, hard dividing lines in nature . . . no stiff, frigid, stony partition walls betwixt us and heaven. There are blendings as immeasurable and untraceable as the edges of melting clouds. Eye hath not seen, nor ear heard, etc., is applicable here, for earth is partly heaven, and heaven earth."[47] Here Muir translates the language of salvation from his conservative Protestant upbringing into a new earthy register: deliverance lies in losing oneself in what one already is, a creature who craves for communion with the beautiful creation God has made. "Everybody at heart loves God's beauty because God made everybody."[48]

---

46. John Muir, letter to Jeanne Carr, in Cohen, *The Pathless Way*, 122.

47. John Muir, Yosemite Journals, 21 August 1872; *John of the Mountains*, ed. Wolfe, 89.

48. John Muir, "Thoughts Upon National Parks," in *John of the Mountains*, ed. Wolfe, 352.

Adrift in the beauty of the Yosemite high country and intoxicated with sequoia blood, Muir blends earth and heaven into an ecological sacrament where a climactic union between spirit and nature, self and other, is passionately consummated.

Muir's erotic and ecstatic earth religion seeks to transform the emptiness of modern urban existence into lifelong cohabitation with the sacred wilderness of God's mountains and forests. For Muir, nature is a living temple where the Spirit is at play in the flora and fauna of the wild. "Every purely natural object is a conductor of divinity, and we have but to expose ourselves in a clean condition to any of these conductors, to be fed and nourished by them. Only in this way can we procure our daily spirit bread. Only thus may we be filled with the Holy Ghost."[49] Muir experienced the ecstasy of worship in the "church of nature," as it were, by regularly practicing the art of heathen vision: by seeing all living things, from the smallest wild animal to the highest mountain peak, as charged with the grandeur of God's Spirit. His nature writing is a fusion between a love of God and a lust for the earth that paves the way for a life-centered theology of the Spirit appropriate to our own time.

JOB, GENESIS, AND THE PROMISE OF BIOCENTRISM

Muir's lusty celebrations of intimacy between humankind and otherkind embody the kind of "composting religion" valorized by Douglas. His wilderness pneumatology, however, upsets the common nature-indifferent, or even antinature assumptions in much of Western Christian thought. Much of the normative tradition argues that the God of the biblical narratives is the Lord of *history* rather than a deity of *nature* (*contra* Muir).[50] The God of the Bible is primarily the guarantor of the historical covenant between God's self and humankind rather than a cosmic force who interanimates the rhythms and cycles of natural life. From the perspective of traditional covenantal theology, the biosphere as such is not the primary abode of the one God of biblical history; rather, the God of the Bible inhabits a heavenly realm that is radically separate from the material world of bodies and matter. Moreover, the sky-God

49. John Muir, Yosemite Journals, 16 February 1873; *John of the Mountains*, ed. Wolfe, 118.
50. For an insightful analysis of this mind-set in the history of Christian thought, see Paul Santmire, *The Travail of Nature: The Ambiguous Ecological Promise of Christian Theology* (Philadelphia: Fortress Press, 1985).

of the Bible is "jealous" of the covenant community's occasional involvement with the fertility deities and agricultural spirituality of other peoples and thus makes war against the many earth-gods and goddesses worshiped by pagan peoples. In this framework, Muir's nature eroticism would be read as having degenerated into "worshipping and serving the creature rather than the Creator" (Romans 1:25), and should be vigorously resisted. "Destroy their altars, smash their images, and cut down their sacred groves," commands God to his servant Moses (Deuteronomy 7:5). The Lord's violent anger is directed against the early Hebrews, who did not fully exterminate the nature spirituality of their enemies; this failure led to dangerous interfaith cross-pollinations between the covenantal people and the agriculture-centered religions of their neighbors. Western theology's indifference or hostility toward nature is an extension of the biblical mandate to the prophets to smash the shrines to the plump fertility goddesses of rural agrarian peoples by brandishing the Word of God as a weapon against pagan animism and idolatry.

This *contemptus mundi* tradition has had enormous practical consequences. The historic biblical contest between monotheism and paganism has helped to normalize the contemporary moral conviction that natural beings should be subjugated to their human caretakers for the benefit of human needs. If nature is not sacred space but a ready and potential site for idolatry, then it is properly regarded as the domain of God's chosen human agents who, because of their innate superiority, have been designated by God to be God's guardians and enforcers of the divine will over all creation. On this basis the case can be made for an anthropocentric ethic of *lordship* and *stewardship* in which nature is valued for its utility for humankind because it is God's gift for the care and preservation of human communities. The problem with this seemingly scripturally sanctioned, human-centered ethic, however, is that it does not tell the whole story concerning the biblical view of nature. In particular, biblical wisdom and creation literature offer a telling counterpoint to the normative paradigm.

Consider in this vein the story of Job. The narrative recounts the life of a religious man who was struck down by Satan for no apparent reason. Job's cry is the perennial complaint of the innocent sufferer, "Why do I suffer, O Lord, if I have done nothing wrong?" Significantly, however, instead of providing an answer to Job's complaint, the Divine responds by situating Job within the diversity of the powerful life-forms that God has made. Job challenges God to answer his cry for justice, and God answers him with vignettes about nature taken from the geography and bestiary of creation. "I will question you and you shall answer me," says the Lord to Job in the book's latter chapters (Job

38:3; 40:7; 42:4). "Where were you when I laid the foundation of the earth?
. . . Did you give the horse his might and clothe his neck with strength? . . . Is
it by your wisdom that the hawk soars and spreads its wings to the sky? . . .
And behold Behemoth—the hippopotamus—which I made as I made you.
. . . His bones are tubes of bronze, his limbs like bars of iron, because he is the
first of the works of God" (Job 38:4; 39:19, 26; 40:15, 18–19).

Why does God respond to Job in this manner? Job asks a perfectly legitimate question about unjust suffering and is right to expect, it seems, a rational
theological answer. He expects, perhaps, a response that logically imputes the
cause of his suffering to some hidden sin or the higher good of character formation, or some other justifiable cause. But God instead reminds Job of his
place in creation—that he was not present at the foundations of the world,
that he did not create the horse and the peacock and the lion. Job is reminded
that he is a member of a wider biotic community, and that he is not superior to
other forms of life; he and his kind are not *the measure of all things*. Moreover,
God tells Job that it is the strong but comical hippopotamus—not his fellow
human beings—that is the first of God's works! From the perspective of the
divine interrogation of chapters 38–41, it seems that Job in his suffering has
assumed that his plight is the center of God's concerns; in fact, however, other
beings, like the hippo, possess the same claim to God's attention as does Job.
Their suffering and their needs are as important to God as humankind's.
Could it be that the Joban God is impartial with respect to the needs of different species because all forms of life deserve the Divine's equal concern?[51]

"I understand your pain and anguish," God says to Job, "but you and your
human friends are not the center of the universe. Indeed, the lowly hippopotamus that some of your kind kill for bloodsport is the 'first of my
works' in the hierarchy of the animal creation. You too are one of those animals. I know that your pain is inscrutable to you, but perhaps if you could
learn the lesson that you too are an earth-creature then your all-too-human
assumption would be tempered that you have a divine right to full creature

51. Bill McKibben makes a similar point in reference to God's care of landscapes apart
from their utility for humans: "Job could not hope to understand many mysteries, including
why 'rain falls on land where no one lives, to meet the needs of the lonely wastes and make
grass sprout upon the ground' (Job 38:26–7). God seems to be insisting that we are not the
center of the universe, that he is quite happy with *places* where there are no people, a radical
departure from our most ingrained notions" (*The End of Nature*, 76). A related exegesis of the
"ecological Job" can be found in Holmes Rolston III, "Wildlife and Wildlands: A Christian
Perspective," in *After Nature's Revolt: Eco-Justice and Theology*, ed. Dieter T. Hessel (Minneapolis: Fortress Press, 1992), 130–36.

comforts and an existence free of pain. I remind you, my friend, that in strength and fitness for life in the wild, you are lower than the ungainly hippo; by the same token, however, you share a deep kinship with the hippo and other plants and animals within the common natural order that I have created. You search for answers to your questions and for meaning in your life. My answer is for you to *resituate yourself* in the fragile economy of the wild and sacred world of creation. Become what you are, Job—an earthling who is of the same biological stuff as other life-forms, including the wide and bumbling hippo. Find your answers to your questions in the powers of life and death you see demonstrated always and everywhere in the cycles of the seasons and the rhythms of the wild."

Not only in Job but also on the basis of the creation hymn of the first chapter of Genesis, the assignment of equal priority to all species, including the wild hippo, makes sense. According to Genesis 1, the first thing the Artisan-Creator did after spinning the waters, plants, and heavens into existence was to generate a teeming diversity of living creatures from the oceans, lakes, and rivers. Only after this was accomplished was humankind created, as Paul Ricoeur argues in his exegesis of Genesis 1:1–2:4a.[52] Ricoeur reads the Genesis story as a sort of polyphonal "creation song" animated by a variety of themes and counterthemes. From this contrapuntal perspective, the text's overall *cosmological* orientation contains within it, but is never superseded by, its *anthropological* counterpoint. Thus, the whole biological order "marks the limits of man, the milieu which precedes and envelops him, the universe which comprises him."[53] Such an interpretation clashes with the historical approach of the neoorthodox biblical theology movement (inspired by thinkers such as Karl Barth and Gerhard von Rad) that relegated the creation account to the role of a prologue within the overall narrative space of the Hexateuch. Apropos of this *heilsgeschichtlich* orientation, the creation of humankind is the crowning point of the creation story. Ricoeur argues, however, that the text is structured according to a series of dynamic oppositions—order and chaos, night and day, plants and animals—and that the creation of humankind emerges from within this overall cosmic give-and-take. Thus, Genesis 1 is best read as a nonanthropocentric ordering of all life-forms into a cosmic, biocentric harmony that precedes and envelops the salvation-history account of the Yahwist redactors.

52. See Paul Ricoeur, "Sur l'exégèse de Genèse 1,1-2,4a," in *Exégèse et herméneutique: Parole de Dieu*, ed. Xavier Léon Dufour (Paris: Seuil, 1971), 67–84.
53. Ibid., 82.

While the order of creation is reversed in the second creation account in Genesis 2, the definition of humankind as a biological creature remains constant with the first chapter. The prototypical human being, Adam, has its origin in the muck and mire of the soil. "Then the Lord God formed the human (ʾādām) of dust from the ground (ʾădāmâ), and breathed into his nostrils the breath of life; and the human became a living being" (Genesis 2:7). Note the pun on ʾādām and ʾădāmâ: the human is an earth-creature fashioned by the Birth God of Genesis from the dust of the ground. The God of Genesis 2 is a primitive potter, who molds humankind out of the clay of the earth. As well, this first earthling becomes a living being through the breath of life (rûaḥ)—an intertextual reference to the breath of God (rûaḥ) in Genesis 1:2, who broods over the face of the waters as a mother hen broods over her young. Like a mother who feeds her baby in utero through her own life and breath, the Mother God of Genesis "breathed into [the human's] nostrils the breath of life" (Genesis 2:7). The God of creation animates all forms of life, including human life, through the vivifying breath of the Spirit. As with the inaugural creation hymn, the second creation narrative suspends humankind within a biological web of interconnected plants and animals—all of which is brought to life by the quickening breath of the Spirit.

Pilgrims or Stewards?

The biocentric worlds of Job and Genesis are uncomfortable places for religious writers and practitioners who aver that human beings possess more intrinsic value than nonhuman organisms.[54] The ethical corollary to this

---

54. The tension among religious and ethical thinkers on the question of biocentric equality is intense. We might label the two positions "soft anthropocentrism" and "radical biocentrism." For a defense of the first view, see John B. Cobb, Jr., and Herman Daly, *For the Common Good: Redirecting the Economy toward Community, the Environment, and a Sustainable Future* (Boston: Beacon Press, 1989), esp. 376–400. Cobb and Daly argue that organisms possess different grades of value depending on their place in the evolutionary chain. Viruses and mosquitoes are not equal in intrinsic worth to human beings and porpoises. For the egalitarian biocentric perspective, where equal value *and* "rights" are extended to all members of the biosphere independent of their level of evolutionary development, see Bill Devall and George Sessions, *Deep Ecology: Living As If Nature Mattered* (Salt Lake City: Peregrine Smith Books, 1985): "The intuition of biocentric equality is that all things in the biosphere have an equal right to live and blossom and to reach their own individual forms of unfolding and self-realization within the larger

"speciesist" assumption is that other creatures, though possessing intrinsic value, are of lesser value and more expendable than human beings in competition for scarce resources and habitats, all other factors being equal. But religious anthropocentrism, even in its "soft" forms, contradicts the basic insight of biblically inspired egalitarian biocentrism, which maintains that all life-forms possess intrinsic value and that no one species, including the human community, enjoys natural priority over any other species. From the perspective of biocentrism, the Spirit is best understood as a natural being who renders fluid the lines of distinction between humankind and otherkind, and empowers all life-forms to exist in greater dependence on one another. In a Spirit-led love for nature, the human is awash in a loss of distinctions between itself and the nonhuman other. This pneumatological loss of identity and difference serves as a negative condition for an ethic of transgressive, boundless openness to all life in which the assignment of moral preference to human needs is permanently suspended. Human chauvinism, in other words, is not possible within an earth-centered model of the Spirit.

Nevertheless, is it possible to formulate an ethic of species-impartiality that would have real practical consequences? Or is such an ethic an ecotopian ideal that has little if any concrete application? In response, let me summarize the argument to this point. I have suggested that an earth-centered model of the Spirit figures creation as a community of biotic interdependence in which each life-form is a bearer of equal and intrinsic value. This premise warrants the move toward erasing the hierarchical distinctions that prioritize the interests of humankind over otherkind since all life-forms are Spirit-animated and codependent members of the biosphere. If this is the case, then it follows that the ethical corollary to this model centers on equal regard for all species populations. Thus, the practical question remains as to which principles should be invoked to guide human conduct toward other living things in the spirit of such equal regard.

Current studies in biocentric moral philosophy are an aid to answering this question. The fundamental insight in this literature is that the dynamism of life *as such* is a value unto itself, and that the realization of this value is the *summum bonum* of environmental ethics. Since all organisms, from single-celled bacteria to highly developed mammals, are goal-oriented centers of

---

Self-realization" (p. 67). Analogously, see Tom Regan, *The Case for Animal Rights* (Berkeley: University of California Press, 1983); and Paul W. Taylor, *Respect for Nature: A Theory of Environmental Ethics* (Princeton: Princeton University Press, 1986), 99–168.

biological activity, the maintenance of healthy environments in which the realization of an organism's life cycle can be sustained is the primary concern of a nature-based ethic. The moral rule that results from this premise is variously formulated as the "duty of noninterference," the "principle of minimum impact," or the "principle of nonmeddling."[55] This rule, then, entails a hands-off, live-and-let-live behavioral norm that would encourage the practice of noninterference in various biotic populations. In conflict situations where humans and other life-forms have competing claims to resources and habitats, the ethical goal would be to develop policies that register *no or as little human impact as possible* on the natural world. Practically, this would entail that in situations where nonessential human interests are furthered by the destruction of plants and animals (for example, in the case of the bulldozing of a coastal wetland in order to make room for a housing development), the decision should be to make little or no provision for such environmental impact. On the other hand, however, in situations where the essential integrity and well-being of a species population is at stake, human or nonhuman, more latitude could be given to measures that will benefit the needy population in spite of the negative effects on the populations not benefiting from the measures in question (for example, in cases where the study and use of some organic specimens are necessary for eradicating certain human diseases). Nevertheless, the same rule applies in both situations, namely, the path of minimum impact on other species.[56]

The practical calculus that results from a consistent life-centered theological ethic would not rule out, for example, the use of antibiotics in the treatment of illness. At first glance this would seem to be the case, insofar as my point is that all life-forms, as codependent members of the ecological order, possess intrinsic and equal worth, and that no one species, including the human species, has the right to secure its welfare at the expense of other life-forms. But this biotic "equality" principle must be balanced against the "minimal impact" principle, which is that if a species needs to use another species

55. The articulation of this rule is quoted from Taylor, *Respect for Nature*, 174; Devall and Sessions, *Deep Ecology*, 68; and Tom Regan, "The Nature and Possibility of an Environmental Ethic," *Environmental Ethics* 3 (1981): 31–32.

56. In the vein of the noninterference maxim, Taylor provides a helpful list of five principles—self-defense, proportionality, minimum wrong, distributive justice, and restitutive justice—for resolving conflicting "claims" between human and nonhuman populations. He also provides a number of case-studies illustrating the relevance of these principles to different hypothetical conflict scenarios. See Taylor, *Respect for Nature*, 256–313.

for its own survival (as in the case, for example, of smallpox immunization) then such use is permissible as long as it registers as little impact as possible on the species being used. In predator–prey relationships, nature allows various life-forms to use one another in the struggle for survival. What human beings have done, however, is enter this life-support struggle with an exploitative attitude: other life-forms are systematically abused in order for humans to enjoy as many creature comforts as possible with little attention given to the environmental degradation that results from such behavior.

In the current climate, however, much of the most original writing in the burgeoning field of theology and ecology is a variation on the "soft anthropocentrism" that takes issue with a full turn toward biocentric species-impartiality. Jürgen Moltmann's work is a case in point. The aim of his powerful *God in Creation* is to rethink the major *topoi* of Christian faith along environmental lines. Nature is valorized as the dwelling place of the Creator God who wills the growth and fulfillment of all living beings. But Moltmann's ascription of special privilege and value to human beings in the cosmic order belies what is an otherwise powerful ecological doctrine of creation and the Spirit. He argues that while the sabbath is the "crown of creation," human beings are the "apex of created things" because they alone are God's image-bearers to the rest of the world. Humans alone serve as God's "proxy" to creation insofar as they mediate God's will toward, and glory over, all creation; in turn, through prayers and good works, human beings act on creation's behalf as they represent all creatures to God.[57] Moltmann avers that only "the human being is able—and designated—to express the praise of all created beings before God. In his own praise he acts as representative for the whole of creation. His thanksgiving, as it were, looses the dumb tongue of nature."[58] In spite of Moltmann's consistent criticism of the normative traditions' insensitivity to the ecological crisis, his anthropocentric rhetoric of the human as the "apex of creation," who is uniquely suited to loosen the "dumb tongue of nature," repristinates the usual Christian inability to celebrate nature *on its own terms and for its own sake*—not as lesser than humankind, or in need of human mediation, but as wild and sacred space possessing its own unique and equally important values and goods.

James A. Nash's *Loving Nature* makes a fuller turn to an integrated "biotic ethic" where all life forms are ends in themselves and not simply means to fur-

57. Jürgen Moltmann, *God in Creation: A New Theology of Creation and the Spirit of God*, trans. Margaret Kohl (San Francisco: Harper & Row, 1985), 187–90.
58. Ibid., 71.

ther human ends. Nash's argument turns on an analysis of the failure of mainstream theology to confront the ecological crisis, on the one hand, and the public policy framework that results from a redefined Christian love for nature, on the other. But Nash hedges his ideal of "ecological love" with the claim that only humans, as image-bearers of the Divine, are superior "creative predators" who can rationally balance their own needs against the interests of other species in the ecosphere.

> Only humans, according to traditional Christian doctrine, have the potential to serve as the image of God and to exercise dominion in creation. Despite historical misinterpretations and abuse, these concepts recognize a basic biological fact: humans alone have evolved peculiar rational, moral, and, therefore, creative capacities that enable us alone to serve as responsible representatives of God's interests and values, to function as protectors of the ecosphere and deliberately constrained consumers of the world's goods. We alone are the *creative predators*. In the light of that fact, it seems unreasonable to put humans on a moral par with other creatures.[59]

Echoing Moltmann, Nash makes a comparable appeal to the *imago Dei* tradition and its legitimation of human beings as God's unique proxy and representative to other kinds. He is nervous about the putative extremism of deep ecologists who maintain that all natural entities possess equal value and should be accorded the moral right to develop their own potential apart from human influence as much as possible. Humans are not "on a moral par with other creatures," as deep ecologists would maintain.[60] Nash takes issue with the postulate of biotic equality—though he defends the principle of intrinsic value for all organisms—and concludes by privileging human interests as superior to the needs of the less "rational" and less "creative" nonhuman creatures over whom we are to exercise our roles as responsible predators. His book, as does Moltmann's, falls prey to the same theological tendency to prioritize human welfare at the expense of other beings, his stated orientation to the contrary notwithstanding.

On biblical and ecological grounds Moltmann's, Nash's and other likeminded theologians' value hierarchy is untenable. Ecologically speaking, it seems odd to claim that humans alone are uniquely equipped to protect the natural order. Given our collective appetite for mass consumption, overpopu-

59. James A. Nash, *Loving Nature: Ecological Integrity and Christian Responsibility* (Nashville: Abingdon, 1991), 149.
60. Ibid.

lation, radioactive energy, fossil fuels, ozone depletion and the like, it would make more sense for us to go to other creatures to learn ecological sanity rather than look to ourselves as responsible guardians of the biosphere. Indeed, we should "go to the ant, observe her ways and be wise," as the sage in Proverbs 6:6 exhorts, rather than resort to human ingenuity to solve the problem of environmental abuse. *Instead of paternalistically arrogating to ourselves the role of being divinely appointed stewards over all living things, we would serve creation better by refiguring ourselves as temporary sojourners on the earth who should practice a "hands-off" ethic toward other life-forms.* We need to grasp how to care for ourselves and others by learning humbly at the knee of our common earth mother, *Gaia*, who subsists in and with the life-giving Spirit. The demand of the moment is for earth-love and earth-healing, not more calls for being "creative predators" over and against other living things, as Nash puts it. We would do well to abandon the regnant rhetoric of protection and stewardship and substitute in its place a new language of humility and caution. Instead of blunting the Spirit's new work by insisting on our dubious roles as divinely ordained exercisers of dominion, all creation would profit from a collective redefinition of ourselves as dangerous travelers on a fragile earth. The earth has had enough of our "enlightened" oversight as it cries out for us to leave it alone before it is too late.

Likewise from a biblical perspective, the approach of Moltmann and others appears equally troubling. The Bible uses mixed discourse to describe the order and relationship between the human and nonhuman spheres. We have seen that while the scriptures do speak pejoratively of other living things as inferior to humankind, the Bible also articulates a high degree of parity between human beings and other beings. For example, God's rebuke to Job is that all life-forms (including the hippo who is the "first of God's works") are candidates for equal treatment and valuation; similarly, the creation of humankind is but one theme in the overall cosmology of Genesis. Exegetes and theologians who oppose biocentrism can and will read the biblical record differently, but that only underscores the point: at worst the Bible offers conflicted testimony to equality between species, and at best it sounds a loud protest against the arrogant human assumption that the original divine command to "subdue the earth and exercise dominion over it" (Genesis 1:28) sacralizes human beings' preferential service of their own desires over and against the needs and rights of other species. Moreover, the reunderstanding of the Spirit in our time as a wild life-form who transgresses boundaries between humans and otherkind, while threatening to our traditional assumptions and identities, embodies the biblical promise of a new nature-intoxicated spirituality that knocks humankind off its hierarchical pedestal and replants it within the great earth mother, vitalized by the Spirit, who gives life to all beings.

CONCLUSION

The *fact* of biological interdependence should entail the *value* of defending the integrity of species life for its own sake. But this particular fact/value dialectic is lost on those of us who do not sense our fundamental cobelonging with nature. The Bible's creation hymns teach us that we are earth creatures, mud people, molded by the cosmic potter out of the clay of the earth. But many of us in the postmodern West construe ourselves differently as denizens of a shopping-mall, temperature-controlled, throw-away world in which we have little need for reidentification with the primitive soil of our ancestral origins. Others, however, hunger for a renaturalized Christianity where the palpable sense of divine presence can be touched and tasted and heard and smelled in the push and pull of natural beings and forces. "This universe itself, but especially the planet Earth, needs to be experienced as the primary mode of divine presence, just as it is the primary educator, primary healer, primary commercial establishment, and primary lawgiver for all that exists within this life community."[61] Without this primal earth connection, however, clarion calls for an ecological spirituality and an earth ethic fall on deaf ears. How can a new vision of the interdependence of all life be restored in a technological age when the umbilical cord between divine, human, and nonhuman life has been snapped long ago?

I have argued that a Muir-like, Job-like ecological pneumatology is the most adequate response to our planetary crisis. If the crisis stems from humans' chronic lack of earth-identity, then the Spirit's erasure of distinctions and creation of solidarity between human and otherkind is the hope of our time. I have sought to show that the Spirit's transgressive and unifying activity is basic to its historic, biblical role as the bond of love within and between the immanent and economic Trinity. The Spirit is the power for convivial unity between all beings through her erasure of the culturally constructed boundaries that separate human and nonhuman life-forms. But what is now needed is the practical application of the Spirit's identity as the *vinculum caritatis* to the crisis situation at hand by refiguring the Spirit as a natural being—as breath,

---

61. Thomas Berry, *The Dream of the Earth* (San Francisco: Sierra Club Books, 1988), 120.

wind, bird, and fire—even if such refiguration runs provocatively close to neo-pagan nature worship. On the question of the environment, Christian theology desperately needs a blood transfusion, and one of the sources for this healing, in addition to rehabilitating the normative trinitarian lexicon, is the provocation of indigenous and neonative folkways and beliefs.[62]

To live in harmony with the earth is to live inspired (*in-spirited, in-the-Spirit*). Recently the Presbyterian Eco-Justice Task Force issued, in an otherwise excellent document, a call for a new model of environmental stewardship, an ideal of "servant lordship," as the hope for a revised Christian ethic of ecological responsibility.[63] But I believe that the time has long passed for the recovery of lordship and responsibility language in crafting a sound ecological ethic. Rather, the hope of our time is the promise of biocentrism as an alternative to the servant-lordship model for an adequate land ethic. When the Spirit inspired the formative pentecostal gathering in the book of Acts to speak in other tongues, an eschatological rupture from the past occurred in which the ancient prophecy was fulfilled that the Spirit would pour out itself onto all flesh. It was said that the fulfillment would be distinguished by excessive and impossible signs of the Spirit's presence: some would have visions, others would prophesy, and blood and fire and smoke would cover the earth (Acts 2:14–21). Today the haunting prospect of mass environmental death bears traces of just such a cataclysm. We too have entered a new era marked by a similar apocalyptic break with the past, where the Spirit is again at work to foment aberrant, unorthodox life-styles ("these ones are full of new wine," Acts 2:13). We are being asked to abandon old mores in favor of a new biocentric and nonconformist theology and ethic. We are being wooed by the Spirit to desert custodial language of dominion and stewardship in favor of an

---

62. In addition to the works cited at the beginning of this chapter on neopaganism and environmentalism, Chung Hyun-Kyung's postcolonial Spirit theology responds to this challenge. She crafts a powerful interreligious mediation between the spirits of indigenous peoples, who cry for justice in the struggle for liberation, and the Holy Spirit, who seeks to renew the integrity of all living beings. See Chung Hyun-Kyung, "Welcome the Spirit; hear her cries: The Holy Spirit, creation, and the Culture of Life," *Christianity and Crisis* 51 (July 15, 1991): 220–23. (This article is from her controversial address on the theme "Come Holy Spirit, Renew the Whole Creation," delivered at the Seventh Assembly of the World Council of Churches, Canberra, Australia, 8 February 1991). See also Chung Hyun-Kyung, *Struggle to Be the Sun Again: Introducing Asian Women's Theology* (Maryknoll, N.Y.: Orbis Books, 1990).

63. See the Presbyterian Eco-Justice Task Force, *Keeping and Healing the Creation* (Louisville: Presbyterian Church U.S.A., 1989), 51–60.

earth-centered religious discourse: all creatures are best served when humans abdicate their identities as overlords and defer instead to the wisdom of the Creatrix who renews and empowers the common biotic order. If we allow the Spirit's biophilic insurgency to redefine us as *pilgrims* and *sojourners* rather than *wardens* and *stewards*, our legacy to posterity might well be healing and life-giving, and not destructive of the hopes of future generations.

CHAPTER SIX

The Spirit and Evil:
Eyeless in Gaza (Again)

[I]f men are to have knowledge of the evil which will result from their actions or negligence, laws of nature must operate regularly; and that means that there will be what I may call "victims of the system."[1]

What the problem of evil calls into question is a way of thinking submitted to the requirements of logical coherence, that is, one submitted to both the rule of non-contradiction and that of systematic totalization.[2]

Gregor was angry. "After what happened to us, how can you believe in God?"
   With an understanding smile on his lips the Rebe answered, "How can you *not* believe in God after what has happened?"[3]

In the first two chapters of Part Two, I have sought to construct a nonsacrificial and earth-centered portrait of the Spirit. Against the philosophical quest for certainty described in Part One, I have crafted a postmetaphysical model of the Spirit as the power of social transformation and ecological renewal. I have envisioned the process of constructing such a model as a thoroughly heuristic and highly imaginative enterprise. Insofar as I have performed this task from the perspective of reconceiving theology as a "rhetorical art" rather than a "philosophical discipline," I have sought to resist the temptation to legitimate the project by fixing it to a philosophical foundation that

---

1. Richard Swinburne, *The Existence of God* (Oxford: Clarendon Press, 1979), 210.
2. Paul Ricoeur, "Evil, A Challenge to Philosophy and Theology," in *Figuring the Sacred: Religion, Narrative, and Imagination*, ed. Mark I. Wallace, trans. David Pellauer (Minneapolis: Fortress Press, 1995), 249.
3. Elie Wiesel, *The Gates of the Forest*, trans. Francis Frenaye (New York: Shocken Books, 1982), 194.

could provide a universal validation structure for my proposals. As I argued in chapter 1, I believe that no such foundation exists, either for theology or any other discipline, because all systems of thought are determined by the perspectival bias of the interpreter. Theologians often write *as if* they have a God's-eye view of reality, but they too are dwellers and detainees within the preserves of language and culture (whether they realize it or not). Thus, to do theology as a type of rhetoric in the aftermath of foundationalism is to be both honest about the historicist origins of one's enterprise, and to be free of the legitimation anxiety that has traditionally plagued modern intellectual inquiry, including academic theology.

But the practice of rhetorically conscious theology has another benefit as well—namely, it frees theology to return to its erstwhile dialogue with its primary documentary source, the Bible, and eschews the need to ground the results of this dialogue on a metaphysical system that is putatively more basic and original, and therefore more "true," than the biblical witness itself. The call to a postmetaphysical *ad fontes* approach to theology is not, however, a call to a narrow biblicism or fundamentalism that flattens out the incongruities within the Bible in an effort to defend its theological integrity. Rather, a postmodern *ad fontes* theology is a call to cultivate a vigorous engagement with the biblical texts in all of their heterogeneity and instability. It is a call to read the Bible by continually tracking the zones of indeterminacy and strategies of concealment that characterize the diversity of biblical discourses. It is a call to read the Bible as an exercise in difference and displacement, as well as a medium of coherence and unity, even when such a reading challenges the theological certainties of received Christian thought.

Two results of a revised *ad fontes* hermeneutic have direct relevance to the task of writing a life-centered theology of the Spirit. First, in relying on the Bible as the primary source for pneumatology, it is clear that there is considerable tension in the scriptures between the affirmation of God's sustaining presence through the Spirit, on the one hand, and the avowal of radical evil as a ubiquitous and permanent feature of everyday existence, on the other. This tension is a recurrent theme throughout the scriptures: the Bible consistently narrates the plight of persons and communities who suffer existence in a world where arbitrary pain and suffering regularly call into question the reality of God's goodness. Second, a life-centered portrait of the Spirit in the face of a world that seemingly denies any such reality can be partially accounted for, if not fully explained, by a return to the Bible's double-edged descriptions of the Spirit as alternately God's agent of healing and renewal *and* the instrument of God's judgment and revenge. Most contemporary pneumatologies ignore this double-edged portrait by privileging the narratives of divine benevolence as the only significant identity descriptions available to the theologian who culls from the Bible source material for a doctrine of the Spirit. My approach, however, seeks to account for the problem of evil by tracing the problem (theologically understood) back to its origins in the stories of divine violence within the biblical texts. A life-centered pneumatology ignores such narratives at its own peril. Unless one travels through, and not around, the Bible's complicity with the structures of violence that still define our own time, no biblically centered nonviolent model of the Spirit is possible. As the previous two chapters spoke to the reality of the Spirit in relation to the problems of violence in culture (chapter 4) and the environment (chapter 5), this chapter's focus falls on the question of the Spirit in a world where violence against the other is seemingly sanctioned, if not perpetrated, by the God of the biblical witness.

The task of this chapter, then, is (a) to analyze the different understandings of the problem of evil and violence within contemporary theology, (b) to evaluate whether these approaches are able to sound the depths of the problem as it has been understood in both biblical and contemporary terms, and then (c) to move to the constructive task of reformulating an understanding of the Spirit in the light of my initial analysis and evaluation of the alternatives. I will conclude that a reformed understanding of the Spirit is possible only when, in the rhetoric of biblical wisdom discourse, God is engaged as *both* lover and betrayer, defender and judge, friend and enemy. On the one hand, to live the life of faith in the face of radical evil is to attune oneself to the life-giving power of the Spirit in all living things—while, on the other hand, always remaining aware of the possibility that this power can engender ruination as well as renewal, destruction as well as healing.

THREE GENRES: SPECULATION, NARRATIVE, WISDOM

The problem of evil—that is, the dilemma of affirming the reality of a loving and powerful God in the face of widespread violence and suffering—is a problem that has long counted against religious belief. Though I have sought up to this point to articulate a model of the Spirit as a benevolent healer and sustainer of life, no theology of the Spirit is finally coherent, either existentially or intellectually, that does not come to terms with the appalling reality of global suffering vis-à-vis the belief in a loving God. A contemporary pneumatology is finally bankrupt if it cannot account for the problem of evil in a world purportedly sustained by the Spirit who works to maintain all forms of life and counter systems of violence. With this concern in the foreground, I begin by analyzing various responses to the problem of evil in contemporary religious thought. Only after this analysis is deployed will I be able to return to the question of whether a life-centered pneumatology is possible in a world scarred by violence and terror and seemingly devoid of any signs of the Spirit's ministry of love and renewal.

Simply stated, the problem of evil is the following: Though God is said to be an omnipotent being who could abolish all evil, and a loving being who would want to abolish evil, evil still exists; therefore, there can be no all-loving and all-powerful God.[4] Various intellectual solutions to this enigma have been formulated in the history of Christian thought; these solutions are referred to as "theodicies" from the Greek words *theos* and *dikē*, which, when placed together, loosely translate as "justifying God's ways to humankind." Such solutions usually argue against the truth of either or both of the first two premises (God is all-good and all-powerful) and/or the third premise (evil exists) in order to deny that the final conclusion (God does not exist) follows logically from the initial premises. The result is that while the argument against God from evil is generally considered to be formally valid, its soundness is questioned in terms of the truth of one or more of its premises.

As *intellectual* exercises in abstract argumentation, the various criticisms of the argument from evil have their merits; but as *theological* strategies for making sense of religious belief in the face of the horrifying evidence to the contrary, they are fundamentally inadequate. In the light of this problem, I will argue here that the most adequate "solution" to the problem of evil is a practical "dissolution" of the problem by way of a rhetorical analysis of the lived responses to radical negation within biblical wisdom discourse. I am especially interested in describing the power of sapiential discourse, in contradistinction to the modes of discourse used in analytic and narrative theodicies, to engender a therapeutic and performative response to the problem of evil. I maintain that this approach has a twofold advantage: it has the potential for being intellectually and emotionally edifying for the victims of unjust suffering, and it is free of the theoretical problems peculiar to philosophical and

4. The problem is similarly stated as a conditional syllogism by David Hume: "Epicurus' old questions are yet unanswered. Is [God] willing to prevent evil, but not able? then is he impotent. Is he able, but not willing? then is he malevolent. Is he both able and willing? whence then is evil?" See Hume's *Dialogues Concerning Natural Religion*, ed. Henry D. Aiken (New York: Hafner, 1948), 66.

narrative theodicies. The wisdom model shows how the speculative aporia of traditional theodicy (either God or evil but not both) can be relocated on the plane of practical (rather than theoretical) knowledge within biblical wisdom literature. This relocation renders the aporia practically productive by setting free a purgative response to evil. In this response, the community of faith is empowered to challenge in catharsis and anger the recalcitrant evil that is not subsumable under any final logic (*pace* speculative theodicy) or master story (*pace* narrative theodicy). In biblical wisdom discourse the aporia of evil is not *answered* (as in speculation and narration) but is *confronted* through the praxis of irony, anger, catharsis, and ritual.

In this chapter I will link the writings of different theodicists to a particular *genre* or *type of discourse*. If theology is a rhetorical discipline, then the question of genre is paramount to understanding the different styles of argument theological writers use to account for the problem of evil. In raising the question of genre, however, I am interested not in *classifying* different theodicies under this or that category but rather in *how* a theodicist (and her readers) create a particular vision of the world through different modes of discourse. Genre understood in this way is not a matter of literary taxonomy but a question of how authors and readers figure reality through style and rhetoric. Attention to genre (now understood as productive of meaning) allows one to step back from the many discursive claims made by an author in order to examine the underlying assumptions that make possible these claims in the first place. (If, for example, the basic assumption is that the problem of evil is a candidate for theoretical solution, then the genre of analytic philosophy might be employed as the form of discourse most homologous to and supportive of this assumption.) Genre analysis of different theodicies takes us "behind the scenes" to the root assumptions and argumentative strategies that underlie the so-called solutions to the problem of evil. Such an approach provides insight into the situated, constructed, and historical character of theological and philosophical inquiry and sets free a better understanding of the rhetorical strengths and limits of proposals in theodicy today.

I have chosen three genres—speculation, narration, and wisdom—because I believe they are fundamental to the mainstream theological response to evil in the contemporary situation. And in combination with this choice I have selected three thinkers—Richard Swinburne, Ronald Thiemann, and Paul Ricoeur—to be representative practitioners of these genres (even though none of these thinkers has made theodicy per se his primary concern).[5] The

5. By theodicy, I do not primarily mean the discipline of providing an ontotheological jus-

advantage of this typological entrée to the problem is that it focuses on three of the more articulate exponents of the different argumentative styles used to generate the theodicies most at issue in the current discussion.[6]

RICHARD SWINBURNE AND THE VALUE
OF MORAL RESPONSIBILITY

In order to describe and evaluate Swinburne's theodicy, it is initially important to situate his project within the overall program of his philosophy of religion. His religious apologetics encompasses a wide oeuvre, but he is perhaps best known for his trilogy *The Coherence of Theism*, *The Existence of God*, and *Faith and Reason*. In these works and others, Swinburne maintains that religious belief is rational and coherent because the weight of evidence (philosophical, historical, cosmological, and experiential) supports the existence of the God of classical Christian theism. Strong *a posteriori* evidence in favor of the existence of God includes, *inter alia*, cosmological harmony, biological design, moral conscience, miracles, and mystical experience. In the balance of probability these confirmatory phenomena lead to the conclusion that it is highly likely, though not incorrigibly certain, that there is a loving creator who sustains the universe in an orderly fashion. Swinburne acknowledges

---

tification of God's ways to humankind (say, in the manner of a Leibniz, though my understanding of the term includes this sort of approach), but rather the broader activity of articulating responses (both theoretical and practical) to the problem of radical evil in our time. For an analysis and defense of this wider use of the term in order to include "theodicies with a practical emphasis," see Kenneth Surin, *Theology and the Problem of Evil* (Oxford: Basil Blackwell, 1986), 1–37, 112–64.

6. Other religious thinkers with similar agendas could be substituted for the authors listed here (including, for example, Plantinga for Swinburne, Moltmann for Thiemann, and Surin for Ricoeur). The list of genres, however, is intentionally exclusive, for while other modes of discourse are critical for contemporary theodicy (especially tragedy), I find them less compelling as responses to the problem of evil for reasons discussed below. The contemporary *locus classicus* for the relationship of genre to theodicy remains Paul Ricoeur's *The Symbolism of Evil*, trans. Emerson Buchanan (Boston: Beacon Press, 1967). See also Larry Bouchard, *Tragic Method and Tragic Theology: Evil in Contemporary Drama and Religious Thought* (University Park: Pennsylvania State University Press, 1989), 1–94, for a profound analysis of genre and its relevance to the problem of evil in Western theology; and Terrence W. Tilley, *The Evils of Theodicy* (Washington, D.C.: Georgetown University Press, 1991), 222–55, for an equally thoughtful discussion of the different forms of discourse that undergird modern philosophical theodicies.

that this probable conclusion is militated against by strong counterevidence, such as the existence of radical evil. But, in the balance, even the problem of evil is not a defeater of the rationality of belief in a beneficent and omnipotent creator God.

But is the world as we now experience it—a world purportedly under the governance of a good God and yet marked by evil—theologically defensible? It is, Swinburne avers, because it is a world in which human agents can have real moral knowledge about the consequences of their actions and thereby realize personal growth in an environment of choice and freedom. Evil is the inevitable detritus of such a world. If there were not the possibility of evil consequences resulting from one's actions, then so-called moral choice would not be choice at all because it would always be limited to the good; and without real choice human beings would be automatons and would never have the potential for becoming moral agents who can shape their own destinies— for good or for ill.[7] Personal destiny, individual virtue, moral responsibility, and meaningful freedom are possible only if God gives to humankind a panoply of options from which to choose. Swinburne writes:

> evil comes with the good—it would be logically impossible for God to give certain benefits (e.g. choice of destiny and responsibility) without the inevitability or at any rate enormous probability of various accompanying evils. . . . A good God would have reason to create a world in which there were men with a choice of destiny and responsibility for each other, despite the evils which would inevitably or almost inevitably be presented in it, for the sake of the good which it contained.[8]

The linchpin of Swinburne's free will defense is his argument from the need for moral *knowledge*. If agents are to have a "genuine choice between bringing about evil and bringing about good" then they must be able to acquire "knowledge of which of their actions will have pleasant consequences and which will have unpleasant consequences for themselves or others."[9] This knowledge guarantees the reality of moral agency. But for this knowledge to be a real possibility, a necessary condition is that the universe be maintained in a ruled fashion so that certain moral actions and natural occurrences produce consistently predictable results. Human beings are free agents who make

7. Richard Swinburne, "Natural Evil," *American Philosophical Quarterly* 15 (1978): 295–301.
8. Swinburne, *The Existence of God*, 200.
9. Ibid., 203.

their own destinies. If I choose to dump toxins into the groundwater, for example, I need to know what consequences will result from this action and who or what will become the "victim" of my decision.

Swinburne acknowledges that something or someone will be victimized by the outworking of this law-governed moral "system": "the above argument illustrates the more general point that if men are to have knowledge of the evil which will result from their actions or negligence, laws of nature must operate regularly; and that means that there will be what I may call 'victims of the system.'"[10] But in the balance, and in spite of the victims, the painful result is worth the price because free moral agents are fashioned in the process, agents who benefit from the knowledge of the logical possibilities that could accrue from their actions:

> it is good that men should have experience of a full range of possible experiences. A world in which we did not know (except in the most formal way) of the logical possibilities of pain and disease . . . would be a world in which we would know little of the logical possibilities. 'It is good for me that I have been in trouble' sang the Psalmist, and he was right.[11]

Swinburne continues that God has not only the power but also the *right* not simply to allow but, moreover, to *impose* pain and suffering upon particular individuals for the sake of their or another's greater good. In a section from *The Existence of God* entitled "God's Right to Inflict Harm," Swinburne argues that God, as the author of our being, has the right to inflict upon his human subjects pain and suffering in order that they might realize the higher good of personal growth and knowledge. His maxim is that God creates "a world in which some suffer [in order] to give others knowledge."[12] Thus, as our creator, God's choice to cause harm to one of his creatures is always for the sake of that person's or someone else's benefit, or both.

In one remarkable passage, Swinburne suggests that even the most heinous of crimes and disastrous natural events in our time are in fact opportunities for growth in knowledge and responsibility. Consider the following:

> Clearly if there is a God he must set a limit to the amount of suffering. Clearly too there is such a limit. . . . *But the objection is that the limit is too wide. It ought never to have allowed Hiroshima, Belsen, the Lisbon Earthquake, or the Black Death. But the trouble is that the fewer natural evils a God provides, the less opportunity he provides for man to exercise responsibility. For the less the natural evil,*

10. Ibid., 210.
11. Ibid., 215.
12. Ibid., 217.

the less knowledge he gives to man of how to produce or avoid suffering and disaster, the less opportunity for his exercise of the higher virtues, and the less experience of the harsh possibilities of existence; and the less he allows to men the opportunity to bring about large-scale horrors, the less the freedom and responsibility which he gives to them. What in effect the objection is asking is that a God should make a toy-world, a world where things matter, but not very much; where we can choose and our choices can make a small difference, but the real choices remain God's.[13]

While the reach of such suffering as Hiroshima and Belsen and Treblinka might seem to be too wide, Swinburne does not flinch in his logic that the value of the knowledge and virtue that can be accumulated by such events outweighs their infernal violence and destruction. "The antitheodicist says . . . it would be wrong to create men able to put each other in Belsen. . . . The theodicist in reply must sketch in detail and show his adversary the good which such disasters make possible."[14] So Swinburne's paraphrase of Paul's dictum ("where sin increases, grace abounds"): the greater the evil, the greater the opportunity for growth and development in the exercise of the higher virtues.[15]

THE PROBLEM OF GRATUITOUS EVIL

Swinburne's "solution" to the problem of evil preserves the value of personal moral responsibility and follows through to its logical conclusion the implications of the biblical and classical understanding of God as the guarantor of human freedom. His basic idea, therefore, is the following: if a necessary condition for individual moral maturity is the possibility of real moral choice, then God has good reason for creating a world in which these choices, for good or evil, can be realized. If God is to enable moral responsibility in a moral universe (not a "toy-world") where human subjects can make lasting decisions, then the horror of the death camps and the prospect of environmental or nuclear mass death must be allowed, if not imposed, by God in order to realize this possibility. Swinburne extricates God from the illogical triad of omnipotence, perfect goodness, and evil by defending the constitution of a world in which individuals learn the values of self-sacrifice, noble suffering, and communal responsibility through sometimes massive pain and

13. Ibid., 219–20, my emphasis.
14. Richard Swinburne, "The Problem of Evil," in *Reason and Religion*, ed. Stuart C. Brown (Ithaca, N.Y.: Cornell University Press, 1977), 100.
15. Swinburne, *The Existence of God*, 219.

misfortune. Since a necessary condition for knowing how to prevent evil in the future is existence in a world in which that evil (or its analogue) does occur, the world as we know it can be justified.

From this perspective, the value of personal growth and future responsibility through adversity outweighs the value of life in a "toy-world" in which the realization of these higher-order moral goods is, by definition, impossible.[16] Of course, Swinburne acknowledges, this universe of learning-responsibility-through-pain does necessarily lead to considerable waste and agony, as many persons must bear horrible suffering in order to be taught the lessons of moral growth. It does inevitably lead to such persons becoming "victims of the system," as he puts it.[17] But he speculates that this inevitable victimage, in addition to the character benefits it yields, may be partially compensated for by certain postmortem rewards (heaven) or by God's willingness to suffer alongside the system's victims (atonement).[18]

The problem with this model, however, is its insensitivity to the pain and death that resist any such solution in the name of "moral responsibility." Swinburne's ascription of utilitarian value to natural and moral evil sounds like the proverbial scoutmaster's call to his troops to endure pain for the sake of winning future merit badges in the great organization of Scouting. There is something cavalier and unfeeling about his response that reflects the deep structural limitations peculiar to all forms of speculative theorizing in theodicy. The problem, in other words, is endemic to Swinburne's choice of genre. This choice commits him to the inexorable logic of all analytic theodicies that drive toward a "solution" to the problem of evil at the expense of the concrete agony of victims.

Swinburne's problem stems from his adoption of certain classical ideas about God and the world (namely, that God is good and powerful and that evil is an instrumental good) now wedded to an analytic mode of discourse that guarantees that on the basis of these presuppositions certain conclusions will follow (namely, that no amount of suffering can weigh in as final evidence against traditional theism). Radical evil, however, is a problem for thought and experience that resists the syllogistic closure foisted upon it by the genre of speculative theodicy. Swinburne's argument is formally valid but painfully irrational to many victims of disabling pain and suffering. For these victims who are the supposed beneficiaries of God's terrifying visitations—the ones

16. Ibid., 220. Also see Surin, *Theology and the Problem of Evil*, 78–86.
17. Swinburne, *The Existence of God*, 210.
18. Ibid.

who are said to experience growth by, or be the occasions for, learning responsibility through pain—there is little comfort in the tight weave of Swinburne's speculation and logic. Thus, the reader questions the soundness of the overall argument: can moral development really be had through the screams of victims of political torture, the cries of children who are ground underfoot by poverty, the destruction of families who are torn apart by the politics of greed and scarcity?

Swinburne's universe is a make-believe world, a speculative preserve that is off-limits to the forgotten and dispossessed of history. His world is the place where landed, privileged individuals have lived through the manly school of hard knocks, have profited accordingly, and now enjoin others to acquire the sense of responsibility they have learned. His ethic is a tidy Victorian calculus that rules out any squeamishness in the face of difficulty and places a high premium on moral knowledge and character development. His God is the Eaton headmaster who paternalistically but firmly pushes his charges beyond the point of endurance so that they might realize higher-order goods.

Though consistent in his logic of justification, Swinburne, along with other speculative theodicists like Alvin Plantinga, fails to make a distinction concerning evil that is important for clarifying the theodicy problem.[19] Etymologically, the modern word "evil" is from the Middle English "evel" with the primary sense of "exceeding due measure" or "overstepping proper limits."[20] Here the connotation is that evil is a problem for thought, a limit idea that is beyond linear reason, a boundary concept outside the horizon of conceptual frameworks. This is the clue to the problematic status of the term in a system of reason (like Swinburne's) that seeks to contain all thought and experience under the canopy of traditional metaphysical theism. *Radical evil, however, is not susceptible to any philosophical sleight of hand that would seek to reduce it to a problem that can be located, mediated, and finally solved within the confines of a thought system.* Fundamental evil is not a problem for thought awaiting the solution of the "right" philosophical vocabulary, but rather a rupture, a fissure, a caesura of thought that resists the final closure foisted on it by any philosophical system.

A distinction, therefore, between two different types of evil is in order. Some forms of evil are reducible to rational adjudication. Evil as a sometimes absence of good or as an occasional aberration of the will is accurately ascrib-

19. See Alvin C. Plantinga, *God, Freedom, and Evil* (Grand Rapids, Mich.: Wm. B. Eerdmans, 1977), 45–73.

20. Etymologies are from the *Oxford English Dictionary*, ed. John Sykes (New York: Oxford University Press, 1971).

able to the limits of the created order, in the first case, and the finitude and fragility of human strength and intention, in the second. But evil as an alien force completely hostile to human intervention and coherent explanation—what Barth labeled *das Nichtige* or Arthur Cohen the *tremendum*—is evil that is not reducible to any particular metaphysical system.[21] I will call this form of fundamental evil "recalcitrant evil" because it is evil that is a surd for thought and, indeed, a surd, a reality, that is not redeemable no matter how many ethical goods or spiritual graces (such as Swinburne's moral knowledge) it produces in the wake of its rapacious destruction. It is a category mistake to blur the distinction between *finite evil* and *recalcitrant evil* and regard the one as belonging to the same conceptual type as the other.[22] The two types of evil are not the same, for while finite evil is a problem within the horizon of thought, recalcitrant evil transcends and shatters thought precisely at that point where thought tries to think the unthought of irredeemable suffering and atrocity. Swinburne's ethical calculus seeks to justify radical negativity by guaranteeing that those who suffer are enabling others (if not themselves) to act responsibly in the future. But the idea that God can redeem the *horror religiosus* of the death camps, Hiroshima, or environmental mass death is an obscene suggestion. Deep into the abyss of recalcitrant evil the human heart finds itself spent and debased by theodicies like Swinburne's that find God at work in the madness, shaping the remains of the victims into the raw materials for the "moral development" of themselves or others. This god is a monster, the god of Goya's *Saturn Devouring His Son,* not the God of religious faith and witness.

RONALD THIEMANN AND THE GOD OF PROMISE

Thiemann to date has not articulated a theodicy as such, but we can discern the outlines for what a theodicy might look like in the light of the theo-

---

21. See Karl Barth, *Church Dogmatics*, vol. 3:3, trans. G. W. Bromiley and R. J. Ehrlich (Edinburgh: T. & T. Clark, 1961), 289–368; and Arthur A. Cohen, *The Tremendum: A Theological Interpretation of the Holocaust* (New York: Crossroad, 1981), 8–42 and passim.

22. On the problem of "category mistakes," where certain phenomena are misidentified as belonging to one logical type when they actually belong to another, see Gilbert Ryle, *The Concept of Mind* (Chicago: University of Chicago Press, 1984), 15–24. My contention is that the antinomy of radical evil has been fundamentally misunderstood by theistic philosophers who attempt to resolve the problem in terms of the putative moral goods occasioned by such evil. From my perspective, "recalcitrant evil" does not belong to the same category of experience as "finite evil."

logical method suggested in his *Revelation and Theology*. In this book Thiemann supplies an intratheological recovery of the doctrine of revelation through a defense of the classical Protestant idea that true knowledge of God is a gift of God's grace. By "intratheological" I mean that he does not provide an extrinsic theory that can prove or ground the book's founding axiom—that God is graciously active in human affairs—because such an axiom qua axiom is a matter of basic belief and not a candidate for rational or empirical demonstration. The task of theology is to consider the meaning of those cardinal beliefs that are always already presupposed by the very logic of Christian faith and not to attempt to prove the truth of these beliefs with the aid of any philosophical system. Thiemann writes that "[a] doctrine of revelation ought not be conceived as an epistemological theory but as an account which justifies a set of Christian convictions concerning God's gracious identity and reality."[23] The justification of these convictions can never be founded on a bedrock of neutral first principles or empirical evidences outside the household of faith.

Contrary to Swinburne, Thiemann does not maintain that there is strong empirical evidence for the reality of God that can provide a sure footing for the witness of Christian belief to the identity of God as an agent of grace and power. Rather, Christian witness functions as a "retrospective" or "abductive" hypothesis that provides a working explanation for a range of beliefs and practices that cannot be adequately understood apart from this hypothesis.[24] A retrospective or abductive hypothesis concerning the reality of God begins not with that reality itself as an evidential probability but with the biblically mediated experience of Christian life and belief, and, on the basis of that experience, argues back to the condition that is implied by, and makes possible, the experience in question. The originating event of God's self-disclosure in Christ, then, is the essential presupposition that is implied by all Christian praxis. This presupposition stresses "the *prevenience* of God's grace, the conviction that we are enabled to have access to God solely through God's prior

---

23. Ronald F. Thiemann, *Revelation and Theology: The Gospel as Narrated Promise* (Notre Dame: University of Notre Dame Press, 1985), 7.

24. Ibid., 72–78. This notion of a third type of argument (abduction) that is different from induction (so Swinburne) and deduction (so Anselm) was originated by Charles Peirce and has recently been developed for theological ends by Francis Schüssler Fiorenza, as well as by Thiemann. See Charles S. Peirce, *Philosophical Writings of Peirce*, ed. Justus Buchler (New York: Dover, 1955), 150–56; and Francis Schüssler Fiorenza, *Foundational Theology: Jesus and the Church* (New York: Crossroad, 1984), 306ff.

action."[25] This presumption cannot be *argued for* on the basis of some other evidence or belief more basic than it; rather, it can only be *argued to* (in a reverse movement) in the light of Christian faith.

Thiemann's theological model "takes its rise from the specific beliefs, rituals, and practices of the Christian community. . . . Like all Christian theology, it is guided by the Anselmian credo 'I believe in order that I may understand.'"[26] This *fides quaerens intellectum* model is consistent with what Barth calls theology as *nachfolgen*; it is theology that eschews any philosophical or empirical defense of Christian belief in favor of the descriptive, interpretive task of "following" or "thinking after" those revelational occurrences that founded the Christian community.[27] But what is the locus of these occurrences and how are they to be appropriated? A Lutheran, Thiemann maintains that the Bible is the place where the definitive expression of the divine identity is located, presumably because the experience of the community and the language of the tradition are parasitic upon the originary witnesses to God's activity within Jewish and Christian Scripture. And he continues that the category of *narrative* provides the most adequate genre for interpreting the biblically mediated identity of God as a prevenient agent in human affairs. Narrative, for Thiemann, does not specify the story-bound nature of generic human experience (though he does not deny that this may be the case) but rather the premier literary style within the Bible for articulating God's gracious activity in the world.

> Theology on this view is the description or redescription of biblical narrative into a coherent language which displays the logic of Christian belief. Narrative highlights both a predominant literary category within the Bible and an appropriate theological category for interpreting the canon as a whole. Theology is primarily concerned with the interpretation of text and tradition and only secondarily, if at all, with speculations about the true nature of the self and the deep structures of human understanding.[28]

---

25. Thiemann, *Revelation and Theology*, 3.

26. Ronald F. Thiemann, *Constructing a Public Theology: The Church in a Pluralistic Culture* (Louisville: Westminster/John Knox Press, 1991), 21.

27. For a clear exposition of Barth's idea of *nachfolgen*, see Eberhard Jüngel, *God as the Mystery of the World: On the Foundation of the Theology of the Crucified One in the Dispute Between Theism and Atheism*, trans. Darrell L. Guder (Grand Rapids, Mich.: Wm. B. Eerdmans, 1983), 152–69. In spite of his telling criticisms of Barth's "objectivist model of revelation," Thiemann is closer to Barth on issues of theological method and the idea of revelation than he is to any other contemporary theologian. See Thiemann, *Revelation and Theology*, 94–95, 177–79, and his "Response to George Lindbeck," *Theology Today* 43 (1986): 377–82.

28. Thiemann, *Revelation and Theology*, 83.

Here and elsewhere Thiemann makes clear that theological considerations play the major role in determining the primacy of narrative in his recovery of the prevenience of God. He accords priority to narrative because, while it is only "one of a number of possible images around which the diverse materials of the canon can be organized," it does have "the advantage of integrating a central literary genre in scripture with an organizing theological theme" [namely, the "promising God" motif].[29] This comment is important for our use of genre analysis to clarify and evaluate the assumptions of an inchoate theodicy in Thiemann. What we observe here is that Thiemann suggests two reasons for his assignment of pride of place to narrative discourse. First, as a literary genre, narrative provides history-like verisimilitude to the actual events witnessed to by the biblical writers. Through a storied plot line, narrative offers the reader a coherent temporal and historical pattern that brings together characters and incidents into a meaningful whole. Thiemann acknowledges, however, that narratives do allow for a measure of ambiguity and discordance in their stories of configured unity. He refers to Frank Kermode's attention to the fractures and ruptures that characterize many figurative texts (including the Gospels), and he recognizes the occasional plot twists and zones of indeterminacy that call into question putative resolutions of the biblical texts' sense in favor of strict concordance.[30] But in the end Thiemann demurs on this point, and argues instead that "good stories" uphold a "configuration of events" that "make sense from the vantage-point of the end."[31]

The grounds for this judgment, however, are less than clear in Thiemann's presentation. His position that the quality of literary art should be judged on the basis of its coherence and closure is less an argument than an assertion. Why should a good story have a certain sequential integrity and a sense of an ending? On the contrary, many literary classics—from the Gospel of Mark and Mallerme's poetry to Beckett's plays and Joyce's later novels—are devoid of seamless connections and final resolutions and, in fact, seem to delight in overturning the very sense of conventional narrative order that Thiemann prizes as essential to a good story. These texts flout traditional conventions of sequential followability and well-closed coherence as they place the burdens of emplotment and order making onto the reader or performer. Such texts

---

29. Ibid., 86.

30. Ronald F. Thiemann, "Radiance and Obscurity in Biblical Narrative," in *Scriptural Authority and Narrative Interpretation*, ed. Garrett Green (Philadelphia: Fortress Press, 1987), 21–28.

31. Thiemann, *Revelation and Theology*, 86.

serve as disturbing counterpoints to Thiemann's presumption that successful narratives are bounded exercises in concordance and closure.

But while it appears that there are not compelling aesthetic reasons for Thiemann's emphasis on narrative discourse, there are important theological criteria at work in his proposal. His second reason for prioritizing narrative follows from the first. Not only does narrative render time coherent and history followable in the crafting of a "good story," but, moreover, it gives the reader structured and reliable access to the centrality of God's prevenience within the biblical accounts. As a mode of theological (as well as literary) discourse, narrative is governed by the centrality of the divine's gracious activity in history. This reassures the reader not merely that the story is coherent with a predetermined ending, but that the God in this story can be relied on and trusted as the reader learns to discern the overarching patterns of theological meaning within the stories. What emerges in these patterns is the identity of God as an agent of promise. In the Gospel stories God is pictured as a gracious initiator and fulfiller of the commitments God has made to different communities. This depiction provides the grounds for the "meta-rule" that should govern all narrative theology in its role as a guide in the formation of Christian character.

> Theology assists this process [of Christian identity formation] by articulating the rules which guide the interpretation of text and tradition and the correlative formation of Christian character. Those specific rules which regulate the development of doctrine and virtue are themselves governed by an overarching "meta-rule." *Let all Christian interpretation proceed in a manner which recognizes the absolute primacy of God's promising grace.*[32]

As a test case for this thesis, Thiemann turns to the Gospel of Matthew as the narrative vehicle for the enactment of God's supreme promise in the mission of Jesus. In Matthew's identification of the God of promise with the Father of Jesus Christ, the Gospel renders the divine character in terms of spontaneous, unmerited graciousness. In this way the text makes a noncoercive appeal to the reader to exercise belief in the biblical narrative's depiction of a God of promise, a God of grace.[33]

32. Ibid., 148–49.
33. Ibid., 112–56. Also see Thiemann, "Radiance and Obscurity in Biblical Narrative," 33–39, and his "The Unnamed Woman at Bethany," *Theology Today* 44 (1987): 179–88.

The Other Face of God

At first glance, Thiemann's narrative theology provides a more adequate rhetorical framework for tackling the theodicy problem than that offered by Swinburne. His deployment of a nonspeculative interpretation of the New Testament's message concerning Jesus as the promise of God to humankind is a corrective to Swinburne's metaphysics. Since Thiemann maintains that his God can be trusted on the basis of the scriptural witness, we have here the outlines for a narrative theodicy rooted in the cardinal biblical themes of election, providence, and covenant. This implied theodicy in Thiemann emerges from his analysis of the genre of narrative, the mode of discourse best suited to reveal the character of a loving and trustworthy God who upholds the fiduciary bonds this God has forged between the divine promise and the people of God.

Though Thiemann's tact is biblically centered, my sense, nevertheless, is that his retrieval of the idea of revelation, which he defines as the disclosure of the character of a God of promise through the narrated identity descriptions within the Gospels, suffers from a homophonic bias toward one divine attribute, namely, the attribute of promise, and cannot adequately account for the polyphony of theological counterthemes within Jewish and Christian scriptures that alternately support and undermine this covenantal description of the divine life.[34] Thiemann, like many other narrative theologians, develops a single-voiced interpretation of the Gospels that is insensitive to the generic alternatives within these and other biblical texts that overstep the neat boundaries of the scriptural covenants.

These transgressive genres include the rhetorics of irony and lament that characterize biblical wisdom discourse. As Thiemann rightly maintains, the Gospels do create narrative space for the reader's faithful response, but, in a contrary gesture, biblical wisdom literature in its ironic and plaintive modes seeks to destabilize and even subvert this space. The rhetoric of divine faithfulness in the Bible's historical books is challenged, in the face of evil, by the anguished cries from the heart in the Hebrew Bible wisdom books of Psalms,

---

34. See M. N. Bakhtin, *The Dialogic Imagination: Four Essays*, ed. Michael Holquist and trans. Caryl Emerson and Michael Holquist (Austin: University of Texas Press, 1981); and George Steiner, *Real Presences* (Chicago: University of Chicago Press, 1989), on the problem of regimenting and flattening the multiple voices of the epic or the novel (and by implication, the Bible) into a single-voiced text.

Proverbs, Job, and Lamentations. Sapiential irony reminds the reader that the Bible's narrated promises are not inviolable safeguards against the terror and death that always question naïve fidelity to the God of the covenant. Indeed, the Bible's wisdom genre is an intentional violation of the reader's trust in the promise-keeping God of Christian theology—a violation that is not accounted for by Thiemann's narratology, in spite of the many other virtues of this approach.

The violation of the reader's confidence in the promising God begins in the cracks and along the fault lines of the regnant biblical accounts of God's faithful activity. Here another picture of God emerges for the reader less sanguine than Thiemann about the promise of Christian narrative theology.[35] Another face of God appears on the margins of the text: a taunting, capricious, and sometimes malign divinity who destroys a family because of a lie (Ananias and Sapphira in Acts), hands over the body of an innocent man to Satan for testing (Job), and unleashes the ultimate violence of sacrificial infanticide (the slaughter of the Egyptian firstborn in Exodus). These stories of extravagant divine violence and vengeance sober the reader who hopes to decipher, through the aid of a Thiemann-like narrative theology, the theological justification of recalcitrant evil within the narrative structures of the Bible.

These accounts of terror in Exodus, Job, Acts, and elsewhere take us to the borderlands of narrative theodicy, to the place where God's benevolent, covenantal identity is mocked by the caprice and malice that seem to lie close to the heart of the divine life itself. Of course we can ignore the borderlands by following instead the straight road of narrative coherence and closure, the road that follows the supreme christological plot line to its predetermined telos in the final triumph of God over all things anti-God and evil. But such a road short-circuits the ambiguity and confusion that lie underneath and alongside the biblical narratives of prevenience and grace, and it runs the risk of depriving the victims of radical suffering of the complete literary space necessary for them to act out their anger against and struggles with God.

Use of narrative discourse as a resource for theodicy can initially appear to be an edifying reading strategy. Such an approach inculcates the reader-

---

35. See Michael Goldberg, "God, Action, and Narrative: *Which* Narrative? *Which* Action? *Which* God?" *Journal of Religion* 68 (1988): 39–56. Also see Maurice Wiles, "Scriptural Authority and Theological Construction: The Limitations of Narrative Interpretation," in *Scriptural Authority and Narrative Interpretation*, ed. Green, 42–58; and Mark I. Wallace, "Parsimony of Presence in Mark: Narratology, the Reader, and Genre Analysis in Paul Ricoeur," *Studies in Religion/Sciences Religieuses* 18 (1989): 201–12.

oriented value of being transported into the world of the text, of learning to be an intratextual inhabitant of the narrative space projected by the stories of Jesus' ministry, passion, and resurrection.[36] But the temptation to this approach is that it will delimit too quickly the possible traversals available to the reader who enters the Bible's literary universe. The temptation is that the narrative approach will ward off the chaos shadowed in the recesses of the Bible's stories because it is embarrassed by their heterodoxical possibilities of meaning. The danger, in other words, is that Christian narrativists will take premature refuge in the comfortable literary space of the Jesus story that they have been taught to trust and rely on. Narrative theologians believe they can trust this story and that its protagonist can be relied on: as Thiemann maintains, herein Jesus' identity (and God's as well) is faithfully enacted through intention-action descriptions of divine forbearance, enduring compassion, and solidarity with others.

But many of us who have struggled to live the grammar of the Jesus story find that something is missing in a singular narrative hermeneutic. What is missing is the power of deep and strong readings of the biblical texts to refigure our *entire* experience as selves in the valleys of the shadow, the power of a vertiginous and sometimes healing freedom to read these texts in all of their plenitude and pathos and heterogeneity. Deep readings risk subscending conventional textual mores and assumptions, and they refuse to cauterize the reader's pain (or anyone else's pain) through a truncated hermeneutic that issues in discipleship to a God whose identity is only on the surface (and not underneath) the narratives. Theodicy in a narrative mode implies that the church-sanctioned mainline stories of God's gracious agency tell the whole story, but those who endure the pain of recalcitrant evil know that the numbing enigma of their suffering remains inscrutable and unanswerable within the plotted framework of this type of narrative theodicy. Something is missing.

PAUL RICOEUR'S THEODICY IN A PRACTICAL REGISTER

Up to this point I have examined the limitations of speculation and narration for addressing the problem of radical evil and have suggested that a retrieval of biblical wisdom is a more adequate mode of discourse for confronting (though not "solving") the question of evil for Christian thought

36. Thiemann, "The Unnamed Woman at Bethany," 179–88.

and experience. My move to wisdom discourse is an extension of Paul Ricoeur's writings on theodicy—a move (in the manner of Ricoeur) that arises in the aftermath of the conceptual finality of speculation and the christological closure of narration. Ricoeur's thought begins with the scandal of implacable, irredeemable suffering as the fundamental reality that is consistently denied by the inherent triumphalism of both speculative and narrative theodicies. He agrees with Kant (against Hegel) that the aporetics of experience undermine all forms of totalizing theodicy, and that the task before the theologian is to relocate the problem of evil on the grounds of practical rather than theoretical knowledge.[37] This transposes the problem of evil to a new register by avoiding the "false clarity" on the problem that all putative theoretical solutions offer. Ricoeur's thought helps us to realize that we have come to the end of an intellectual epoch on the question of how to understand the problem of recalcitrant evil as a candidate for theological "solution." It now seems that the received root assumptions and ideas about this question are fundamentally exhausted because they appear, on the one hand, *unable* to resolve the speculative aporia of God's goodness, power, and evil, and, on the other hand, they appear *irrelevant* to the intractable practical difficulties of *living* a life of faith after the *loss* of faith in the biblical God of covenant and election. Evil in our time has emerged as a terminal aporia, a vanishing point that escapes the conceptual closure foisted upon it by speculative and narrative theodicies. The problem of suffering cannot be adequately addressed if the debate is forced to operate once again on the same intellectual terrain of traditional philosophy and theology. This recognition forces a relocation of the problem of evil onto new topography.

Ricoeur maintains that theodicy in a new key illuminates resources in the biblical traditions that were always there but were not recognized as such. In this regard, his hermeneutical retrieval of sapiential rhetoric is fundamental to my attempt to forge an alternative account of evil for Christian thought. By way of comprehending how Ricoeur's theodicy is engendered through his study of the biblical texts, I will restrict my attention to the tensional cross-fertilization between two of the biblical genres, narrative and wisdom, that he examines in his biblical commentary.[38] Ricoeur maintains that a synchronic

37. Paul Ricoeur, "Naming God," in *Figuring the Sacred*, ed. Wallace, 217–35. Also see Immanuel Kant, *Critique of Pure Reason*, trans. Norman Kemp Smith (New York: St. Martin's Press, 1965), 487–531.

38. See Paul Ricoeur, "Toward a Hermeneutic of the Idea of Revelation," in *Essays on Biblical Interpretation*, ed. Lewis S. Mudge (Philadelphia: Fortress Press, 1980), 73–118.

study of these modes of discourse illustrates the *intertextual dynamics* that generate wisdom theodicy. We begin with narrative and then turn to wisdom discourse.

Narrative discourse is structured by its powers of emplotment, whereby disparate events are organized into a coherent story with a predetermined telos.[39] This genre is successive, cumulative, anticipatory, chronological. The plotmaker combines and arranges her data into a single overarching chronology—an account with a beginning, a middle, and an end—in order to persuade the reader that this narrative uncovers the untold story waiting to be told, the hidden temporal logic that underlies the random occurrences of everyday existence. The narrative understanding of reality, then, is totalizing and chronological: it depends on the power of the productive imagination (in Kantian terms) to *schematize* into a meaningful whole the seemingly unrelated data of temporal existence. Narrative transforms all history into tales about the flow of time. Quoting from Kant's first *Critique*, Ricoeur contends that our capacity for narrative configuration is "an art hidden in the depths of the human soul" that organizes events into a history-like *Zeitroman* of successive plot and character.[40]

The narrative temporality of the Bible projects a world of coherent events and meanings. The Yahwist, for example, uses the theological devices of genealogies and covenants in order to generate a narrative identification of the God of the Hebrew tribes. A "cumulative comprehending" of God is accomplished by tracing the acts of God within time and space.[41] Israel's God is a God of the fathers and mothers, a God who, generation after generation, provides continual support through the community's "time" of testing and suffering. Like Rahab's scarlet thread, clues are given in history that can guide the struggling community to safety in spite of the dangers that surround it. In this respect, Ricoeur agrees with Thiemann that the biblical writers use such devices as the promise and the covenant in order to generate a narrative identification of the divine life. This-worldly existence is now charged with sacred

39. Paul Ricoeur, "The Narrative Function," in *Paul Ricoeur: Hermeneutics and the Human Sciences*, ed. and trans. John B. Thompson (Cambridge: Cambridge University Press, 1981), 274–95.

40. Ibid., 287. See Ricoeur's discussion of three novels about time—Virginia Woolf's *Mrs. Dalloway*, Thomas Mann's *Magic Mountain*, and Marcel Proust's *Remembrance of Things Past*—as paradigmatic of the temporality of narrative discourse, in Paul Ricoeur, *Time and Narrative*, trans. Kathleen McLaughlin and David Pellauer, 3 vols. (Chicago: University of Chicago Press, 1984–88), 2:100–160.

41. Paul Ricoeur, "Biblical Time," in *Figuring the Sacred*, ed. Wallace, 173–76.

purpose because it is the place where the divine faithfulness is being worked out—in spite of the prima facie evidence to the contrary.[42] The events of Exodus and Sinai offer a certain temporal security to the Hebrews, who, without these events, would have found themselves adrift as victims of someone else's history and chronology. In this way the terror of the eternal return of the same, the terror of forever being relegated to the role of bit players within another nation's autobiography, is stemmed by Israel's collective memory of a God whose abiding presence guarantees the community's safe passage through the chaos of mundane history and the meaninglessness of cyclical time.

Ricoeur's biblical narratology makes a similar claim with reference to the Gospel stories. His exegesis of Mark highlights the interpretive function of this version of the Jesus story. He borrows from Robert Alter the classification of the Bible's narratives as "historicized prose fiction."[43] Like the other biblical story traditions, the Gospels use a particular verisimilitude to create a history-like account of Jesus' mission and identity. This feature is evident on the surface planes of Mark's narrative, where elements of episodic history and theological necessity are continually crisscrossing. In Mark, Jesus is both the innocent victim of Judas's treason and the disciples' abandonment who *does* suffer as a contingent consequence of their betrayal and the heavenly Son of Man who *must* suffer on behalf of humankind in keeping with the divine master plan. "[T]o explicate this gospel means looking for the indications of the equation it posits between its Christology of a suffering Son of Man and the story of the betrayed Jesus."[44] In a manner analogous to the "Who is Yahweh?" question of the Hebrew Bible, Mark's narrative art "foments" (*fomentent*) a story-based identity description of Jesus: he is the fully human *and* divinely promised suffering servant. Ricoeur argues that this twofold identity of Jesus as eternal Christ and historical human being is generated by the complicated temporality of Mark's Gospel, in which aspects of historical contingency (Jesus suffers) and eschatological necessity (Jesus must suffer) are fictively interwoven.[45]

As the Hebrew Bible is structured according to the tick-tock rhythm of its narrative temporality, so the Christian Bible is rooted in a configuration of events that renders Jesus' identity historically credible as well as a fulfillment of the divine promise. The monumental time of the master biblical story

42. Ibid.

43. Paul Ricoeur, "Interpretive Narrative," in *Figuring the Sacred*, ed. Wallace, 182.

44. Ibid., 192–93.

45. For an analysis of this dialectic, see my "Parsimony of Presence in Mark: Narratology, the Reader and Genre Analysis in Paul Ricoeur," *Studies in Religion/Science Religieuses* 18 (1989): 207–12.

grounds the identity of the biblical communities of faith and interpretation by bringing together the Hebrew Bible's narratives of divine deliverance and the Christian scripture's double description of the God-human Jesus.

From one perspective, Ricoeur (like Thiemann) says that "narrative constitutes the encompassing genre" of the Bible insofar as it locates the various biblical traditions and characters on a "unique time line" that imposes temporal and theological coherence onto the different accounts.[46] Ricoeur accords narrative literature a certain primacy in the polysemy of biblical revelation because it functions to identify the founding events that trace the divine presence at the origins of Israel and the church. "In this sense, we must say that naming God is first of all a moment of the narrative confession. God is named in 'the thing' recounted."[47] Narrative is the literary form that organizes the "polyphony of count and counterpoint" within the other modes of discourse into a "fragile analogical unity."[48]

But (unlike Thiemann) Ricoeur avers that the *heilsgeschichtlich* mind-set that is born by narrative is dangerous and seductive for a community that now considers history a present-at-hand "possession" under its control. The danger lies in the community's confidence that its future is secure because it has the occult knowledge of the divine master plan. The danger lies in the community's inability to acknowledge the discordant, the novel, and the chaotic which always threaten to undermine its attempts to domesticate the divine identity through comfortable stories of sequential narrative coherence.[49] *To engage the Bible solely from the perspective of its putative mainstream genre—narrative—is to compress the tensions and surplus of biblical meaning into a totalizing master story immune from the irony and pathos of daily experience.* Disconnected from its collision with other literatures, the time of progressive narrative can degenerate into a disengagement from the forces of history that result in the victimization and destruction of individuals and communities. And religious communities formed by narrative can often slip into an insensitivity toward the specific and the heterogenous—those events that resist subsumption under the logic of the supreme plot.

---

46. Ricoeur, "Biblical Time," in *Figuring the Sacred*, ed. Wallace, 171–76.

47. Ricoeur, "Naming God," in *Figuring the Sacred*, ed. Wallace, 225; cf. Ricoeur, "Biblical Time," in ibid., 173–76.

48. John W. Van Den Hengel, *The Home of Meaning* (Lanham, Md.: University Press of America, 1982), 233.

49. Paul Ricoeur, "Time and Narrative in the Bible: Toward a Narrative Theology" (unpublished Sarum Lectures, delivered at Oxford University, 1980), 15–22.

Wisdom discourse is the genre that challenges this quiescence. Unlike narrative, wisdom writings are not interested in history, but, like narrative, they are concerned with the meaning of time.[50] The temporal structure of wisdom is the time of the everyday and the immemorial, which are, in some respects, uninterested in the emplotted time of the narrative. Wisdom does not offer a time line that is punctuated by sequential events. Instead, it offers genric space for the reader's confrontations with ageless limit questions: What is the meaning of death? Why is joy so transitory? How should one live one's life? Why do the innocent suffer? Where is God amidst the vagaries of existence? The ubiquity of death, the suffering of innocents, the slaughterbench of history, the transience of joy, the absence of God—these are the realities and events that cannot be subsumed under the temporal logic of the master narrative. Through proverbs, wise sayings, and cries of lamentation, wisdom provides spiritual and affective resources for the perennial questions that are not accounted for by the "great events" of history and narrative.

This mode of discourse is not confined, Ricoeur contends, to a body of writings we technically refer to as "wisdom literature"; rather, the questioning of the sages and prophets conveys a sensibility about the meaning of existence that permeates all scriptural literature.

> Wisdom is not just contained in the wisdom writings. Overflowing the framework of the Covenant, its mediation bears on the human condition in general. It is directly addressed to the sense and nonsense of existence. It is a struggle for sense in spite of nonsense. Unjust suffering has a central place here to the extent that suffering itself poses its enigma at the juncture between the order of things and the ethical order.[51]

The pain and bewilderment articulated by the wise ones—Qoholeth, Job, Jeremiah, Jesus—are summarized in terse questions such as Why me? and How long? which supersede the boundaries of the covenants remembered in the community's sacred stories. This gives wisdom temporality a universal and ahistorical character because the problems it addresses are the concerns of all people at all times.

Sapiential discourse engenders interest not only in the time of the everyday but also in the time of the arbitrary and peculiar. In the Bible, the anonymous occurrences that erupt and shatter lives often cannot be accounted for by the incipient triumphalism of narrative coherence. The specific and ironic out-

---

50. Ricoeur, "Biblical Time," in *Figuring the Sacred*, ed. Wallace, 176–78.
51. Ricoeur, "Naming God," in *Figuring the Sacred*, ed. Wallace, 227.

breakings of radical evil within the life of the people who had trusted their God to deliver them from such evil overflow the bounds of narrative identity. Unwarranted suffering, therefore, exposes the insufficiency of the deutero-nomic or evangelical reassurance that living the Torah or following the gospel will guarantee the faithful person's safe passage through the terrors of time and history. On the contrary, wisdom insinuates that all forms of existence—even a life of obedience and fidelity—carry no assurances except that benign trust in a formulaic obedience undergirded by a master story is destined for disappointment and disillusionment. Thus, sapiential discourse performs the abrasive function of questioning the sometimes facile assumptions of narra-tive writings by honestly attesting to the specific and ironic irruptions of rad-ical evil within the life of a people who had trusted their God to deliver them from such evil. In the face of concrete negations of divine protection, history is now no longer the space for God's interruptive activity (as in narrative time), but the Joycean nightmare from which the community struggles to awake.

In narrative discourse God is named as the Deliverer who saves the people from their enemies; in wisdom God is a problem to be struggled with and against in the light of the Divine's prima facie abandonment of the commu-nity in times of trial. Thus, the speculative aporia of philosophical theodicy (either God or evil but not both) that emerges in reaction to unmerited suf-fering and evil is answered not by a formal theological solution but by the practical and cathartic responses offered by wisdom. "[W]isdom does not so much speak of what ought to be done as of how to endure, how to suffer suf-fering."[52] Wisdom relocates the theodicy aporia on the level of practical expe-rience (rather than theoretical knowledge), and thereby dissolves (rather than solves) the aporia and renders it "productive." "It is to this aporia [the prob-lem of evil] that action and the catharsis of feelings and emotions are called upon not to give a solution but a response, a response able to render the apo-ria productive."[53]

The theoretical aporia is made practically productive because its dissolu-tion liberates a therapeutic and purgative response to radical negation. The hope of wisdom is that one will discover some comfort in a life wagered on the temporal and religious values embodied in sapiential writings. The praxis of mourning one's losses, expressing anger toward God, learning solidarity

52. Ibid.
53. Paul Ricoeur, "Evil, A Challenge to Philosophy and Theology," in *Figuring the Sacred*, ed. Wallace, 258.

with other victims of suffering, and discerning the overturning power of irony in all things provides a modicum of solace in a life fractured by suffering and violence. Wisdom permits those who are alienated believers on the fringes of the synagogue and the church to belong again even if they cannot believe again in the interruptive God of biblical narrative salvation history.

The time of wisdom, then, is different from the time of narrative. Wisdom resists the narrative temptation to provide a supralapsarian temporalization of evil where evil is located at the origins of creation as a punishment of sin and, by virtue of that location, the problem of evil is thereby solved (theoretically speaking) in terms of the logic of punishment. This logic of punishment (evil and death are the outcome of an originary fall from grace) provides a temporal archaeology that is linked to a temporal teleology in the Bible's narrative genre.[54] In this fashion radical evil is assigned not only a beginning but also an end: it is the power of the original enemy, and it is a power that will be destroyed when the covenantal community is vindicated by God in the preordained endtime. Evil is no longer a surd when it can be emplotted on a time line that explains its first occasion and its preestablished fate; it is no longer inscrutable when it can be inserted into the plot of a totalizing narrative. And yet, as we have seen, it is this very totalization that wisdom resists: narrative's episodic structuring of evil into a meaningful whole is insensitive to the grief and pain that cannot be subsumed under any divine master story, even the master story of the Bible.

In a three-way conversation between Swinburne, Thiemann, and Ricoeur, it is clear that for the latter two the task of theodicy is best handled not through inductive arguments from experience (*pace* Swinburne) but through rhetorical analyses of the patterns of meaning within the biblical text-worlds. But on the question of the content of the text-worlds prioritized in their reflections, Thiemann and Ricoeur basically differ insofar as Ricoeur demonstrates a wider sensitivity to the texts' surplus of meanings and zones of intertextual conflict than does Thiemann. Ricoeur resists the perennial theological temptation to short-circuit the working of the texts on themselves through a monological hermeneutic of one particular genre and one particular form of characterization. For this reason Ricoeur does not accord (as does Thiemann) special privilege to one mode of discourse (the genre of followable narrative) and one particular theological identity description (God as promise-keeper) as the singular clues to understanding human experience in the light of the

---

54. Ricoeur, "Time and Narrative in the Bible: Toward a Narrative Theology" (unpublished Sarum Lectures), 33–36.

biblical message. Rather, he maintains that it is in the interpretation of the interanimating conjunctions between the Bible's many and diverse forms of discourse that a well-rounded picture of the discontinuities of lived existence is brought to light.

In the confluence of narrative and antinarrative, the biblical understanding of suffering and violence is generated by discourses that are both illuminating and obscure, coherent and dissimulating. Neither narrative nor wisdom alone is sufficient to the task of constructing a theodicy attuned to the irruptions of gratuitous evil in our time. In the point–counterpoint movement between story and wisdom within the Bible, the reader can learn to figure reality as an elegiac tale of occasional hope and sometimes chronic despair in the presence of the evil and absurdity always crouching just outside the door of the household of faith. Job's irrational punishment at the hands of Satan and Jesus' cry of dereliction from the cross are accounts of what Ricoeur calls "narrativized wisdom," whose destabilizing message serves as a warning against the naïveté of a faith unwilling to engage the discontinuities of existence as witnessed to by the biblical texts.[55] Like Kafka's unfollowable parables, the Bible for Ricoeur refuses to allow the reader to take comfort in a seamless depiction of a benevolent God whose identity is fully transparent to the reader and secure against the vagaries and brokenness of life.[56] Against the grain of our love for literary coherence and the need for final meaning, we are forced to ask, painfully, whether paradox and irony, even divine betrayal, lie at the heart of the narrative schemas valorized by Israel and the early church. In putting this difficult question to the reader, wisdom discourse deprivileges, challenges, indeed subverts any totalizing and homophonic approach to an engagement with biblical literatures. In spite of their similarities, I regard Ricoeur's model as more appropriate than Thiemann's to the heterogeneity of the biblical witness and to the complexity of our discordant-concordant lives as readers.

We have also seen that Ricoeur's thought concerning wisdom discourse is a fundamental challenge to Swinburne's orientation as well. Through its awareness of the crippling power of radical evil, wisdom accuses speculative theology of a totalizing and rationalistic impulse that cannot account for the pain and discontinuity at the center of our historical existence. "What the problem of evil calls into question is a way of thinking submitted to the requirements of logical coherence, that is, one submitted to both the rule of non-contradiction

---

55. Ricoeur, "Interpretive Narrative," in *Figuring the Sacred*, ed. Wallace, 181–99.
56. Ibid.

and that of systematic totalization."[57] Though sapiential theodicy is not governed by the same standards of logic and reason that guide other modes of inquiry, it is not therefore devoid of a certain intellectual credibility. Put positively, Ricoeur's point is that theology sensitive to radical evil will be (*eo ipso*) more paradoxical than systematic, more practical than theoretical, and will risk abandoning "the requirements of logical coherence" in favor of nourishing a cathartic response to those forms of suffering and incoherence that cannot be subsumed under any rational system, theological or otherwise.

IS THE SPIRIT FRIEND OR ENEMY?

For the believing community, the problem of God's complicity with, or absence in the face of, suffering and violence is at the heart of the problem of evil. Is it possible that the divine life itself is responsible for some or much of the evil that has destroyed people's lives for generations? Is God guilty of perpetrating violence against humankind and otherkind either because of human sin or for reasons known only by God? Or is God merely absent and unmoved in the face of pain and suffering, either unwilling or unable to intercede on behalf of the victims? In either case, God has evolved for many into being either a malignant force in the universe who visits bone-crushing judgment onto human societies for their disobedience, or a distant and unfeeling spectator who cannot or will not stop the violence that plagues all forms of life on the planet. The notion that God is a conspirator with, or indifferent toward, global suffering appears to shatter the biblical portraiture of the divine life as the advocate for the forgotten and dispossessed of history.

In the face of widespread pain and evil, God appears to be either guilty or unmoved, and it would seem that the most consistent response to this realization is to pronounce the death of the interruptive and intercessory deity of biblical faith. If God ever *had* saved the victims of unjust suffering from their captors, it appears that God *cannot* or *will not* perform such feats of deliverance today. Too many lives have been crushed; too much damage to the ecosystem has been sustained, for most people, even members of believing communities, to take seriously any longer the time-honored belief that God is willing and ready to break into history and protect innocent life, human and nonhuman alike. It is written that God cares for all life in the most inti-

---

57. Ricoeur, "Evil, A Challenge to Philosophy and Theology," in *Figuring the Sacred*, ed. Wallace, 249.

mate fashion—even the hairs on our heads have all been numbered, and not a single sparrow can fall to the ground without God's knowledge (Matthew 10:29–31)—but what sense do such proverbs make except as nursery rhymes for a world-weary culture now jaded by the violence about which God appears to express no concern and no remorse? Richard Rubenstein was right, I believe, when he stated almost thirty years ago that we live in the time of the death of God.[58] In the sense that belief in the interruptive God of the exodus, Sinai, the cross, and the resurrection is no longer tenable given the tenacity of gratuitous evil, it appears that the most authentic response to such evil is to abandon the naïveté of biblical faith once and for all.

Many post-Holocaust Jewish thinkers, including Emil Fackenheim, Richard Rubenstein, Arthur Cohen, and Elie Wiesel, and a number of contemporary Christian thinkers, such as Paul Ricoeur, Kenneth Surin, Terrence Tilley, and others, argue that the traditional theological lexicon used in theodicy debates is now passé after the Shoah and other such events that point to God's guilt or indifference. I believe they are right in their assessments. Living amidst the wreckage left over from the eruptions of radical evil in our time, we find ourselves left with the divine terror and dread (*mysterium tremendum*) in Rudolf Otto's famous formula concerning religious experience (*mysterium tremendum et fascinans*), but without the alluring and life-renewing fascination (*fascinans*) toward God, the "Wholly Other," that Otto argued was a hallmark of spiritual life.[59] We are left with the terrifying mystery of religious experience in a world seemingly stripped of divine goodness. Cohen remarks that the numinous confronts us today after the Holocaust as a *tremendum,* yes, but as a demonic *tremendum,* a malign divinity who destroys hope and possibility, rather than as the *tremendum* of the biblical covenant, the Sinaitic God of compassion and deliverance.[60] Ricoeur agrees, observing that events such as the Shoah project a "negative revelation, an Anti-Sinai" that sets before the reader/believer a new and monstrous disclosure of the numinous as Un(w)ho(l)ly Other.[61] These and similar attempts to face the full implications of radical evil would seem to undermine the integrity of faith in our time.

Nevertheless, the loss of biblical faith need not be the consequence of an honest confrontation with the problem of evil. Though many people of faith

58. Richard Rubenstein, *After Auschwitz* (Indianapolis: Bobbs-Merrill, 1966), 151.

59. Rudolf Otto, *The Idea of the Holy*, trans. John W. Harvey (London: Oxford University Press, 1958), 12–59.

60. Cohen, *The Tremendum*, 27–38.

61. Ricoeur, *Time and Narrative*, 3:188.

now acknowledge that trust in the agential and historical God of the Bible has been shattered by the irreparable forces of Anti-Sinai, it does not necessarily follow (though it may for some) that faith *as such* must be abandoned. For the person who has wagered her life on the basis of religious conviction, God, in the wake of gratuitous violence and evil, may be silent, God may even be guilty; but it does not follow that God is dead. Consider Nietzsche in this regard. For the person of faith caught between belief and unbelief, hope and despair, she will most likely be unable to concede to Nietzsche's madman the final verdict that God is dead and we have killed him. It is premature (and impossible for tortured faith) to abandon the struggle of belief in and against the divine life, and it is the height of arrogance to celebrate the dance of death on the tomb of God in a self-congratulatory paroxysm of self-divinization. For Nietzsche, by performing the act of supreme parricide, we have all become gods, *Übermenschen*, who rule the world in the twilight of God's death.

> "Whither is God" [the madman] cried. "I shall tell you. *We have killed him*— you and I. All of us are his murderers. . . . How shall we, the murderers of all murderers, comfort ourselves? What was holiest and most powerful of all that the world has yet owned has bled to death under our knives. . . . Is not the greatness of this deed too great for us? Must not we ourselves become gods simply to seem worthy of it?"[62]

To say that Nietzsche's atheistic hubris arrives too early with its obituary concerning God is not to say, however, that the task of forging a coherent theology that accounts for both the sometimes benevolent God of the Bible and the malign Power of the *tremendum* is a task that can be accomplished at this time in history. It is to say, rather, that it is this aporia that the believer, the one who can neither abandon hope nor take comfort in its traditional expressions, must live with and think about, and that the difficulty cannot be resolved by resorting to Nietzsche's human, all-too-human murder of God.

The aporia of biblical faith played out against the terrors of history is given moving expression in the wisdom literature of anger and complaint. In the elegiac cries of sadness and desolation that resonate throughout the book of Lamentations, for example, the person of faith comes to understand the divine life as a hateful enemy.

---

62. Nietzsche, "The Gay Science," in *The Portable Nietzsche*, ed. and trans. Walter Kaufmann (New York: Viking Press, 1980), 95–96.

> The Lord has become like an enemy, he has destroyed Israel; he has destroyed all its palaces, laid in ruins its strongholds; and he has multiplied in the daughter of Judah mourning and lamentation. (2:5)

> He is to me like a bear lying in wait, like a lion in hiding; he led me off my way and tore me to pieces; he has made me desolate; he bent his bow and set me as a mark for his arrow. (3:10)

In these texts God is tropologically figured "like" an enemy, a destroyer, a rapacious wild beast—like a bear or a lion that attacks and devours its prey, or an archer who uses human subjects as his targets. And yet the Lamenter oscillates between *acknowledging* God's role in laying waste to the covenant people, on the one hand, and *indicting* God for brutally crushing the people for their foibles, on the other. The author's use of simile (God is *like* an enemy) rather than metaphorical predication (God *is* an enemy) underscores the despair as well as the ambiguity of his cries: Is God a judge who severely, but justly, punishes persons for their transgressions, or is God a cosmic enemy, a monstrous predator who spitefully tears individuals and communities apart in fits of rage and disgust that are disproportionate to anything human beings could do to provoke such eruptions of anger? The author does not answer this question; instead, he gives vent to an agony deeply rooted in the pathos of faith. This agony remains forever suspended between the inescapability of religious belief and the most deeply held religious anxiety that the referent of belief may be a God whose goodness and anger are tied together in a knot that is inseverable and inscrutable.

A cursory reading of the Bible might indicate that the problem of divine violence is a problem specific to God the Father or God the Son but not to God the Spirit. Theologians have often noted this problem with reference to the sometimes monarchical and warlike portrayals of God *as Father*, or with reference to God *as Son* who judges the world on behalf of the Father and punishes sinful persons through his righteous anger. In Judges, for example, Yahweh is a Man of War who commands the Israelites to ambush the Benjaminites, and twenty-five thousand are killed in one day. Or in Revelation, the Son of God, the one who will "tread the wine press of the fury of the wrath of God," arrives in judgment with the armies of heaven behind him, and together they gorge themselves on the flesh of their victims in the final marriage feast of heaven. But I am not aware of instances where contemporary theologians have traced the question of divine violence back to the biblical models of the Spirit. Yet although the Spirit is primarily the agent of healing and renewal in the scriptures, the Spirit is also the source of divinely inspired wrath and vengeance against the enemies of God. In three different instances in the book of Judges, for example, the Spirit "visits" various rulers of Israel in order to sow the seeds of violent intratribal and intrafamilial conflict. In chapter 3, the Spirit comes upon Othniel and inspires him to make war against Israel's aggressors; in chapters 6 and 7, the Spirit takes possession of Gideon and empowers him to kill the princes of Midian, Oreb and Zeeb, and then present their decapitated heads to the Hebrews as trophies of victory; and in chapter 11, the Spirit takes hold of Jephthah and inspires him to make a vow to sacrifice his daughter as a "burnt offering" in gratitude for his victory over the Ammonites.

The stories in Judges that attest to the Spirit taking possession of tribal heroes and leading them to war are stories that many people of faith are repulsed by and would rather ignore. Michael Welker, for example, writes that while the "Spirit is indirectly involved in militaristic actions," God's Spirit is not "a spirit of war."[63] I am not convinced by Welker's attempts to mitigate the Spirit's military conduct. The biblical attestations to the Spirit's involvement in armed conflict are all prefaced with the claim that the "Spirit came upon" this or that individual in order to lead that person to do battle against the Lord's enemies. A theology that tries to sidestep these biblical witnesses to the Spirit's warrior identity is a theology that falsely projects a truncated portrait of the Spirit. Such a theology denies to the reader the right faithfully to confront the biblical God as "guilty" for this God's complicity in acts of war and terror against other communities. If such a faithful confrontation is denied to the reader through a sanitized biblical hermeneutic, then the problem of evil cannot be authentically wrestled with by the person of faith deeply disturbed by God's martial activities. Without this existential wrestling, the problem of evil is rendered frozen and abstract; it becomes a philosopher's puzzle to be "solved" by appeals to logic and argument. In reality, however, this problem is a living dilemma for people of faith who are genuinely troubled by a religious tradition that has at its center a God who is alternately benevolent and warlike, peace-loving and vengeful. *A living confrontation with the problem of evil must include the frank recognition that evil is a mystery within the divine life itself.* When this recognition is made, the potential arises for the reader/believer cathartically to come to terms with the *horror religiosus* that the God who seeks to overcome suffering and oppression is also the God who engenders much of the same as well.

---

63. Michael Welker, *God the Spirit*, trans. John F. Hoffmeyer (Minneapolis: Fortress Press, 1994), 56.

The biblical portrait of the Spirit's violent visitations is not, however, limited to the Hebrew scriptures. In the book of Acts, for example, the story of Ananias and Sapphira is recounted as a cautionary tale to warn members of the early church not to lie to the Holy Spirit lest they suffer the deadly consequences. Two Jerusalem Christians, a husband and wife named Ananias and Sapphira, conspire with one another to deceive the apostles concerning the proceeds from the sale of their property that they plan to donate to the church. When Ananias appears before Peter and attempts to give to the church less than the full amount produced by the sale, Peter responds, "'Ananias, why has Satan filled your heart to lie to the Holy Spirit and to keep back part of the proceeds of the land? . . . You have not lied to men but to God.' When Ananias heard these words, he fell down and died. And great fear came upon all who heard of it" (Acts 5:3–5). After Ananias's death, Sapphira appears before the church elders and Peter queries her about whether the proceeds from the property sale were accurately reported by her husband. She says that they were, at which point Peter, with icy prolepsis, makes the following response: "'How is it that you have agreed together to tempt the Spirit of the Lord? Hark, the feet of those that have buried your husband are at the door, and they will carry you out.' Immediately she fell down at his feet and died. . . . And great fear came upon the whole church, and upon all who heard of these things" (Acts 5:9–11).

It may seem that this text is ambiguous as to whether the Spirit is directly responsible for slaying Ananias and Sapphira, or whether the two disciples, independent of one another and in the same manner, coincidentally collapse and die immediately upon learning that their deception is well known. But the drift of the narrative's meaning is clear: directly or indirectly, through attempting to deceive the Spirit by holding back an honest response to Peter's interrogation, the couple have sinned against the Spirit and have incurred God's judgment and anger as a result. The text makes unlikely a reading that Ananias and Sapphira, completely independent of each other and at different intervals, simply drop dead from natural causes upon hearing that their ruse has been exposed. Rather, the text points to the Spirit's violent complicity with the apostles in bringing about the sudden death of the couple as a terrifying reminder of the consequences of attempts to deceive either God or the disciples or both. It is unlikely that the "great fear" that came upon the crowds after hearing this news, in verses 5 and 11, would have occurred if it had been assumed that Ananias and Sapphira had died from natural causes, albeit suddenly, after their deception had been exposed. It seems, rather, that the text wants to convey to the reader that the terror of the crowd is well grounded in their legitimate collective fear of God's judgment. The response of the crowd, then, is intended to engender a similar response in the reader: to offend the Spirit is to run the risk of incurring God's mortal wrath against the offender. *Here the Spirit functions as the divine avenger who punishes the guilty parties for their duplicity.* Searching out the deep motives and hidden secrets of religious pretenders, the Spirit in Acts, much like the Spirit in Judges and other biblical texts, is an ill wind that blows over anyone who would challenge its authority, leaving in its wake the bodies of the victims of God's terrible anger.

Earlier I suggested that a genric recovery of biblical wisdom serves as a corrective to the traditional tropes of God as guarantor of moral order (speculative theodicy) or agent of narrated promise (narrative theodicy). We have seen, however, that the model of God that emerges through such a recovery is disturbingly contradictory and polyvalent: alternately and at the same time, God is both a source of steadfast love and support for the sufferer *and* an avenging judge who crushes friends and foes alike with terrible anger. This tension in the heart of the divine life itself can be obviated by relegating these disparate scriptural figures for God to the level of an ornamental discourse that is finally irrelevant to the task of thematizing a rationally coherent doctrine of God. But such obviations reflect a certain kind of dishonesty because they ignore the instabilities within the biblical texts. The frank recognition of these instabilities is not well served by hermeneutical attempts to flatten out the diversities of biblical rhetoric in order to serve the theological interests of normalizing, totalizing thought. The normative approach both studiously ignores the dark and discordant underside of the biblical portraitures of the divine life, and it denies to the reader the full range of aesthetic space within which she can cathartically act our her rage and sorrow, as well as her love and devotion, toward God.

The wager of my *ad fontes* project has been that a retrieval of the diversities of biblical rhetoric is the most adequate approach to understanding God for our time—and, by implication, for an understanding of God as Spirit. It may seem that the double-edged figuration of God as advocate and enemy is a problem not endemic to the biblical representation of the Spirit. But this is not the case. Rather, I have sought to show that the question of divine violence is a question that cannot be answered by absolving the Spirit of complicity with the forces of violence and destruction with which God as Father and Son is similarly allied. To whitewash the triune God (including the Holy Spirit) of the charge of perpetrating violence is to deny the full range of possibilities projected by the text in dialogue with the reader attuned to the discontinuities within historical existence as well as the biblical witness. From my perspective, the person of faith must learn to live with both horns of the dilemma regarding the Spirit's double identity as friend and foe.

An equally problematic response to the double-edged divine portraiture, however, is to try to resolve this practical and conceptual tension by singularly stressing the Spirit's role as destroyer and ignoring or denying the Spirit's identity as healer. That is, if the normative response has been to snap the dialectical tension between the two tropes by denying the violence of the Spirit, a similarly one-sided response to this tension is to erase the traditional focus on divine goodness by an overemphasis on the Spirit's collusion with the debilitative forces that blunt and frustrate the well-being of humankind and otherkind. The burden of faith in suspension between these seemingly contradictory scriptural tropes for God cannot be resolved by finding a false security in isolating *either* of the two figures as normative for making sense of the reality of God in the face of recalcitrant evil and violence. If the problem with *speculative* and *narrative theodicies* has been that they have sought conceptual order at the expense of accounting for the fractured significations for God within scripture, the obverse danger of *tragic theodicies* is that they overemphasize the fated character of the cosmos in order to explain how it is that God cannot or will not intercede on the victim's behalf. Instead of compromising the biblical picture of divine violence by overly stressing the singular notion of God's goodness, tragic theologies can sometimes err at the opposite extreme by isolating divine vengeance at the expense of a full consideration of the complexity of biblical meaning.

Consider in this regard the understanding of God and evil in classical theater. The Greek spectacles, for example, articulate the ineluctable fatedness of individuals who are blind to the gods' will (or are blinded by the gods' whims). Whereas in biblical rhetoric, as we have seen, God is alternately portrayed as unlimited in ability to act either compassionately or malevolently, the divine reality in Greek tragedy is determined to punish and destroy persons who knowingly (or unknowingly) flout sacred law and the order of nature. The tragic hero plays out his or her predetermined destruction on the stage of history, and the gods who observe this drama are either unwilling or unable to do anything about it. Whether through hubris or the innocent violation of prohibitions, the tragic protagonist is both victim of inhuman cosmic forces and object-lesson to his or her earthly peers. Recent theological retrievals of the tragic vision for the purpose of theodicy have played down the "wicked-God" motif in classical tragedy in order to investigate the meaning of evil as a limit concept and problem for religious thought and experience.[64] Here tragedy is understood not as divine malevolence and fated destruction but as the arational eruptions of evil within communities of biblical faith.

Two problems arise, however, from this redefinition of tragedy for theological purposes. First, the term "tragedy" is redefined so broadly that it runs the risk of losing its analytic power; second, and related to this, is the problem that when the term is more narrowly defined in the interest of explanatory precision, it becomes reattached to its etymological provenance in the Greek idea of *fate*: human subjects inevitably fall prey to the malevolence and wrath of the gods. In this second instance the tension between the destruction of life and the inconstancy of biblical hope is snapped, and tragic theology sinks back into the comfort of an overarching master narrative—namely, that the one who violates the universal, moral law is destined for a disastrous end. Such a narrative (once again) "explains" the problem of evil in a manner similar to the rationales given for this problem in speculative and narrative theodicies. If it is inevitable that everyone is fated to offend the gods at some point, then the destruction of particular individuals is a sensible outworking of this inevitability. Tragic theology is not, therefore, sufficiently dialectical. Kierkegaard, for example, argues that a wide gulf separates the tragic hero and the knight of faith, for while there is no comprehensive rationale that can ground faith, the tragic hero can "find rest in the universal" knowledge that her actions are justified by the socially approved assumptions that underpin the tragic system.[65] As ideal types, then, wisdom is a hope-against-hope struggle against the darkness, while tragedy is acquiescence to the fated destruction that awaits all of us. As Ricoeur observes, the gossamer thread hope of biblical faith and the logic of tragic necessity are incommensurable: "Explicit formulation of the tragic theology would mean self-destruction for the religious consciousness."[66]

CONCLUSION

In this chapter, I have taken issue with the demand for "victims" in Swinburne's philosophy, and the singular emphasis on the "promising God" in

64. See Bouchard, *Tragic Method and Tragic Theology;* and Wendy Farley, *Tragic Vision and Divine Compassion: A Contemporary Theodicy* (Louisville: Westminster/John Knox Press, 1990).
65. Søren Kierkegaard, *Fear and Trembling/Repetition*, ed. and trans. Howard V. Hong and Edna H. Hong (Princeton: Princeton University Press, 1983), 54–81.
66. Ricoeur, *The Symbolism of Evil*, 226.

Thiemann's theology, in favor of a sapiential approach to the problem of evil. My case is that theodicy in the twilight of the twentieth century must begin at the place where we all stand and should avoid soaring beyond the crisis of belief into the ether of speculative theorizing or totalizing narratives. Where we stand, I believe, is in the midst of chronic global suffering and violence, and it is this hard fact that should be the *norma normata* of theological work on the problem of evil. Anything less is no longer credible. If we forget that the owl of minerva often arrives too late (and especially for theologians it seems), we will continue to be satisfied with elegant solutions to the theodicy problem, only to discover (after it is too late) that our solutions ring hollow to a generation that is increasingly tone-deaf to traditional theological approaches to this issue.

With an eye toward Ricoeur, I have maintained that theodicy right for our time is a theodicy with a practical and emancipatory intent, a theodicy that manifests itself less in propositional solutions and triumphal narratives than in rituals of mourning and anger, on the one hand, and in works of charity and justice on behalf of other victims of evil and violence, on the other. Such a theodicy will be seen by some as an assault on agreed-upon standards of rational theological inquiry, while others will find it provocatively honest and attuned to the reality of that which is a limit and a scandal to reason, namely, gratuitous evil. Sapiential theodicy is indebted to scriptural wisdom discourse and contains a number of salient features: it is biblical in origin, ironic in style, and restorative in function. It is biblical: while it is rarely comfortable with the optimistic rhetoric of victory and triumph in Paul's theology, it is amenable to the various scriptural stories of struggle with and against God embodied, for example, in Jacob's wrestling with the angel at the Jabbok, or the synoptic Jesus' cry of dereliction from the cross. It is ironic: while it places in abeyance apodictic belief in an omnibenevolent God after the horrors of our time, it does not abandon the cathartic struggle to live a religious life in a world where the traditional idea of divine covenant seems meaningless and the hallowed doctrines of election and providence appear untenable. And such a theodicy is regenerative: it abandons the application of totalizing reason to the task of justifying God's ways to humankind, but it does not deny that theodicy in the mode of broken hope and compassionate action can restore a fractured meaning to a world that appears brute and unfeeling, even Godless.

Theodicy that enacts a living confrontation with the limit idea of recalcitrant evil is the theodicy best able to address the conscience of our time. Such a theodicy would shift the center of gravity concerning this problem onto another plane of understanding and experience, one that is therapeutic and practical in orientation rather than theoretical and speculative. Wisdom theodicy offers a rich and complicated biblical vocabulary to the reader/sufferer; it gives not a *solution* but a *response* to the aporia of irredeemable horror —a response that renders the aporia practically productive (not theoretically solvable) for the person who suffers the burdens of faith and hope in the hollows of the abyss. Wisdom theodicy provides not new answers but age-old resources for an immemorial problem, and thus it is theodicy in the register of feeling: it validates and engenders the release and catharsis of those emotions that can nourish a vigorous and ironic faith in a world that is evacuated of God's (traditionally understood) presence.

Tethered between the God of biblical witness and the phenomenon of evil, the practitioner of wisdom occasionally finds release in the accusation of faith and the impatience of hope. This praxis is the *vita activa* in the mode of anger and irony, the enactment of a life of protest and catharsis that must remember but longs to forget its existence in the divine abyss, the mystery of recalcitrant evil. It is the praxis of prayer and liturgy while belief in and worship of God are held in abeyance; it is the mad dance of Elie Wiesel's Hasidim, who, *in spite of God* and *in order to spite God*, throw themselves into the liturgy of revolt and blasphemy. "You don't want me to dance; too bad, I'll dance anyhow. You've taken away every reason for singing, but I shall sing."[67] Wisdom theodicy is not the cynicism that announces the death of God after the *tremendum*, but rather the realization that we must all wait in broken hope for a healing Other that can help us to address the terror of ultimate evil. We are all eyeless in Gaza (again) but not completely so: we have lost our capacity to see fully the divine presence, but we resist to the end the verdict that the darkness has forever extinguished the light.

67. Wiesel, *The Gates of the Forest*, 198.

CHAPTER SEVEN

Prospects for Renewal

Historically, thought in the West about the Spirit has been speculative and philosophical. In such discussions the Spirit has been defined in terms of the "ground of Being" or the "principle of consciousness," transforming the dynamics of the earth-centered *reality* of the Spirit, as witnessed to in the Bible, into an abstract *idea* that says little to the current struggles for communal health and ecological well-being. The philosophical determination of the Spirit as the ground of Being has consistently removed the topic of the Spirit from the concerns of culturally engaged theological reflection. Metaphysical pneumatology undermines a biblical understanding of the Holy Spirit as the renewing power of God in a world suffering from chronic violence toward humankind and otherkind. The "metaphysical captivity" of the Spirit, coupled with the christocentric, even christomonist, orientation of historic Christian thought, has meant that pneumatology continues to be the "orphan doctrine" of Christian theology.[1]

The burden of this book has been to retrieve the role of the Spirit as cosmic healer and sustainer of all forms of life on the planet. Through the use of countermetaphysical and biblically attuned rhetoric, I have sought to reenvision the Spirit as the power of transformation and renewal within a violent cosmos. The goal of the project has been both to suggest a change in our

---

1. Adolf Harnack, quoted in Alan M. Olson, *Hegel and the Spirit: Philosophy as Pneumatology* (Princeton: Princeton University Press, 1992), 15. See also Welker's thoughtful criticism of Aristotelian and Hegelian metaphysics for understanding the biblical attestation of the Holy Spirit in his *God the Spirit*, trans. John F. Hoffmeyer (Minneapolis: Fortress Press, 1994), 279–302.

understanding of the Spirit away from its status as a concept within speculative thought and to provide imaginative and spiritually rich resources for the
related tasks of earth-healing and Christian theology. When confined to
being either a philosophical idea or a christological afterthought, the Spirit's
unpredictable power to "blow where it wills" (John 3:8) and challenge our
violent, ecocidal habits cannot be accounted for. My hope is that by reimagining the Spirit as the divine agent for renewal within creation the freedom
and alterity of the Spirit's life-giving power can again be celebrated.

In a remarkable commentary on Heidegger's evolving notion of "spirit"
(*Geist*), Derrida seeks to preserve the wholly-otherness of spirit, which is "not
first of all this, that, or the other" but is the "most originary, the pre-archi-
originary" basis upon which philosophy, religion, and politics should be
based.[2] Indeed, insofar as deconstruction seeks to track the caesurae that
mark our failed attempts philosophically to enclose all reality in a totalizing
thought system, the task of deconstruction and the recovery of spirit-
language are fundamentally compatible, even necessary: "Rather than a value,
spirit seems to designate, beyond a deconstruction, the very resource for any
deconstruction and the possibility of any evaluation."[3] Spirit is the unname-
able name for the "origin-heterogeneous" that is the apophatic source for the
possibility of philosophical and theological reflection as such.[4] At this "origin" of thought which cannot be thematized, one traverses the "path of the
entirely other," a path that is the "most vertiginous and abyssal" of all pathways because it travels back to the originary spirit which cannot be determined, conceptualized, quantified, or thingified.[5] Derrida's Heideggerian
spirit philosophy is not, of course, equivalent in meaning to the understanding of the Spirit proposed here under the tutelage of the biblical witness.
(This difference is obvious on the basis of appellations: I and many other theologians name the Spirit by using the article and capital *S,* while Derrida and
most philosophers prefer the singular designation "spirit.") Nevertheless,
Derrida's attempt to secure the free, indeterminate, and wholly different reality of (the) S/spirit represents a philosophical orientation that shares deep
affinities with the postmetaphysical, biblical model of the Spirit suggested in
this project. In this respect, deconstruction and revisionist pneumatology

2. Jacques Derrida, *Of Spirit: Heidegger and the Question*, trans. Geoffrey Bennington and
Rachel Bowlby (Chicago: University of Chicago Press, 1989), 112.
3. Ibid., 14–15.
4. Ibid., 113.
5. Ibid.

share a common agenda: an understanding of S/spirit as the "entirely other" and "origin-heterogeneous" basis on which all forms of inquiry into God, self, and world are possible.

From the perspective of earth-centered pneumatology, Derrida rightly understands spirit as anterior to ontotheological determination. And yet, and understandably so, Derrida is hesitant to specify further the identity of spirit—other than to say that spirit is neither this nor that—because he fears the perennial temptation to reify the spirit as a thing or object in the process of further articulating its identity. For the theologian, however, it is not enough to say what the Spirit is not; the theologian must press the inquiry across the apophatic borders erected by Derrida and travel further to the place where the Spirit has been named and identified. For this theologian, in any event, that site where the divine life is named, a site that is always more complicated and contested than is generally recognized, is the Bible. After acknowledging the signal importance of various deconstructions of metaphysical attempts to substantialize the Spirit's identity, the theologian must move on to the constructive task of *risking a positive interpretation* of the Spirit's work in the world within and among all forms of life. From my perspective, this hermeneutical risk is best run by attending to the unstable portraitures of the Spirit within Jewish and Christian scriptures.

BIBLICAL PORTRAITURE

We have seen that the reader of the Bible confronts a panoply of imagery for the Spirit. In the opening hymn of Genesis the *rûaḥ* is a brooding water spirit who oversees the creation of all life; in Samuel the Spirit is simultaneously the agent of order and chaos in a society at odds with the divine legislation; in the prophets the Spirit is the power of prophecy and justice for the fatherless and widows; in Luke, Jesus is anointed with the Spirit to bring good news to the poor and liberty to captives; in John, the Spirit restores the community's hopes and advocates for victims of religious violence; in Acts, the Spirit inaugurates a multicultural church through the mediation of different languages; in Paul, the Spirit is the agent of transformative speech for those with little or no formal rhetorical training; and in Revelation, on some readings, the Spirit in chapter 12 is the courageous woman who gives birth to the savior in the face of the dragon who seeks the destruction of her son.

What unifies these texts is their portrayal of the Spirit as God's power to disrupt the social hierarchy in order to engender healing and renewal among the victimized and disadvantaged. Throughout the Bible, the Spirit is the divine agent for radical social change; the Spirit is never a present-at-hand object under human control, a subservient force at the disposal of human needs. As liberating power, movement for change, agent for peace, healing wind, and secret advocate for the poor, the Spirit is God present in the world: a catalyst for community and a champion for the marginal and oppressed.

In Johannine literature the Spirit is figured as the silent healer and advocate for victims. In Jesus' farewell discourses in John 14 the Spirit is described as the inner counselor who invisibly dwells within the community as a nurturing replacement for the absent Jesus. Jesus says he cannot remain with his followers, and he offers the Spirit in his stead as an occult comforter who will mend troubled hearts and banish all fears. It is clear on the basis of John's realized eschatology that Jesus' promise to return to the community is fulfilled by the gift of the Spirit and not in a physical return of Jesus to earth. The promise of the parousia is realized spiritually, not literally; the divine presence remains with the community but now through the agency of the Spirit. In John 14 this presence is worked out through the ministry of healing the disciples' memories: the Spirit restores to Jesus' troubled community a sense of peace and equanimity because she reminds them of all that Jesus has taught them.

In John 15 and 16 the Spirit is the advocate for victims of socially sponsored violence. The Spirit is the *Paraclete*, which literally means "one called to the side of another."[6] The Spirit paraclete is alternately an "advocate" who testifies on behalf of her followers against their detractors, and a "comforter" who strengthens and aids those who are unjustly persecuted, even murdered, because of their witness to the truth. John's account is a powerful statement of the Spirit's work of solidarity with those who suffer from mob violence. As "the Spirit of truth" who will "guide [the community] into all the truth" (John 16:13), the Spirit renders public all that can be known about the instances and structures of collective violence. The Spirit carefully tracks the patterns of violence against Jesus' followers and then empowers them to speak out with candor and courage about what they have seen and heard. Even as the Spirit refuses "to speak on his own authority" (16:13), so also friends of the Spirit are those persons who deflect attention away from themselves in order to direct attention to the plight of group-sponsored, and in our time

---

6. See *A Greek-English Lexicon of the New Testament and Other Early Christian Literature*, ed. William F. Arndt and F. Wilbur Gingrich (Chicago: University of Chicago Press, 1957), s.v. *paraklētos*, pp. 623–24.

state-sponsored, violence. These friends are reassured that they can register effective protests against the disenfranchisement and destruction of others by relying on the Spirit's advocacy on behalf of the marginalized and falsely accused.

FINAL SUGGESTIONS

In the light of this biblical sketch of the Spirit's identity, I would like to conclude with four final thoughts that have emerged over the course of this project. Each of these ideas is meant to serve the purpose of providing practical resources for a committed life-style that is nourished by a nonviolent and earth-identified pneumatology. These points are intended both to summarize the lineaments of the argument and to suggest the ethical implications of appropriating a life-centered model of the Spirit.

Truth as Inner Testimony

Truth is the performance of what one discerns to be the Spirit's interior testimony concerning the needs of the other. Attuning oneself to the Spirit's promptings enables the practice of the truth so that one's concern for the other's welfare is deepened and transformed. Discerning the Spirit's inner persuasions enables compassionate engagement with the other, even though this moral engagement does not have the security of a philosophical theory or foundation upon which to base the rationality of such an engagement. There are no extra-communal warrants outside the process of Spirit-discernment—what the Reformed tradition calls the *testimonium Spiritus Sancti internum*—that can apodictically ground the gesture of compassion toward the other. Theories such as realism (truth is correspondence to mind-independent reality) or antirealism (truth is a matter of choice in relation to incommensurate conceptual schemas) are inadequate to living out theological claims that are both *basic* to one's orienting worldview and yet *revisable* in the light of further experience and reflection. Wittgenstein is right to argue that claims to "truth" in particular networks of belief specify the flexible ability of the networks in question to facilitate a generous understanding of a wide range of experiences. In this regard, theological approaches to truth share a family resemblance to cosmological reality claims: both models are culturally embedded attempts to provide broader and deeper understandings of the world than would be possible apart from such models. Since there are no bias-free standards for adjudicating which models are best able to explain the relevant problems at hand, Wittgenstein stresses that it is a model's potential for ever-widening and more fruitful applications that makes it a candidate for truth.

This Wittgensteinian sensibility undergirds my thesis that theology is a rhetorical enterprise with an emancipatory intent rather than a metaphysical inquiry into the ground of all knowledge and experience. If truth in religion is a never-ending discernment of the Spirit's promptings rather than a philo-sophical quest for universal certainty, then the process of making theological truth-claims is fraught with fundamental ambiguity and instability. The redefinition of theology as rhetoric makes this point clear: there is no stan-dard of absolute reason outside the play of interpretations that can guarantee the interpreter has correctly intuited the Spirit's inner testimony in the moment. Glossing Levinas, I have suggested that the divine Spirit's interior ministrations consistently lead the interpreter to live a life of service toward the other. Claims to religious truth are vacuous unless they help to enact transformed social relations between self and other. "There can be no 'knowl-edge' of God separated from the relationship with men."[7] Nevertheless, while the Spirit consistently summons the subject to take up the other's welfare, the subject should guard against converting this summons into a fixed axiom within a universal calculus for ethical decision making. In his exegesis of the *Akedah*, Kierkegaard's thought serves as a resource for cautioning us against attempts to secure the Spirit's witness on the basis of a rationally justified moral system. The Spirit calls us to the wager of vertiginous faith, to take the leap of obedience into the void of uncertainty, to follow its demands even at the risk of a "teleological suspension of the ethical," as Kierkegaard says.[8] The ethical demand of postmetaphysical pneumatology is to follow the Spirit's promptings wherever they might lead, even if the eventual destination con-founds the received understandings of reason and morality. Truth in religion, therefore, begins with the willingness to travel the unmarked path plotted by the Spirit in the heart of each person.

The Spirit and Boundary Crossing

The practice of nonviolent care for the other is modeled after the Spirit's moral insurgency and erasure of cultural boundaries. At first glance, it may appear that

---

7. Emmanuel Levinas, *Totality and Infinity*, trans. Alphonso Lingis (Pittsburgh: Duquesne University Press, 1969), 78.

8. Søren Kierkegaard, *Fear and Trembling/Repetition*, ed. and trans. Howard V. Hong and Edna H. Hong (Princeton: Princeton University Press, 1983), 54–67.

the moral demand to seek the other's welfare can be easily taken up by the subject who attends to the Spirit's inner voice. But the practice of other-regard is more complicated than it first appears. The subject is not, as we would like to think, a self-directed and self-controlled agent coincident with its own and others' best interests, but rather a perpetual imitator of the wider culture's value preferences, rendering its attempts to practice disinterested other-regard forever partial and self-defeating. In traditional theological parlance, the self's inability to follow the Spirit's impulses and seek the other's welfare has been labeled "the bondage of the will." In a contemporary idiom, Girard's astute analysis of the servile will through the mimesis-violence dialectic sets forth the self as both responsible for, and captive to, the culturally mediated desires that define postmodern subjectivity.

Girard argues that the subject's desires are never self-generated but are formed by the preferences of the other, the mediator of desire. As the mimetic subject becomes better adept at obtaining the objects of the other's desires and begins to erase the distinctions that have separated subject and mediator, she finds herself caught in the double bind of all mimetic rivalry—the double bind of the mediator's mixed message, "Imitate me!" and "Do not imitate me!" The concomitant loss of defining differences between subject and mediator, and the bitter rivalry that is the consequence of this loss, generally results in violent attempts by the wider society to reassert the once-dominant moral codes and prohibitions that supported the culture's system of distinctions. Chaos and confusion are the by-products of the breakdown in social order; peace and stability are the results of successful attempts to reassert the familiar taboos so that everyone knows their "place" in the social hierarchy.

Many persons and groups, however, challenge unjust social hierarchies in the interest of forging novel and egalitarian alliances across the cultural boundaries that give the wider society its sense of stability and identity. When people with AIDS, on the one hand, and prophets of racial justice, on the other, are vilified and persecuted for challenging the "natural" order of society, they are accused of leveling the sacrosanct *differences* (sexual and racial differences, respectively) that keep Western society from disintegrating into a supposed "cross-gendered" and "mixed-race" miasma of confusion and non-differentiation. The collective reaction to such leveling and confusion is the all-against-one violence of the mob against the outsider, the scapegoating of the other as the insidious instigator of cultural disorder. The "prophylactic" of violence against the "virus" that has spawned cultural confusion checks the dangerous "contagion" that might yield more boundary erasures and loss of differences.

The Girardian dialectic of mimesis-violence paves the way for a revised understanding of the Spirit as the power of God to challenge and subvert the mainstream reassertions of cultural order at the expense of the victims of that order. When violence breaks out against the marginal other who is blamed for the dissolutions of social hierarchy, the Spirit comes to the aid of the oppressed and empowers them to resist and undermine the regnant social order. The Spirit works on behalf of the oppressed in order to enable the dispossessed to subvert the structures of capital and control that block the inclusion of all persons as full and productive members of society.

The challenge of the Spirit to the guardians of the dominant culture is the Spirit's celebration of *differences* vis-à-vis the wider society's increasingly violent attempts to preserve sameness, order, and tradition. The story of Pentecost in the book of Acts, for example, narrates the origins and formation of a Spirit-filled countercommunity that celebrated its cultural and linguistic diversity in the face of an imperial government of occupation that persecuted nonconformists as instigators of social unrest. Few of us today are willing to take the risks undertaken by the early disciples at Pentecost. The early followers of the Spirit found unity in a common vision while still preserving the integrity and value of each member's distinctive language and culture. In Western culture we pride ourselves on championing the values of *democracy*, but the Spirit calls us to a more radical political vision, a *heterocracy* of sorts, to paraphrase Foucault's notion of "heterotopia," in which the unity of common values and commitments is never purchased at the price of scapegoating any person or group as the "demonized other" who has caused the breakdown in social order. Unity is not the same as unanimity, and the quest for common values is not equivalent to the legislation of one group's favorite taboos and prohibitions at the expense of another group's deeply held moral principles. Analogous to the dynamics of growth and decay in the wider biotic community, it is important, then, to recognize the importance of change, even revolution, within human societies as well. The Spirit is the divine catalyst for social transformation in communities where difference and dissent are suppressed by the administration of state-approved violence. For present-day apprentices to the Spirit's work of renewal, the ethical burden is to resist the subtle machinations of the scapegoat mechanism and to seek the welfare of persons and groups who have been ground underfoot by the culturally approved apparatuses of coercion and violence.

To reconceive Christian identity as a subversive challenge to the wider society has direct political implications for American congregational life. But a political understanding of church life is in tension with the postliberal model of the church articulated by theologians such as Stanley Hauerwas, William Willimon, William Placher, George Lindbeck, and others.[9] Hauerwas, to borrow a phrase from Placher, argues that Christians should be "tribalists" whose first priority is to preserve the distinctive biblical values of their own church congregations before they enter the public fray in the fight against poverty and injustice. Hauerwas questions the presupposition of liberal theologians that direct political action on behalf of disenfranchised persons should be the first task of the Christian community. He avers that the basic responsibility of the church is to put its own house in order and then worry about the larger issues of social and political injustice.

> Christians must again understand that their first task is not to make the world better or more just, but to recognize what the world is and why it is that it understands the political task as it does. . . . In developing such skills [i.e., for understanding the world] the church and Christians must be uninvolved in the politics of our society and involved in the polity that is the church.[10]

Hauerwas maintains that until the church has secured its biblically centered identity it cannot responsibly move into the public arena and address wider social problems. Only when the church has reinforced its own polity can it offer a countercultural alternative to a dysfunctional society. "[T]he church must recognize that her first social task in any society is to be herself."[11] What I find disturbing about Hauerwas's model of the church, though I do not think he intends this consequence, is the implication that internal housecleaning and external social witness entail different sets of priorities and levels of commitment. From my perspective, reaffirming the biblical foundations of American congregational life and reaching out to a divided world consist of the same gesture. It is impossible, I think, to seek to inculcate biblical values within congregations without at the same time raising a prophetic voice against the culture of prejudice and violence that all of us inhabit—Christian and non-Christian alike. It is impossible to nurture church families in the

9. For postliberal ecclesiologies that offer alternatives to political-liberal models of church and society, see Stanley Hauerwas and William H. Willimon, *Resident Aliens* (Nashville: Abingdon Press, 1989); William C. Placher, *Narratives of a Vulnerable God: Christ, Theology, and Scripture* (Louisville: Westminster John Knox Press, 1994); and George A. Lindbeck, *The Nature of Doctrine: Religion and Theology in a Postliberal Age* (Philadelphia: Westminster Press, 1984).

10. Stanley Hauerwas, *A Community of Character: Toward a Constructive Christian Social Ethic* (Notre Dame: University of Notre Dame Press, 1981), 74.

11. Ibid., 83–84.

biblical traditions without simultaneously struggling against the syste
inequities and structural violence that undergird our public life.

The mission of the church in the struggle for justice has been driven ho
to me by my involvement with other clergy and academics from the Philac
phia-New York area in requesting a stay of execution and a new trial
Mumia Abu-Jamal, an activist journalist and author who is currently awa
ing execution of a death sentence for his conviction in the murder of
Philadelphia police officer in 1982.[12] In the case against Abu-Jamal, mar
people feel his original trial was marred by a hostile court; his supporte
argue that he deserves a new, fair trial. His trial and sentencing in July 198
now appear to be riddled with police and prosecutorial misconduct, testi
mony that may have been coerced from witnesses, and the inability of a
stand-in attorney to represent fairly Abu-Jamal's interests in the case. The
court's refusal to order a new trial has convinced me, with reference to
Girard's analysis of sacrificial violence, that Abu-Jamal is a political scapegoat
who is being blamed for crimes he most likely did not commit because of his
political views and activist history (he was a former member of the Black Pan-
ther party). In other words, his "kind" is regarded as a mortal threat to society
and needs to be punished accordingly.

The Commonwealth of Pennsylvania's unwillingness to give Abu-Jamal a
new trial further demonstrates that many of us are convinced that public executions are necessary for maintaining law and order in society. Paroxysms of
legalized violence are necessary for restoring order even when the evidence
against a defendant like Abu-Jamal is manufactured at worst and questionable at best. Girard is right: we are a culture that worships violence.[13] We
believe that ritualized public executions restore the health of the body politic
by eradicating the human "viruses" that infect our society with violence and
lawlessness. We believe that the eradication of such viruses deters future
crimes. To use religious language, we believe in blood atonement, namely,
that by putting to death a person who has killed another we have somehow
righted the moral imbalance by exchanging one life for another. Our sacrificial logic is inexorable: periodic executions of convicted felons are just punishment for the commission of certain capital crimes.

12. See Leonard I. Weinglass et al., "Petition for Post-Conviction Relief for Mumia Abu-
Jamal," Court of Common Pleas, Philadelphia, Pennsylvania, 1995; and Mumia Abu-Jamal,
Live From Death Row (New York: Addison-Wesley Publishers, 1995).

13. René Girard, *Things Hidden Since the Foundation of the World*, with Jean-Michel
Oughourlian and Guy Lefort, trans. Stephen Bann and Michael Metteer (Stanford: Stanford
University Press, 1987), 32.

But this way of thinking, I believe, is demonic in the extreme. On the basis of the biblical witness, it appears that God alone has the right to give life and to take it away (Job 1:21; cf. Luke 8:1-11); it is not our prerogative to kill people for crimes they may or may not have committed. Particularly in cases like Abu-Jamal's, where the evidence is highly questionable, we run the risk of robbing an innocent person of life in a rush to judgment. Moreover, we deceive ourselves in thinking that we restore the moral and social order by killing off persons convicted of capital crimes. In public executions of scapegoats like Abu-Jamal, we join the fellowship of the lynch mob and we are all dehumanized and diminished in the process. No matter what the *other* person has or has not done, we suffer the loss of our *own* dignity and humanity whenever we participate in the bloody ritual of public executions. We have become the society of the spectacle: people convicted of serious crimes are publicly put to death in order, we are told, to deter future criminal activity. But public executions do not deter crime; instead, the cycle of violence continues to spiral out of control, and we reenergize the cycle whenever we cry out for more vengeance and more blood.

We inhabit a culture divided by deep problems—problems that stem from some persons' ethic identity, sexual orientation, or criminal standing. What does it mean to be the church in such a society? What does it mean to be the church in a society where many people of color remain disenfranchised, where people with AIDS are publicly shunned and ridiculed, and where the spectacle of state-sponsored executions is held up as a deterrent to crime when its real effect is to further erode the basic humanity that binds us all together as a society? Surely the scandal of inclusivity engendered by the Spirit's insurgent activities in Luke-Acts runs counter to an ecclesiology based on race, sexual preference, and legal vengeance. Thus, in the current social crisis, I regard the tribalist call to attend first to the church's internal problems to be hollow unless that call also directs our attention to the fundamental injustices that separate all members of the wider culture from their fellow and sister citizens and neighbors. Our proclivities to scapegoat and demonize other persons because of their ethnic background, sexual orientation, or criminal status are problems not external but internal to the life of the church insofar as the church seeks to follow the Spirit's subversive mission of fostering inclusion and diversity. The alternative to sacrificial violence is the celebration of difference and the renunciation of the use of violence to suppress difference. True Spirit-filled churches and communities celebrate their members' heterogeneity and struggle to abandon the time-honored hatreds and divisions that beset mainstream societies caught up in ritual victimage.

Sojourner Ethic

Since the Spirit is the "vinculum caritatis" who labors against nature-hostile structures and values, our ethical orientation should include a sojourner, rather than a stewardship, stance toward nonhuman life-forms. I have suggested that the Spirit's interior witness empowers the subversion of the cultural boundaries that scapegoat the other and blame the other for the social ills that characterize postmodern cultures. Societies bitterly resist the erasure of culturally sanctioned boundaries because without these boundaries the process of identity formation is undermined by instability and plurality. Nevertheless, bearers of the Spirit's prophetic witness must take the risk of crossing such borders in order to co-engender in the other—including the nonhuman other—the realization of everyone's potential.

One such boundary that is now being crossed because it has been especially pernicious in contemporary culture is the rigid distinction between humankind and otherkind at the center of our Western worldview, including our theological worldview. This culturally constructed distinction has long served the interests of Western societies and economies in their efforts to maintain dominance over nonhuman life-forms. Christianity is partly responsible for the ideological maintenance of this partition between humankind and otherkind. Normative Christian thought has positioned the human being as the lord over all creation; on the basis of our powers of reason, it is argued that we are God's chosen wardens and stewards of the created order. This seemingly benign understanding of the human–nonhuman relationship betrays, however, a residual commitment to a monarchial and feudal notion of a great Chain of Being in which human beings function as the hierarchs over a natural world that is at their disposal. At the behest of the Spirit, it is time for a reversal of this convenient hierarchy: rather than placing nature at *our disposal*, it is now the natural world itself, in all its power and poverty, its grandeur and fragility, that *disposes us* to interact with it as equal copartners. The Spirit is calling us to become friends of the earth rather than stewards of its resources.

The theological basis of a green ethic of equality and friendship with the earth begins with a revisioning of the Spirit as a *life-form* who indwells and sustains all things. Historically, the Spirit has been understood either theocentrically as the principle of unity in the triune Godhead, or anthropocentrically as the power of regeneration and sanctification in the human person. In the light of the environmental crisis, I have proposed a shift in emphasis toward a *biocentric* redefinition of the Spirit as God's agent of interdependence and unity within all creation. This biocentric focus recovers two trajectories in the history of Christian thought about the Spirit that are especially powerful resources for addressing the current crisis. First, the biocentric approach retrieves the scriptural tropology of the Spirit that is based on nature imagery. In the Bible, the Spirit is alternately figured as vivifying breath, healing wind, living water, purgative fire, and ministering dove. All of these images underscore the Spirit's reality as a living being, a life-form, who breathes the breath of life into all living beings and sustains them through her ministry of healing, refreshing, and reconciling love. Second, the biocentric approach recovers the classical idea of the Spirit as the *vinculum caritatis*, the power of perichoretic union between Father and Son, as the basis for the more expansive notion of the Spirit as the biotic enactment of the unity and kinship that characterize the relations between *all* members of the ecosystemic whole. The Spirit is the bond of love not only within the intratrinitarian life of God but also within the whole biosphere. The Spirit is the *vinculum caritatis* who indwells and sustains both the "inner economy" of the divine Trinity and the "outer economy" of all life in the cosmos. The recovery of these two pneumatological traditions within the history of Western religious thought—the Spirit as the biblical agent of life and renewal, on the one hand, and the Spirit as the *vinculum caritatis* within the Godhead and creation, on the other—provides a solid foundation for a nature-based ethic that is both appropriate to the Christian tradition and a constructive ally in the struggle for ecological justice and renewal.

The historic biblical contest between the deities of pagan agricultural traditions and the covenantal God of biblical faith has set the stage for our own ambivalence toward nature spirituality today. This contest between paganism and monotheism evacuates nature of its power to function as a medium of the divine presence and twists the natural world into a dangerous site for heathenism and idolatry. The biblical indictment of nature religion reaches a fever pitch in Paul's writings against the Gentiles: "[They] exchanged the glory of the immortal God for images resembling mortal man or birds or animals or reptiles . . . they exchanged the truth about God for a lie and worshiped and served the creature rather than the Creator" (Romans 1:23, 25). Paul inveighs against any attempts to compromise the inviolate distinction between the divine life and other life-forms by showing reverence toward the creation rather than the Creator. Such acts of religious observance reverse the order of creation in which God alone, as the invisible and disembodied source of all life, is singularly worthy of worship and devotion, while the rest of the created order is relegated to the status of something to be used, perhaps even protected, but never worshiped for its own sake as the embodiment of the Spirit of Life itself.

The Pauline dictum, while understandable for its time, is partly responsible for the *contemptus mundi* legacy of Western culture that has had such debilitating environmental consequences. We must challenge this legacy. The theological retrieval of life-centered models for reconceiving God and God's relation to the earth is a productive starting point for such a challenge. Insofar as we are able to reconceive the Spirit as the giver and sustainer of all life, rather than as the principle of intratrinitarian unity only within the divine life, then we will see that the erstwhile biblical distinction between nature-based spirituality ("the worship of creation") and scriptural religion ("the worship of the Creator") is a false and pernicious distinction that has divided what should have been held together, namely, God and the earth. *The distinction, therefore, between love of God and love of nature trades on a false alternative.* Insofar as we revalue the Spirit as the enfleshment and embodiment of God through and within particular natural forces and forms of life—as set forth in the biblical Spirit-language of breath, fire, wind, water, and dove—we cross over the supposed boundary that separates God from otherkind and realize that we are now standing on the sacred middle ground where we have *always* been and where God has *always already* been, namely, the rich and fecund earth of our common inheritance. From this perspective, love of God and love of nature are conterminous expressions of passion and adoration for the Earth-Spirit whose unifying power is the basis for our kinship and common existence. From this perspective, reverence for the Spirit-filled earth and the praise of God's glory in all creation are complementary acts of worship and devotion.

John Muir's ecofundamentalism regularly crossed the false boundaries separating love of God and love of nature. Muir attuned himself to the pulsating rhythms of the Spirit throughout nature; he developed an earthlust spirituality that was both deeply Christian and robustly pagan at the same time. He practiced a "composting religion," to borrow the felicitous phrase of Mary Douglas, in which the culturally distinguished realms of the divine life, human life, and nonhuman life were wonderfully mixed together in heathen vision and nature ecstasy.[14] Since the Spirit is present everywhere as the life-force that interanimates creation, nature becomes the new church for the activist-believer who lives within and among the different life-forms within the biosphere—the very life-forms that the wider culture has sought to relegate to a lower plane of being than that occupied by humankind.

The practical import of a pneumatology inspired by Muir results in a

14. Mary Douglas, *Purity and Danger: An Analysis of the Concepts of Pollution and Taboo* (London: Routledge, Ark Paperbacks, 1966), 167.

sojourner ethic of equal regard for otherkind rather than a stewardship ethic of managing the created order. Traditionally, when religious environmentalists have thought about their relationship to nature, images of caretaking and conservation have come to mind. While these images have solid biblical warrants in their favor, they nevertheless betray a residual anthropocentric bias in which the human person is seen as the rational arbiter of what is most worthy of preservation and value within the natural world. Indeed, Muir was a lifelong conservationist, but his life and thought provide a resource for another environmental model as well, that is, a land-based ethic in which the human person is just one more fellow traveller with other life-forms in the common evolutionary journey. The human person is a temporary passerby on a fragile planet, not God's handpicked warden of nature's bounty. Muir's random, errant wanderings in the Yosemite high country embody an awe of and a love for nature *in and for itself* and apart from the need for human oversight and control. For Muir, the natural world is not a resource for the service of human needs but humankind's biotic partner in the struggle for environmental integrity and wholeness. Since all life-forms are equal members of the Spirit-imbued biosphere, each community of life-forms should be allowed to attain its own teleological fullness with as little human interference as possible. Rather than the ageless attempts to order "rightly" the natural world according to what we deem to be its (and of course our) "best interests," I suggest that the Spirit is asking us at this time to practice a "live and let live" policy of thoughtful nonmeddling in our relationships with other forms of life. The Spirit is prompting us to tread lightly on a billions-of-years-old planet to which we have arrived only a few seconds before midnight on the overall evolutionary clock, so to speak.

Aporia of Biblical Faith

Finally, scriptural wisdom reminds us that the practice of nonviolent love (for humankind and otherkind) has an unstable and aporetic theological basis since the biblical God is alternately portrayed as the defender of victims and the perpetrator of violence. The double-edged portrait of the divine life in the Bible— God is the source of both comfort *and* terror for the sufferer—poses a disturbing challenge to persons who seek to overcome the structures of evil and violence in our time. The conventional theological obviation of this challenge is to deny or ignore the scriptural texts concerning divine violence by ascribing the origin and purpose of evil to the soul-making designs of the God of the biblical covenant. This is the project of classical theodicy and its modern variations: evil is justified because it serves the value of character-formation in a world where God is always good and faithful to the divine promise. Evil is the liquid fire the Refiner uses to hone and perfect the created order; it is not the surd character of reality, as I have suggested, that refuses the totalizing impulses of rational thought and experience. I have argued, however, that the traditional theodicy project fails in the face of irruptions of a hostile power that shatters the confidence of thought systems, including theodicist systems, which seek to render conceptually coherent the reality of gratuitous suffering with the belief in an all-good and all-powerful God. The theodicy project fails in the wake of the human waste and environmental degradation that characterize contemporary existence. Moreover, it fails particularly for the *religious* sufferer when she is forced to confront the biblically sanctioned complicity of God—including God as Spirit—with the powers of violence and vengeance that destroy life and community.

It is at this juncture that Paul Ricoeur's writings on suffering and evil become especially relevant. In his analysis of the play of biblical genres, Ricoeur notes that narrative discourse, in spite of its pride of place in the overall biblical schema, suffers from a totalizing bias in which the outbreakings of radical evil are subsumed under the logic of the master story. Ricoeur's use of wisdom discourse vigorously objects to this narrative homologization of evil to the supreme plot. In *Time and Narrative*, he discusses the power of wisdom to challenge narrative hegemony by way of a new understanding of the interdependence of time and narrative. In this study he maintains that time is humanized to the extent that it can be thematized in a narrative mode, and that narrative is meaningful insofar as it sheds light on our temporal experience.[15] This working thesis is highly elucidative of certain aporetics of time that Ricoeur examines in this work. But in the last few pages of *Time and Narrative*, through a brief consideration of wisdom literature, Ricoeur offers his own immanent critique of this thesis that orients the whole project. Wisdom, according to Ricoeur, challenges the impulse to systematization characteristic of narrative discourse because it questions, in the final analysis, whether the mystery and incoherence of temporal existence can be fully explained on the basis of master stories. Wisdom challenges the chimera of the supreme plot that binds together disparate events, including radically negative events, into a homogeneous totality. Consider the following:

15. Paul Ricoeur, *Time and Narrative*, trans. Kathleen Blamey and David Pellauer (Chicago: University of Chicago Press, 1988), 1:3 and passim.

There is another way for time to envelop narrative. This is by giving rise to the formation of discursive modes other than the narrative one, which will speak, in another way, of the profound enigma. There comes a moment, in a work devoted to the power of narrative to elevate time to language, where we must admit that narrative is not the whole story and that time can be spoken of in other ways, because, even for narrative, it remains inscrutable.[16]

Ricoeur continues that wisdom literature is best equipped to express the "grief that is ceaselessly reborn from the contrast between the fragility of life and the power of time that destroys," because wisdom "goes right to the fundamental without passing through the art of narrating."[17] After interweaving narrative and time into a near seamless whole, Ricoeur, with remarkable honesty and humility, pulls apart the fabric by inserting the temporal problematics associated with wisdom writings. He concludes that narrative meaning is only partly successful because wisdom reminds us that time, finally, remains opaque and inscrutable. In this way the reader of wisdom is taught that grief and irony, even divine betrayal, lie close to the heart of the narrative schemas within the Bible.

Using Ricoeur, my argument is that biblical wisdom provides the most adequate genre for addressing the problems of evil and violence for a rhetorically conscious theology. In the face of a distant God and an unfeeling universe, the appeal of wisdom is simple and profound: cathartically confront suffering by following the way of the lamenters and sages, not the way of the philosophers and theologians. No theoretical justification for the way of wisdom can or should be offered as a ground for this invitation. *Rather, wisdom encourages the existential wager that one will discover a measure of self-renewal in practicing a spirituality of anger toward God, of mourning one's losses, of finding meaning in solidarity with other victims of evil and oppression.* Since no purely speculative or narrative system can ground this wager, the disciple of wisdom discovers her own practical justification for following the way of catharsis and anger. She discovers, it is hoped, the performative value of a theology of lament that refuses to be subsumed by any theology of triumph.

THE GREEN FACE OF GOD

My conviction is that the role of theology in the current situation should be to reconstitute a biblical rhetoric that will serve the desires of all species to

16. Ibid., 3:272–73.
17. Ibid.

survive and flourish. In this project, under the rubric "life-centered pneumatology," I have sought to perform this task by crafting a model of the Spirit as the revivifying and healing power of God in a world in need of restoration. The Spirit comes with healing in her wings to a world that cries out for transformation and renewal. The Spirit comes to a world in need of refreshment as the breath of God and the water of life. The Spirit comes to a world fragmented by violence and suffering with the promise of health and wholeness for all creation.

"Wholeness" and "integrity" are the watchwords for a life-centered theology adequate to the crises of our times. The English word "whole" is a derivative of a constellation of old Teutonic and old English terms that signified well-being, health, and healing. Etymologically, the word "whole" stems from the Germanic *Heil* which is associated with vitality, integrity, strength, soundness, and completeness. The many senses of *Heil* as "good health" and "sound body" gave rise to its use in a variety of salutations in Northern Europe. Likewise, the English word "holy"—derived from *heilig* (a cognate of *Heil*)—historically also had the meanings of well-being and integrity in addition to its denotation as consecrated and set apart. Wholeness, the whole, and the holy, therefore, are terms that have historically cross-pollinated with one another, with the result that the sense arrangement for the word "whole" carries a triple valence: the quality of wholesomeness or being in good health; the character of completeness, fullness, integrity; and that which is set apart and invested with ceremonial dignity and sacred power. To uphold, then, the integrity of the *whole* is to experience the *holy* through living a life of personal and communal *healing* and *well-being*.

The interrelated meanings of wholeness, healing, and the holy signify the kinship between religion and the art of practicing sound and healthy relations with others. Too often we have thought of religion in terms of beliefs and doctrines, but true religion consists rather in the care and maintenance of other members of the life-webs that make up everyone's existence. True spirituality is to seek the integrity of the *whole* in one's everyday relations with others, to find the *holy* in attuning oneself to the Spirit within all life-forms, to be a *healer* in one's interactions with other members of the life-world. On the way to a life-centered spirituality, one travels the road to lasting personal and communal fulfillment, even salvation. Like the word cluster wholeness/holiness/healthiness, the etymology of the word "salvation" is also an index to its original connection to the practice of good health and sound relations with others. "Salvation" shares a common semantic root with the archaic English term "salvatory," a small surgeon's box used for medicinal ointments, and the modern word "salve," by way of the Old Teutonic *salba* ("butter"), which means a healing paste for application to wounds and sores.[18] The state of "being saved," therefore, consists of the practice of spiritual and bodily nurture, toward oneself and the other, in a world that suffers from a pathological disregard for the health and vitality of other beings.

Unfortunately, however, terms such as the "holy" and "salvation" have become so freighted with narrow dogmatic meanings that they have lost their original rootedness in the practice of healing and transformation. Still, many voices in the current conversation have called for a therapeutic understanding of religion, and it is to these voices that I believe the hope for religious practice in general, and for Christianity in particular, best lies. The collective insight is that in spite of the sometimes debilitating teachings and strictures of professional religious organizations, true religion is an exercise in physical and emotional transformation and renewal. The Buddha said his practice was to pull out of people the poisoned arrow of wrong desire and restore the balance in their relations with themselves and others. Jesus taught that his mission was to heal the sick and promote health and well-being among those to whom he ministered. Thomas Aquinas wrote that the function of *gratia*, God's power in the world to bring salvation, is a medicine that heals the will at odds with itself and restores the will to desire its own and the other person's spiritual welfare. The Lakota shaman Black Elk believed that a restoration of the nation's hoop, the symbolic source of all life, was possible when the two-leggeds and four-leggeds learned to live harmoniously among and between one another. Jewish theologian Emil Fackenheim writes that *tikkun olam* (healing the world), that is, the practice of concrete acts of solidarity with victims of ethnic violence, is the common responsibility of all persons—Christians, Jews, and others—whose lives have been shattered by the event of the Shoah. Christian theologians such as Moltmann and McFague stress that the crisis of life on the planet provokes a rethinking of God, humankind, and otherkind as coparticipants with one another in the realization of an ecologically sustainable future. Neopagan practitioners of modern Wicca emphasize the healing of Mother Earth as the primary desideratum at a time in history when the dualisms of Western thought and culture—the dualisms between mind and body, man and woman, and human beings and other beings—have reaped the ugly fruit of social disintegration and environmental squalor. And deep ecologists call for all of us to tread lightly on the earth as we struggle to

---

18. Definitions and etymologies for these terms are drawn from *The Oxford English Dictionary* (New York: Oxford University Press, 1971).

mend the ecosystems we have damaged and preserve the biotic future for humankind and otherkind.

Where are the fragments of the Spirit in our world today? I believe the Spirit is present in the eyes of our neighbor, in the green fuse that drives the growth of trees and plants, in the ebb and flow of the life cycle within which all of us live and move and have our being. The Spirit is alive and active whenever and wherever committed persons and communities work to bring reconciliation and healing to members of the life-web that have been denied the basic means for sustaining a fruitful existence. The Spirit is the green face of God, the intercessory force for peace and solidarity in a world saturated with sacrificial violence, the power of renewal within creation as the creation groans in travail and waits with eager longing for environmental justice for all God's creatures. Like the dance of the sun's light across the surface of the earth, the Spirit in fragments shines with bright hope in anticipation of a time when the original unity and integrity of creation will again be realized.

Index